THE ROMAN EMPIRE

History in a Nutshell

Eric Rump

CONTENTS

Title Page
Introduction   1
Chapter 1: The Origins of Rome and the Royal Period (c. 753–509 BC)   6
Chapter 2: The Roman Republic – Rise to Power (509–264 BC)   32
Chapter 3: Rome as a Great Power – Punic Wars and Mediterranean Dominance (264–133 BC)   51
Chapter 4: Crisis of the Republic and Civil Wars (133–27 BC)   66
Chapter 5: The Principate – Augustus and the Golden Age (27 BC–68 AD)   89
Chapter 6: The Roman Empire under the Flavians and Adoptive Emperors (69–192 AD)   114
Chapter 7: Culture, Religion and Everyday Life in the Roman Empire   139
Chapter 8: Christianization and Religious Transformation (1st–5th Century AD)   167
Chapter 9: Late Antiquity and the Division of the Empire (284–476 AD)   188
Chapter 10: The Eastern Roman Empire (Byzantium) and the Roman Legacy   208
Chapter 11: The Roman Legacy in Europe and the Reception of Antiquity   233

Closing Words

INTRODUCTION

The history of Rome is one of the most fascinating and consequential chapters in human civilization. Few other cultures have shaped the political, legal, linguistic, and cultural foundations of Europe as profoundly as the Roman Empire. From its legendary origins as a community of shepherds along the banks of the Tiber River to its rise as a world power spanning three continents, Rome was not merely an empire built of stone—it was an idea, a system, a myth. Its influence extended far beyond the formal end of its political structures. Even today, centuries after the fall of the Western Roman Empire, we encounter Rome daily—whether in Roman law, Latin-derived vocabulary, urban planning principles, or the Christian religion, which, under Roman patronage, developed into a global faith.

The population of the Roman Empire reached a remarkable size for the ancient world. At its zenith under Emperor Trajan around 117 CE, the empire encompassed approximately 70 million inhabitants—about one quarter of the world's population at the time. Its frontiers stretched over 10,000 kilometers, from Scotland to Mesopotamia, and from the North Sea to the Sahara Desert. Rome governed a multitude of peoples speaking dozens of languages and practicing a diversity of religions and cultural traditions. Despite this diversity, the empire succeeded in establishing a coherent administrative structure, a shared identity, and an expansive network of roads, laws, and ideas that endured for centuries. It was an empire that expanded through military might but also excelled in integration and organization. The concept of *Romanitas*—the sense of belonging to the Roman way of life—was as much an export commodity as the Roman legions, architectural techniques, or legal institutions.

Rome, however, was never a static entity. The history of Rome is a narrative of transformation, transition, crisis, and renewal. This book follows that dynamic trajectory. It begins with the origins of Rome—a city said to have been founded in 753 BCE, whose earliest centuries lie more in the realm of myth and archaeology than in securely attested historical sources. Nevertheless, the preserved accounts depict a Rome that, from the outset, oscillated between monarchy, religious symbolism, and military expansion. The replacement of kings with a republic marked a pivotal moment, laying the groundwork for Roman political culture over the following centuries: a mixed constitution integrating aristocratic, democratic, and monarchical elements—admired even into the modern era.

Yet the Republic was far from a stable political model. It was marked by internal power struggles, social tensions, and recurring political upheavals. The so-called Conflict of the Orders between patricians and plebeians illustrates the profound social inequalities within Roman society—and the considerable resistance to reform. At the same time, Rome emerged as the dominant power on the Italian peninsula and began to confront other great powers of the Mediterranean world. The Punic Wars against Carthage, both a masterpiece of military strategy and a human catastrophe, ultimately elevated Rome to a naval superpower. In the Second Punic War alone, over 500,000 people perished—a figure that, by ancient standards, was apocalyptic. Yet Rome survived, adapted, and grew stronger. The path to global dominance lay open—but it came at an enormous cost.

This book does not treat this development as merely a chronological sequence of military conquests. Rather, it demonstrates the intricate interweaving of politics, society, religion, and culture. Rome's expansion was not solely territorial—it was cultural as well. The conquest of Greece brought not only wealth and slaves but also philosophy, art, and scientific knowledge. Roman elites adopted Greek educational ideals and fused them with Roman pragmatism. The famous line *Graecia capta ferum victorem cepit*—"Captive Greece took captive her fierce conqueror"—aptly captures this cultural exchange. Rome developed its own ideal of education, a literary language, and an architectural style that would serve as a benchmark for millennia to come.

Yet failure is as much a part of Roman history as triumph. The late Republic collapsed under the pressure of internal contradictions. Reform attempts were violently suppressed, and personal loyalty began to override institutional norms. Figures such as Sulla, Pompey, Caesar, and Octavian fundamentally reshaped Roman politics—away from republican ideals and toward personalized rule. The assassination of Julius Caesar in 44 BCE was not the tragic demise of a reformer, but a harbinger of change: the Republic could no longer be saved. With Augustus began a new era—the Principate. Rome became a monarchy with a republican façade. The Senate formally remained in place, but real power was concentrated in the hands of the emperor.

The imperial period forms the core of several chapters in this book—not only due to the compelling personalities involved, but also because it reveals the true character of the empire. The administration was streamlined, the provinces systematically integrated, and communication significantly improved. Rome became a network: of roads, couriers, tax offices, and military outposts. At the same time, it was a realm of abundance and stark contrasts. While hundreds of thousands in the capital enjoyed bread, games, and public baths, tribal societies still existed in other parts of the empire. And yet all were unified by the idea of being part of "Rome"—as citizens, allies, or subjects. This shared identity was cultivated through symbols, rituals, and language. Over 60,000 inscriptions from the Roman world survive to this day—a linguistic treasury attesting to Rome's pervasive presence in daily life.

Religion also occupies a central place in this book. For centuries, Roman religion was polytheistic, functional, and politically charged. Priests served as state officials, and the gods were considered partners in Rome's destiny. Yet with the spread of Christianity, this model began to crumble. What began as a provincial sect evolved into a revolutionary movement—precisely because it resisted co-optation. The persecutions under Diocletian, the dramatic reversal under Constantine, the Council of Nicaea, and finally the elevation of Christianity to the status of state religion—all of these developments profoundly altered the Roman Empire. What had once been a religiously pluralistic state became a doctrinally uniform one, marked by theological disputes, heresy trials, and the growing influence of the institutional Church.

The decline of the empire is likewise a major focus. This book does not portray it as a sudden collapse, but rather as a prolonged process of transformation. Economic crises, internal power struggles, and external threats from Goths, Huns, and Vandals all interacted in a complex interplay. The symbolic fall of Rome in 476 CE did not mark the end of Rome per se, but rather the end of a particular form of Rome. In the East, the empire persisted—under a new name, with a new capital, but still grounded in a Roman identity. The Byzantine Empire preserved many elements of Roman tradition, even as it evolved culturally, religiously, and politically.

This book does not seek to glorify Rome. It also highlights the darker aspects: slavery, colonization, the suppression of uprisings, and the brutality of the legions. But it also presents Rome's extraordinary achievements: in engineering, law, infrastructure, and statecraft. Rome was far from a perfect society—but it set standards that have endured. Its legacy is visible even today—in the design of our cities, the structure of our institutions, and the symbols of our authority. Anyone seeking to understand how Europe became what it is cannot ignore Rome.

At the same time, this book looks not only to the past, but also to the present and future—asking what Rome's legacy means today. Why do politicians, jurists, and historians still invoke Rome? Why does the splendor of antiquity captivate us, as much as its decline? Why is Latin still spoken in medicine, science, and the Church? Why do television series, films, and video games centered on Rome continue to attract vast audiences? Rome is not merely history—it is a cultural reservoir. And this book seeks to offer a key to that reservoir.

The structure of the book follows a chronological order while also addressing thematic focal points such as religion, culture, daily life, and administration. It is intended for readers who not only wish to know when particular battles were fought, but who seek to understand how a small village on the Tiber evolved into an empire that continues to shape our world to this day.

CHAPTER 1: THE ORIGINS OF ROME AND THE ROYAL PERIOD (C. 753–509 BC)

1.1 Founding Myths: Romulus and Remus, the Legend of Aeneas

The origins of Rome are deeply intertwined with mythological narratives that penetrated the collective memory of Roman culture and extended far beyond the boundaries of historical fact. These founding myths—most notably the stories of Romulus and Remus and the legend of Aeneas—fulfilled an identity-forming function for the Romans and served to link their past to divine destiny and heroic origins. Modern historians largely agree that these accounts are not to be interpreted as literal historical records. Nevertheless, they reflect certain historical realities and perceptions of their time. They mark the starting point of Rome's political, social, and cultural development and usher in the first phase of its history: the Regal Period.

Chronologically, the legend of Aeneas constitutes the earliest element in the corpus of Roman origin myths. According to the version presented in Virgil's *Aeneid*, composed between 29 and 19 BCE, Aeneas was a Trojan prince and son of Venus who, after the fall of Troy (traditionally dated to 1184 BCE), sailed westward across the Mediterranean with a group of survivors. His goal was to establish a new homeland in Latium. This narrative connects Roman history to the heroic age of the Greeks and, in particular, to Homer's *Iliad*. Through this connection, the

Romans did not perceive themselves as just another people but as the legitimate heirs of a venerable and fallen civilization.

After numerous wanderings, Aeneas eventually landed on the coast of what is now Italy. There, he encountered King Latinus, who offered him his daughter Lavinia in marriage. From this union arose a new dynasty known as the Kings of Alba Longa, who ruled the region of Latium. Alba Longa, a city located southeast of what would later become Rome, is regarded as the center of this early royal lineage, even though its historical existence remains archaeologically unconfirmed. Nevertheless, multiple ancient sources—including Livy, Plutarch, and Dionysius of Halicarnassus—report a 300-year rule by this line, beginning with Ascanius (also known as Iulus), the son of Aeneas. This dynastic lineage later assumed great symbolic significance for the Julii—the family of Gaius Julius Caesar—who claimed direct descent from Iulus.

The last king of this line was Numitor. Around the year 800 BCE, he was overthrown by his brother Amulius, who usurped power in Alba Longa. To secure his position, Amulius forced Numitor's daughter, Rhea Silvia, to become a Vestal Virgin—a priestess of Vesta who had to remain celibate. In doing so, he sought to prevent her from bearing children who might one day lay claim to the throne. According to legend, however, Rhea Silvia was impregnated by Mars, the god of war, and gave birth to twin boys: Romulus and Remus. The mythological nature of this account is evident, yet it also conveys a potent political message: the foundation of Rome was divinely ordained and guided.

Amulius ordered the infants to be abandoned in a basket on the Tiber River, but they were discovered and suckled by a she-wolf—the *lupa*—an iconic image that would be repeatedly depicted in Roman art and symbolism. The twins were then found by a shepherd named Faustulus and raised by him and his wife, Larentia. Upon reaching adolescence, Romulus and Remus learned of their true origins, confronted Amulius, and deposed him. Numitor was reinstated as king, an act often interpreted as a condemnation of illegitimate rule and a model for the rightful restoration of order.

The founding of Rome itself is traditionally dated to 753 BCE. This date was established by the scholar Varro (116–27 BCE), who developed a systematic chronology of Roman history. According to tradition, after the overthrow of Amulius, Romulus and Remus resolved to found a new city. However, they quarreled over who would be the city's founder and namesake. They sought divine guidance through *augury*, a form of divination that interpreted the number and direction of flying birds as signs from the gods. Remus allegedly saw six birds first, but Romulus later saw twelve, which was considered the clearer omen. The dispute escalated. Romulus began construction of the city on the Palatine Hill. When Remus mockingly leapt over the city wall, Romulus killed him. This motif—the fratricidal origin of the city—cast a long shadow over Roman self-perception: violence was not merely a component of Rome's expansion, but present from its very inception.

Romulus became the city's first king and established the basic framework of its society. He is said to have founded the *Asylum* —a refuge for men of no origin, including criminals, slaves, and the homeless. This measure, though mythologically framed, likely reflects a demographic reality common to many ancient cities: population growth was crucial to political strength. Due to a shortage of women, Romulus purportedly organized the "Rape of the Sabine Women"—a coordinated abduction of women from the neighboring Sabine tribe during a festival. This action sparked a war with the Sabines, which was ultimately resolved through the mediation of the abducted women themselves. The Sabines were incorporated into the new city, significantly expanding Rome's population and power base. This event points to a pragmatic political strategy: integration first through force, then through inclusion.

After Romulus's death—according to some accounts, he was taken up into the heavens during a storm—six additional kings succeeded him, shaping Rome's development as an urban society. Yet in the foundational narrative, Romulus occupies the central role: he was not only the city's eponym, but also embodied the archetype of the Roman leader—assertive, militarily capable, divinely appointed, and willing to subordinate even familial ties to the needs of the state. The construction of this figure was no accident: it provided a model for future political leaders, both as a source of legitimation and as a standard for emulation.

The story of Romulus and Remus left numerous traces in Roman culture and art. Already in the 4th century BCE, visual representations of the twins beneath the she-wolf had been created. The famous bronze statue known as the "Capitoline Wolf"—once believed to date to the 5th century BCE, but now more likely from the medieval period—testifies to the enduring symbolic power of the myth. The twins represented more than just the act of founding; they embodied dualistic opposites: order and chaos, fraternal loyalty and fratricide, divine providence and human hubris.

The connection to the Aeneas legend remained vital throughout antiquity and was particularly emphasized in contexts of political self-presentation. When Augustus came to power, he deliberately promoted the image of Aeneas to underscore the divine legitimacy of his rule. The myth was not merely transmitted, but continually reinterpreted, elaborated, and updated. Especially in times of crisis, the founding myths were invoked to promise stability and affirm a connection to a higher destiny.

During the Regal Period—from the legendary founding in 753

BCE to the transition to the Republic in 509 BCE—the legend of Romulus and Remus remained a central point of reference. It marked not only a chronological beginning but also an ideological foundation: Rome was not a product of chance but the result of divine will, heroic action, and determined leadership. This self-perception contained a political force that later enabled Rome to present itself as a world ruler—not as a usurper, but as the rightful guardian of a divinely ordained order.

From today's perspective, it is difficult to determine to what extent the founding myths are based on historical events. However, archaeological findings on the Palatine Hill show that as early as the 10th century BCE, initial settlements existed on the site. These were simple hut villages that gradually established close ties with other Latin communities. Around 750 BCE, the first urban structures can be identified, particularly in the area of the Roman Forum, which developed into a social and political center. The legendary foundation date of 753 BCE thus falls into a period of actual transformation—from pastoral village to urban settlement.

Ultimately, it is this blend of myth, symbolism, and archaeological evidence that makes the origins of Rome so compelling. The stories of Romulus and Remus, and of Aeneas, are not mere fabrications, but cultural constructs imbued with profound ideological significance. They helped the Romans understand themselves—as a chosen people, destined for power through struggle, sacrifice, and divine guidance. In these narratives, Rome laid the foundations for its political culture, religious symbolism, and conception of history as a directed process. The beginning of Rome was thus not merely a historical moment, but a foundational myth that endured through the centuries.

1.2 The Seven Kings of Rome: Power Structure and Society

The so-called regal period of Rome represents a formative era in early Roman history, which, despite the considerable uncertainty of the sources, played a central role in shaping Roman self-perception. This period spans from the legendary founding of Rome in 753 BCE to the expulsion of the last king in 509 BCE. According to Roman tradition, seven kings ruled the city during this time: Romulus, Numa Pompilius, Tullus Hostilius, Ancus Marcius, Tarquinius Priscus, Servius Tullius, and Tarquinius Superbus. Each of these figures is associated with specific stages in the political, social, religious, and military development of Rome. Whether these kings were historical individuals or symbolic representations of broader structural transformations remains a matter of scholarly debate. Regardless of their historicity, the transmitted narratives provide valuable insight into how the Romans understood their own origins and which elements they considered foundational.

The first king, Romulus, is traditionally considered the founder of Rome. He was succeeded, according to legend, around 715 BCE by Numa Pompilius, a Sabine. In contrast to his martial predecessor, Numa was portrayed as a pious legislator who established religious institutions and thus laid the sacred foundation of the city. He is credited with introducing the Roman calendar, founding various priestly colleges—such as the *pontifices* and *flamines*—and building numerous temples. Historians generally regard Numa as a symbolic representation of an era of institutionalization, a conceptual counterweight to the militaristic Romulus. It is telling that the Romans already distinguished between war and peace, between expansion and internal organization, in their portrayal of early rulers. Numa thus embodies a period of internal consolidation during which religion was used as a tool for social integration and control.

Numa was followed by Tullus Hostilius, who became king around 673 BCE. Under his reign, the martial spirit returned. His rule was marked by military conflicts with neighboring cities, particularly Alba Longa, the mythic mother city of Rome's royal line. The war with Alba Longa is most famously illustrated through the tale of the Horatii and the Curiatii—three Roman brothers who fought three brothers from Alba on behalf of their respective cities. While this narrative is likely fictional, it highlights Rome's early emphasis on warfare as a vehicle for political expansion. Tullus is said to have destroyed Alba Longa and relocated its population to Rome. This not only increased the city's population but also had institutional consequences: the Roman Senate expanded, new cults were introduced, and the integration of conquered tribes became a political strategy.

The fourth king, Ancus Marcius, is said to have begun his reign around 641 BCE. Tradition portrays him as a synthesis of Numa's piety and Tullus's militarism. He is credited with founding the port of Ostia at the Tiber estuary—a major step in Rome's economic and maritime development. He also reportedly built the *Pons Sublicius*, a wooden bridge over the Tiber, marking a significant infrastructural achievement that extended Roman influence across the river and improved connectivity. Ancus is also associated with the first integration of the Latins into the Roman polity: conquered settlements were incorporated into the Roman state, and their populations were granted limited citizenship (*civitas sine suffragio*), lacking the right to vote. This foreshadowed Rome's later expansionist policies, characterized by the incorporation rather than the destruction of conquered peoples.

With the accession of Tarquinius Priscus around 616 BCE, the so-called Etruscan phase of the Roman monarchy began. He was the first non-Latin king of Rome, likely of Etruscan origin, reflecting the city's growing interaction with the culturally advanced northern neighbors. Tarquinius Priscus is credited with introducing Etruscan techniques, religious rites, and political structures to Rome. His reign saw the construction of the *Forum Romanum* as a central public space, the initiation of the *Cloaca Maxima* (a massive drainage system), and the beginning of the Temple of Jupiter on the Capitoline Hill. These projects suggest an increasing urbanization and centralization, supported by a monarchy that had evolved beyond a tribal chieftainship into a more complex administrative apparatus. He also introduced cavalry units into the Roman army and implemented broader military reforms, indicating an expanding military capacity and increasingly complex conflicts.

The sixth king, Servius Tullius, likely began his reign around 578 BCE and is considered one of the most important reformers of early Roman history. Although his origins remain shrouded in legend—he is said to have been born in a household of slaves and called to power through divine signs—his attributed reforms had lasting significance for the Roman Republic. His most famous achievement is the Servian Constitution, which reorganized the Roman citizen body according to property classes. This military classification—based on the ability to equip oneself for war—became the foundation for political participation. Five wealth-based classes were established, forming the *comitia centuriata*, a new popular assembly. Although this did not displace the influence of the patrician elite, it marked an initial move towards broader political engagement. The physical structure of the city also evolved: the first city wall, the so-called Servian Wall, was built, reflecting a growing need for security and an expanding urban footprint. Servius is also regarded as the first king to conduct a census (*census*), an essential step toward rational governance.

The final king, Lucius Tarquinius Superbus, is said to have ruled from 534 to 509 BCE and is portrayed as the archetypal tyrant. He allegedly seized power through the murder of his father-in-law Servius and ruled without the Senate's consent. Historical narratives, especially in Livy's writings, depict him as arrogant, cruel, and autocratic—a portrayal likely crafted retrospectively to legitimize the establishment of the Republic. Nevertheless, significant public works were completed during his reign, most notably the completion of the Temple of Jupiter on the Capitoline. The decisive turning point, according to tradition, was the crime of his son, Sextus Tarquinius, who raped the noblewoman Lucretia. Her subsequent suicide provoked a revolt led by Lucius Junius Brutus, culminating in the expulsion of the Tarquins and the foundation of the Republic. Whether historically accurate or not, this narrative became the foundational myth of the Roman Republic and symbolized the end of monarchy.

The power structure of the regal period was highly personalized, yet not without checks. The king (*rex*) held military, religious, and political authority. He was supreme commander, chief priest, and chief judge. His power was not hereditary but was formally ratified by the Senate and the people—a remarkable aspect that presaged republican principles. Between reigns, the Senate—composed of the leading patrician families (*patres*)—played a significant role. Although its powers were limited, it held advisory and symbolic authority. A popular assembly, the *comitia curiata*, also existed, organizing citizens into 30 *curiae*. This body mainly performed religious functions but represents an early form of political participation.

Socially, Rome in the regal period was divided into two principal classes: the *patricians* and the *plebeians*. The patricians claimed descent from the first families that had allegedly accompanied Romulus and held exclusive rights to the Senate, priesthoods, and political power. The plebeians were commoners—artisans, farmers, and merchants—who lacked political rights. This social tension between the patriciate and the plebs would become a central issue during the Republic, but its origins lay in the monarchy.

Religiously, the era was characterized by a strong fusion of politics and cult. The king, as *pontifex maximus*, was the supreme religious authority. He offered sacrifices, consecrated temples, performed rituals, and declared festivals. The introduction of the twelve Olympian gods, the interpretation of omens (*auspicia*), and the establishment of priestly colleges and religious calendars can be traced, at least partially, to this period. These developments underscore how religion functioned as a means of legitimizing and exercising authority.

By the end of the regal period, Rome had transformed from a collection of settlements into a structured, populous city with formal institutions, a standing army, developed infrastructure, and a complex social order. The seven kings of Rome—whether historical or symbolic—represent not only a political transition in Roman memory but also a cultural maturation. Each one personified a particular phase of development: foundation, institutionalization, expansion, urbanization, integration, reform, and finally the abuse of power. For the Romans, this narrative was more than mere history; it served as a moral and political lesson. It illustrated how power could be constructed, organized, and ultimately become dangerous. The regal period thus marked not only the beginning of Roman history but also offered a reflection of Rome's political identity.

1.3 Social Order and Religion in Early Rome

The early period of Rome was not merely a phase of political and military consolidation; it was also a formative era in which foundational social structures and religious beliefs emerged—structures and beliefs that would shape the essence of Roman civilization for centuries. The social order and religious practices of the Regal Period (ca. 753–509 BCE) formed a tightly interwoven fabric grounded in ancestry, tradition, power dynamics, and the conception of a divinely sanctioned cosmos. Roman society during this time was one in which group affiliation significantly outweighed individual achievement, in which religious rituals permeated daily life, and in which belief in a divine order served not only spiritual needs but also political and ideological functions.

Roman society in its early stages was strictly hierarchical and fundamentally divided into two major classes: the *patricians* and the *plebeians*. This distinction was not merely social or economic but extended to the political and religious spheres, with far-reaching consequences for the entirety of Roman public and private life. The patricians were the descendants of the purportedly first one hundred families who had, according to tradition, founded the city alongside Romulus. These "fathers," or *patres*, composed the Senate and claimed exclusive rights to the highest political offices and religious functions. They owned land, had privileged access to the priesthood, exerted influence over political decisions, and commanded military authority. Their elevated social position was intimately linked to the concept of the *mos maiorum*—the "custom of the ancestors"—which was regarded as an inviolable guide for all actions and decisions.

The plebeians, by contrast, constituted the majority of the population. They included farmers, craftsmen, laborers, merchants, and other free citizens who lacked political and religious privileges. While not slaves, plebeians were excluded from holding office and participating in sacred rites. This exclusion was not necessarily based on wealth—some plebeians could indeed be affluent—but rather on lineage. Roman society in this era was structured according to descent, not merit. At this stage, plebeians had no institutional representation—no tribunes of the people, no popular assemblies on their behalf. Their influence was limited to personal connections with patricians, economic activity, and the opportunity to serve in the military.

A crucial mediating institution between these two groups was the system of *clientela*, or patronage. This entailed a reciprocal relationship of dependency and protection, whereby a patrician —referred to as a *patronus*—acted as protector and benefactor to one or more *clientes*, usually plebeian citizens. In return, clients owed loyalty, political support, labor, or military service. Though not codified in law, the client relationship was deeply rooted in Roman society. It granted patricians influence over the wider population while offering plebeians a form of social security. Patron-client relationships permeated all levels of Roman life and would remain a defining feature of Roman social structure into the Republican and even Imperial eras.

The institution of the *gens*, or extended family clan, was likewise of central importance. A *gens* was a large familial group that traced its origin to a common ancestor—often mythologized or deified. Within each *gens*, a rigid patriarchal order prevailed. The *pater familias* held supreme authority over his household, which included his children, wife, slaves, and even adopted members. This authority, known as *patria potestas*, theoretically extended to the power of life and death, though in practice it was tempered by societal norms. The *pater familias* represented the family publicly, performed religious rites, decided marriages and inheritances, and served as custodian of the family's ancestral cult.

These ancestral cults were not merely private eccentricities but integral components of Roman religious life. Each family honored their *lares* (household spirits), *penates* (gods of the pantry and household stores), and *manes* (spirits of the dead), to whom offerings were regularly made. These domestic deities were not symbolic abstractions but were venerated as real and protective beings who safeguarded the family's well-being. The domestic cult was a cornerstone of Roman social order: one who honored their ancestors, conformed to the divine structure, and upheld tradition was considered virtuous. This fulfillment of religious duty, known as *pietas*, was a core Roman value—not merely piety in the Christian sense, but a holistic obligation to gods, family, and state.

Beyond the sphere of private devotion, a public religion began to emerge during the Regal Period under the auspices of the state, playing a vital role in legitimizing authority, maintaining stability, and exercising power. The king served not only as political leader but also as the chief religious figure. It was his responsibility to interpret the will of the gods, perform rituals, construct temples, and regulate religious festivals. These functions were supported institutionally through the establishment of priestly offices that originated in this early era. Among the earliest priesthoods were the *flamines*, each assigned to a specific deity—such as Jupiter (*Flamen Dialis*), Mars, and Quirinus. Likewise, the *college of pontifices* was founded during this time, later including the *pontifex maximus* as the chief priest. These religious officials advised the king, managed the calendar, oversaw ritual regulations, and maintained sacred records.

Particularly significant was the office of the *Vestal Virgin*. These priestesses of the goddess Vesta tended the eternal flame in her temple. Selected from patrician families at a young age, Vestals took a vow of chastity and served for thirty years. Despite their restricted personal freedoms, they enjoyed high social status and unique legal protections. Their ritual purity was believed to safeguard the city itself; any violation of their vow was punished by brutal ritual penalties. The Vestals exemplify the

Roman connection between religion, public morality, and civic well-being—the spiritual health of the city was mirrored in their lives.

Another critical component of Roman religious practice was *divinatio*, or divination. Of particular importance were *auspicia*, the interpretation of bird flight patterns, and *haruspicium*, the reading of entrails from sacrificed animals. These methods were not dismissed as superstition but were considered integral to political decision-making. No war was declared, no office assumed, and no major construction project undertaken without prior consultation of divine will through auspices. This ritual formalism—often perplexing to outsiders—provided a structured framework for Roman life. Decisions were perceived as reflections of divine intent, and any error in ritual performance was regarded as a serious offense.

The Roman pantheon of this era reflected the polytheistic worldview of early Rome. In addition to major deities such as Jupiter, Mars, and Quirinus, there existed a multitude of lesser gods associated with specific aspects of life. Janus, for instance, god of doors and transitions, was invoked at every beginning and was closely associated with the state, symbolizing time, change, and thresholds. Saturn represented sowing and agriculture, Faunus presided over forests and animals, and Ceres governed fertility. Roman religious belief was pragmatic and functional—worship was directed toward what was perceived as beneficial. What mattered was not inner faith but the correct performance of ritual. The core principle was *do ut des*—"I give so that you may give"—a transactional concept at the heart of Roman sacrificial thought.

Public festivals and religious celebrations were not solely spiritual occasions; they were also major social events that fostered political cohesion. The *Lupercalia*, a fertility rite dedicated to Faunus, featured ritualistic races of young men through the city, while the *Saturnalia* festival temporarily reversed social roles—slaves were symbolically equal to their masters, and a spirit of generosity and relaxation prevailed. These festivals served to ease social tensions and reinforce collective identity. In a society otherwise marked by hierarchy and authoritarianism, these ritual exceptions created moments of communal integration.

The role of women in early Roman society was closely tied to family, religion, and societal expectations. Although women held no political rights, they played a central role in religious life—most prominently as Vestal Virgins. Within the household, their responsibilities centered on marriage, motherhood, and domestic management. Female virtue was idealized, especially chastity (*castitas*), fidelity (*fides*), and industriousness (*industria*). These values were not confined to private life but were also communicated through public morality. Women could exert indirect influence on society through their relationships with prominent male figures, such as husbands from leading families.

In conclusion, the social order and religious structures of early Rome were inseparably linked. The Roman worldview rested on a divinely ordained hierarchy in which every individual had a designated place—from king to slave. Religion was not a private creed but a public mechanism of order. Social roles were legitimized through religious function; political power was reinforced through ritual; and social mobility was constrained by lineage. This was a system grounded in continuity, ritual, and ancestry—one whose core features would persist throughout the Republic and into the Imperial era. Thus, the early period of Roman history was not merely the cradle of political institutions, but the bedrock of a comprehensive Roman understanding of the world.

1.4 Transition to the Republic

The transition from the Roman monarchy to the Republic represents one of the most pivotal turning points in Roman history—a moment of profound political transformation that not only produced a new form of government but also laid the long-term foundations of Rome's self-conception: liberty (*libertas*), the rule of law (*ius*), and the rejection of autocracy. While the regal period, spanning from 753 to 509 BCE, gradually developed into a more complex, urban-centered power structure, a series of political and societal tensions ultimately led to the downfall of the monarchy and the emergence of the Roman Republic. The causes of this transition cannot be traced to a single event but rather constitute a chain of developments and crises that culminated in the symbolic expulsion of the last king, Lucius Tarquinius Superbus. The repercussions of this change extended far beyond the 6th century BCE and continue to shape our understanding of Roman politics and culture.

The final decades of the monarchy—particularly under the rule of the seventh and last king, Tarquinius Superbus (r. 534–509 BCE)—were marked by an increasing centralization of power, the erosion of traditional political institutions, and an authoritarian mode of governance. Tarquinius' rise to power was itself characterized by violence: he orchestrated the assassination of his predecessor and father-in-law, Servius Tullius, to usurp the throne. In doing so, he disregarded the established procedure for royal succession, which required at least the formal approval of the *comitia curiata* (the Curiate Assembly) and the Senate. This illegitimate seizure of power already constituted a fundamental breach of constitutional norms.

In the years that followed, Tarquinius governed without consulting the Senate or acknowledging the authority of the Roman people. He appointed judges without popular ratification, ignored religious auspices in political decision-making, and surrounded himself with a personal bodyguard. Roman sources portray him as a typical "tyrant"—arrogant, cruel, ambitious, and disrespectful of religious and social order. Livy, in particular, characterizes his reign as one of arbitrariness and fear. Although these portrayals are often heavily moralized in retrospect, they point to genuine societal tensions: growing dissatisfaction among the aristocratic elites with monarchical autocracy, increasing marginalization of traditional political bodies, and the erosion of patrician autonomy.

A key element of Tarquinius' political strategy was his ambitious building and infrastructure policy—most notably, the completion of the Temple of Jupiter Optimus Maximus on the Capitoline Hill, a prestige project designed to underscore both his personal authority and the divine legitimacy of his rule. To finance these undertakings, he is said to have imposed heavy levies and conscripted labor from the population. His foreign policy was similarly aggressive: he waged campaigns against the Latins and Etruscans, including the important city of Gabii, which he subjugated through deceit. He allegedly sent his son Sextus Tarquinius to infiltrate Gabii, gain the citizens' trust, and eventually deliver the city into his father's hands.

The decisive rupture occurred in 509 BCE, when a personal crime acquired political explosiveness: the rape of Lucretia by Sextus Tarquinius. Lucretia, the wife of the patrician Lucius Tarquinius Collatinus, was threatened and assaulted by Sextus. In despair, she disclosed the violation to her husband and to his friend Lucius Junius Brutus. To preserve her honor, she subsequently took her own life. This tragic act was not perceived merely as a private tragedy but as a symbol of the moral corruption inherent in monarchy. Lucretia's death became a rallying cry: Brutus, previously considered a relatively obscure aristocrat, now stepped into the political spotlight as a leader.

Under his leadership, an uprising against the Tarquins took shape. The populace—especially the patrician families—rose in open defiance of the king. Brutus convened a public assembly, which declared the monarchy abolished and the Tarquins exiled. The Senate, itself increasingly marginalized by Tarquinius' rule, supported this decision. Thus, in 509 BCE, the Roman monarchy came to an end—not through a spontaneous popular revolution but via a carefully orchestrated initiative by the aristocratic elite seeking to reclaim their political rights.

Following the expulsion of the king, a new form of government was established: the *Res publica*, literally "the public matter." Authority was no longer vested in a single ruler but in annually elected magistrates—primarily the consuls—and in advisory institutions such as the Senate. The first consuls were Lucius Junius Brutus and Lucius Tarquinius Collatinus, Lucretia's widower. However, due to the lingering association of his family with the detested royal house, Collatinus was forced to resign within the same year. He was replaced by Publius Valerius Publicola, who emerged as a key architect of the new republican order.

The constitution of the nascent Republic was shaped by several fundamental principles that directly responded to the experience of monarchy. First was the principle of annual tenure: no magistrate was to hold office for more than one year, thereby preventing the accumulation of long-term personal power. Second was the principle of collegiality: all major offices were held by at least two individuals, who could veto each other's decisions (*intercessio*) and thus act as mutual checks. The consuls, as the highest magistrates, were required to consult each other and agree on significant matters. Third, accountability to the people was essential: after leaving office, magistrates could be held legally responsible for their actions.

Nonetheless, the new system had its limitations. Although monarchy was abolished, power remained concentrated in the hands of the patricians—the hereditary aristocratic class. The *plebeians*, the majority of free Roman citizens, were largely excluded from meaningful political participation. This imbalance soon gave rise to internal tensions that would test the resilience of the fledgling Republic.

As early as 509 BCE, Tarquinius Superbus attempted to reclaim the throne with the support of Lars Porsenna, the Etruscan king of Clusium. The attack on Rome was ultimately repelled—most famously through the legendary actions of Horatius Cocles, who defended a bridge against enemy forces, buying time for the Romans to destroy the Pons Sublicius and secure the city. Other mythical figures, such as Gaius Mucius Scaevola—who burned his own hand after a failed assassination attempt on Porsenna—became part of the emerging republican mythology. These tales symbolized the young Republic's self-image of heroic sacrifice and resistance to tyranny.

Tarquinius Superbus continued his efforts to regain power through alliances with the cities of Veii and Tarquinii. Rome responded with military campaigns between 507 and 504 BCE. Only after the decisive defeat of Tarquin's forces at the Battle of Lake Regillus—probably around 496 BCE—did the ex-king's hopes of restoration come to an end. Roman tradition held that the Dioscuri, Castor and Pollux, appeared during the battle in support of the Republic. As a result, they were venerated as protectors of Rome, and a temple dedicated to them was erected in the Forum Romanum, consecrated in 484 BCE.

The consequences of the transition to the Republic were profound—institutionally, socially, and ideologically. On the one hand, monarchy was rejected as a form of government and became synonymous with tyranny in Roman political thought. The title *rex* became politically taboo—even powerful later figures such as Caesar and Augustus avoided the term and sought alternative legitimations. On the other hand, a new political culture emerged, based on law, consensus, and participation—albeit initially restricted to the patricians. The religious system adapted as well: the king's former role as chief priest was transferred to the *pontifex maximus*, now an elected position that played a central role in the state cult.

Furthermore, the transition to the Republic marked the beginning of a new political dynamic: the struggle between patricians and plebeians. Already in 494 BCE, the first major social conflict erupted when the plebeians seceded to the Mons Sacer in protest, demanding political equality—a pivotal event that led to the establishment of the tribunes of the plebs. These conflicts would not have occurred without the structural exclusion embedded in the early Republic, and they illustrate that the events of 509 BCE did not end power politics, but merely shifted its level and form.

In conclusion, the transition from monarchy to republic was not a spontaneous uprising by the masses, but rather a reconfiguration of power within Rome's ruling elite—triggered by a combination of dynastic overreach, institutional erosion, and a moral scandal that galvanized the aristocracy. In the decades following 509 BCE, the Republic gradually stabilized, continually invoking its foundational myths: the protection of *libertas*, the avoidance of tyranny, and the subordination of power to collective institutions. These ideals would accompany Rome throughout its republican history—sometimes as genuine principles, sometimes as rhetorical tools, and sometimes as political façades. Yet their origin lay in the dramatic and conflict-ridden events of a single symbolic year: 509 BCE, the birth year of the Roman Republic.

1.5 Archaeological Evidence and the Historical Reality of Early Rome

The early history of Rome, particularly the period from the 10th to the 6th century BCE, is not solely preserved through literary sources, but also substantially corroborated by a wide range of archaeological discoveries that have been systematically investigated and evaluated over the past 150 years. These archaeological findings serve as a crucial counterbalance to the heavily mythologized narratives presented by Roman historians such as Livy and Dionysius of Halicarnassus. While these literary sources were predominantly composed centuries after the purported events and are imbued with ideological motivations, archaeological traces offer a more immediate and tangible window into the material reality of Rome's formative centuries. They portray a gradual evolution from scattered small settlements on the hills that would later form the city of Rome into a centralized urban entity. The evidence reflects emerging social structures, economic transformations, religious practices, and the overall transition from a pastoral village to a royal city with urban characteristics.

The earliest traces of settlement on the territory of what would become Rome date back to the 10th century BCE—thus predating the legendary founding by Romulus in 753 BCE by several centuries. Excavations on the Palatine Hill, traditionally considered the site of Rome's foundation, have revealed posthole remains of early dwellings from this period. These houses were constructed of wood and clay, erected on stone foundations, and typically had oval floor plans—a form also observed in other early Latin settlements such as Lavinium and Alba Longa. These findings indicate that the first inhabitants of Rome were sedentary agriculturalists engaged in farming, animal husbandry, and basic handicrafts. Though simple, these dwellings were functional and laid the groundwork for the later topography of the city.

Particularly noteworthy are the discoveries of burial grounds dating from the 9th and 8th centuries BCE in the area of the Roman Forum and on the Esquiline Hill. These graves contain urns—sometimes biconical in shape—alongside grave goods such as weapons, fibulae, ceramics, and modest items of personal adornment. A striking feature is the coexistence of cremation and inhumation practices, suggesting diversity in social or cultural customs among Rome's early inhabitants. Certain grave goods point to emerging social stratification: while many tombs contain only modest objects, others—such as bronze belt plaques or swords—indicate the presence of a nascent social elite. This differentiation marked the initial steps toward the formation of an aristocratic upper class, later institutionalized in the patriciate.

One of the most significant locations for understanding the early phases of Rome is the Roman Forum, the oldest center of civic life. Originally a marshy valley between the Palatine, Capitoline, and Esquiline Hills, archaeological evidence demonstrates that this area underwent systematic drainage during the 7th century BCE. This was accomplished through the construction of a network of drainage canals, the most prominent of which was the so-called *Cloaca Maxima*. Initially an open channel, later covered, this drainage system represents one of the earliest and most impressive feats of engineering from early Rome. Its construction was no ad hoc solution but part of a deliberate urban planning strategy, suggesting that by the 7th century BCE, Rome possessed the political and organizational structures necessary to undertake large-scale infrastructure projects. The reclamation of the Forum marked a significant act of urban transformation—turning a no-man's-land into the political and economic heart of the city.

The redevelopment of the Forum was accompanied by the construction of public buildings, the remains of which have been archaeologically confirmed. Among these is the so-called *Regia*, a complex believed to have functioned either as a royal residence or as a cultic-administrative center. It was constructed no later than the 7th century BCE and was closely associated with the religious offices of the *rex sacrorum* and, later, the *pontifex maximus*. The *Regia* was remodeled several times and remained a central location of religious administration well into the Imperial period. Likewise, the *House of the Vestal Virgins*, situated near the *Regia*, has foundations dating back to the regal era. These structures provide clear evidence that the regal period was not a phase of primitive tribal governance but rather an era of organized urban development.

Another vital piece of evidence for early urbanization is the discovery of the so-called *Servian Wall*, named after King Servius Tullius, although its final construction phase likely dates to the 4th century BCE. Archaeological findings indicate that defensive walls already existed in the 6th century BCE. Remains of such walls have been uncovered on various hills, including the Palatine, Esquiline, and Quirinal. Built from large tuff stone blocks, these walls were fitted together with remarkable precision and without the use of mortar—a technique indicative of Etruscan influence. The construction of such fortifications required not only technical expertise but also considerable labor, suggesting centralized coordination and resource mobilization.

The increasing urban character of Rome during the regal period is further illustrated by the emergence of public spaces and sanctuaries, such as the *Lapis Niger* shrine located within the Forum. This enigmatic site consists of a black-paved area bearing one of the earliest known Latin inscriptions, dated to the 6th century BCE. Though the inscription is fragmentary, it is thought to be a religious or political decree—possibly a legal prohibition or sacred warning. This site underscores the early intertwining of religious and civic life, a feature that would later become foundational to both the Roman Republic and the development of Roman law.

Additional evidence for early religious practices is found in other architectural remnants. One of the most prominent examples is the Temple of Jupiter Optimus Maximus on the Capitoline Hill, traditionally attributed to the reigns of Tarquinius Priscus or Tarquinius Superbus and consecrated in 509 BCE. Although the structure was repeatedly rebuilt over the centuries, excavations have revealed tuff stone foundations indicative of a grand-scale construction project with strong Etruscan influence. The temple was *tripartite*—with three cellae dedicated to Jupiter, Juno, and Minerva—reflecting a layout typical of Etruscan temple architecture and providing further evidence of Rome's cultural interconnection with its northern neighbors.

Indeed, Etruscan influence is one of the most prominent aspects of Rome's archaeological record from this era. Contrary to later Roman literary traditions that emphasized distance from Etruscan heritage, archaeological data clearly show that Rome maintained close contact with northern Etruscan cities such as Veii, Tarquinia, and Clusium during the 7th and 6th centuries BCE. Etruscan funerary architecture, metalwork, artistic motifs, and religious symbols have been definitively identified in Rome. Particularly in the Esquiline necropoleis, higher-status tombs contain Etruscan-influenced objects—such as painted ceramics, bronze mirrors, and weapons—suggesting a cultural elite that distinguished itself from the general population through imported goods and stylistic preferences.

Developments in ceramic production further reflect growing urbanization and specialization. In the earliest layers, archaeologists have found simple hand-molded vessels with smoothed surfaces—known as *impasto* pottery. From the 7th century BCE onward, however, wheel-thrown ceramics and imported wares from Etruria and Greece became more common. The presence of Attic black-figure pottery in the Forum and in tombs is a clear indication of long-distance trade networks. These imports were not merely luxury items but evidence of a Roman elite actively participating in a broader Mediterranean cultural and political milieu.

From an economic perspective, archaeological data reveal increasing specialization and division of labor. Evidence for early workshops—devoted to metalwork, leather production, or pottery—has been found in various parts of the city. Slag deposits and casting molds suggest the local production of tools and weapons. Agricultural implements such as plowshares, sickle blades, and grain mills have also been uncovered, pointing to a predominantly agrarian economy that was nevertheless becoming increasingly professionalized.

Early street systems also merit particular attention. The paving of main thoroughfares within the city, the construction of embankments and terraces, and the building of bridges—such as the *Pons Sublicius* across the Tiber—demonstrate that Rome already functioned as a coordinated organism during the regal era. These infrastructural undertakings were not haphazard developments but the result of centralized planning and governance, characteristic of an urban society with organized rule.

Archaeological finds also confirm a rising militarization during the latter half of the 6th century BCE. The abundance of weaponry—swords, spearheads, shields—as well as depictions of armed warriors on ceramic fragments, underscores the prominence of military elites. Funerary rites involving weaponry indicate that martial roles and social status were closely intertwined. This development is directly connected to the emergence of an early state elite, which derived power not only from landownership and political influence but also from control over military force—forming the nucleus of the later Roman aristocracy.

In sum, the archaeological record demonstrates that early Rome was not an isolated mythical foundation but part of a larger network of Latin, Etruscan, and Greek influences. The city's development from a cluster of villages into a complex urban center was a centuries-long process marked by cultural exchange, social differentiation, and growing political centralization. Rather than fundamentally contradicting literary accounts, the archaeological evidence complements and corrects them, offering a vivid and nuanced picture of historical reality. Rome, in its earliest phases, emerged from a matrix of diverse influences, developed dynamically, and acquired a distinct urban identity well before the advent of the Republic. This reality was far more intricate, layered, and non-linear than later Roman historians would have us believe—but no less fascinating for its complexity.

CHAPTER 2: THE ROMAN REPUBLIC – RISE TO POWER (509–264 BC)

2.1 The Constitution of the Republic: Consuls, Senate, and Tribunes of the Plebs

Following the overthrow of the last Etruscan king, Tarquinius Superbus, in 509 BCE, a new era commenced in Rome—the era of the Republic. The term *res publica* referred to the "public affair" or "commonwealth," symbolizing the collective responsibility of the Roman people. While Rome formally adopted the republican system, political power initially remained concentrated in the hands of a few aristocratic families. Nevertheless, this transition marked the beginning of a complex and unique political order, one that evolved continuously over the following two and a half centuries in response to both internal and external challenges. It laid the institutional foundations for Rome's eventual transformation into the dominant power of the Mediterranean world. At the core of this new system were three key institutions: the consuls, the Senate, and the representatives of the people—most notably, the *tribuni plebis* or tribunes of the plebs.

Unlike modern constitutions, the Roman Republican constitution was not codified in a single document. Rather, it was an organic framework rooted in tradition, customary law, religious norms, and political consensus. It reflected a profound distrust of the concentration of power in a single individual—a direct reaction to the perceived tyranny of the monarchy. Accordingly, the supreme executive authority, once monopolized by the king, was now distributed between two annually elected consuls, who held equal power and could veto each other's actions (a principle known as *collegiality*). This office was instituted in the very year of the monarchy's fall, 509 BCE, when Lucius Junius Brutus and Lucius Tarquinius Collatinus became the first consuls. The latter, however, resigned within the same year due to his familial ties to the ousted royal house, illustrating the young Republic's hypersensitivity to any associations with autocracy.

The consuls possessed extensive civil and military powers. In times of peace, they presided over the Senate and the citizen assemblies, administered the state's affairs, and held the highest judicial authority. In times of war—frequent during Rome's early expansion—they commanded the Roman army, a role that greatly enhanced their prestige and influence. Their imperium, the authority to issue commands, was constrained by both the one-year term limit and the requirement of collegial decision-making. No consul could act unilaterally.

The Senate, originally an advisory council composed of former magistrates and members of the patrician elite, became a central institution despite its formal lack of legislative power. During the monarchy, the Senate had advised the king; now it emerged as a permanent, influential body within the Republic. Typically consisting of around 300 members, the Senate was appointed either by the sitting consuls or, from the fourth century BCE onward, by the censors. Membership was generally for life. Though the Senate could not pass laws, its resolutions (*senatus consulta*) carried significant weight, especially in matters of foreign policy, finance, and military campaigns. The Senate supervised state expenditures, allocated funds for military campaigns, and managed the provinces once Rome began to annex territories outside Italy.

In the early Republic, political power was tightly held by the *patricians*—a narrow class of aristocratic families who claimed lineage dating back to the city's foundation. This exclusivity generated growing discontent among the *plebeians*, the broader class of Roman citizens who were excluded from high office despite their civic duties. This tension culminated in 494 BCE in the *first secession of the plebs* (*secessio plebis*), a mass withdrawal in which the plebeians retreated to the Mons Sacer (Sacred Mount) outside the city. The ruling elite, fearing a collapse of civic order, conceded to plebeian demands, resulting in the creation of a new office: the *tribune of the plebs* (*tribunus plebis*).

The tribunes were magistrates of exceptional status. Elected exclusively by plebeians and drawn only from their ranks, they wielded the *ius intercessionis*, the right to intercede and veto the actions of other magistrates if deemed harmful to the people's interests. Furthermore, they were deemed *sacrosanct*, meaning that any act of violence against them was considered a religious offense. The office rapidly became a critical mechanism for safeguarding plebeian rights and served as an institutional counterweight to patrician dominance. It provided a channel for political participation and served as a balancing force within the republican system, curbing aristocratic overreach without undermining the state's foundational order.

This development initiated a long period of social and constitutional reform during the 5th and 4th centuries BCE. In 451–450 BCE, responding to plebeian pressure, the Roman state issued the *Law of the Twelve Tables* (*Lex Duodecim Tabularum*), the first codification of Roman law. These laws, publicly displayed on bronze tablets, formed the bedrock of Roman legal culture and enshrined the principle of legal transparency and, to a limited extent, equality under the law. Although they did not dismantle the existing social hierarchy, they represented a significant move toward rule of law.

Despite such reforms, the conflict between patricians and plebeians persisted for decades. A second secession occurred in 449 BCE in response to the abuses of the *decemviri* (ten-man commission), who had been entrusted with compiling the Twelve Tables but exceeded their mandate. It was not until the *Lex Licinia Sextia* of 367 BCE that plebeians gained access to the consulship. Gaius Licinius Stolo became one of the first plebeian consuls, marking a major milestone in the political emancipation of the non-aristocratic citizenry and permanently altering the composition of Rome's ruling class.

Further reforms opened additional offices to plebeians. These included the praetorship, responsible for judicial matters, and the censorship, which conducted the census and appointed senators. By the early 3rd century BCE, the legal distinction between patricians and plebeians had largely faded, though a new elite, the *nobiles*—families who had achieved high office—now dominated Roman politics.

Another key element of the Republican constitution was the system of citizen assemblies, or *comitia*. These assemblies enabled Roman citizens to pass laws, elect magistrates, and rule on legal cases. Several types of assemblies existed. The *Comitia Centuriata* was organized along military lines and primarily responsible for electing senior magistrates. Its structure favored wealthier citizens, who were overrepresented in the voting groups (*centuriae*). In contrast, the *Comitia Tributa* and the *Concilium Plebis* offered greater influence to the common citizen. Over time, especially after the *Lex Hortensia* of 287 BCE, which made plebiscites (resolutions passed by the plebeian assembly) binding for the entire Roman populace, these institutions gained in legislative significance.

The political functioning of the Republic was characterized by a sophisticated system of checks and balances, term limits, and accountability. Magistrates were held responsible for their actions after leaving office and could be prosecuted for misconduct. Most offices were held for only one year, ensuring regular turnover and, at least in theory, promoting political mobility. In practice, however, a small elite monopolized the highest offices, though the system remained resilient and adaptable. In times of crisis, the Republic could appoint a dictator with near-absolute authority for a maximum of six months. This temporary role was designed to allow rapid, decisive action in emergencies such as war or civil unrest. A paradigmatic example was Cincinnatus, who in 458 BCE was appointed dictator, swiftly defeated the Aequi, and then voluntarily relinquished power to return to his farm—a lasting symbol of republican virtue.

Religion was inextricably intertwined with Roman politics. Many magistrates held religious roles as augurs or pontifices and were responsible for securing divine approval for political decisions. Virtually every phase of public decision-making was accompanied by religious rites, such as interpreting the flight of birds before assemblies or consulting the Sibylline Books during crises. The integration of religious observance into civic life reinforced the legitimacy of the Republican order and instilled a sense of divine sanction in political institutions.

The cultural impact of these institutions was profound. The republican ethos—marked by the belief that power should be shared, limited, and serve the common good—shaped Roman political thought for centuries. It manifested in Rome's value system: virtues such as *virtus* (valor), *pietas* (duty), *fides* (reliability), and *gravitas* (seriousness) became standards for public behavior. Oratory, legal expertise, and military service were considered essential qualifications for public life. These ideals were cultivated in the education of the Roman elite and gave rise to a political culture grounded in competition, prestige, and public visibility.

By 264 BCE—the conventional endpoint of this formative period—Rome had developed into a sophisticated republic, internally stable and externally assertive. Its constitutional framework was not static but evolved dynamically in response to changing needs and challenges. This structure laid the groundwork for Rome's ascent to imperial power, a trajectory soon to be realized in the Punic Wars against Carthage. Yet this later expansion was only made possible by the political innovations, institutional mechanisms, and social compromises forged during the early Republic, from 509 to 264 BCE.

2.2 The Struggle of the Orders: Patricians versus Plebeians

The so-called *"Struggle of the Orders"* (*Conflictus ordinum*) constituted one of the most central domestic political issues in the early Roman Republic. This was not a brief or isolated conflict, but rather a centuries-long, often bitter process of social and political negotiation between the patricians—an aristocratic elite of large landowners—and the plebeians, the broad mass of Roman citizens who were economically, legally, and politically disadvantaged. The confrontation began shortly after the expulsion of the kings in 509 BCE and, with intermittent phases of intensity, persisted until the end of the 3rd century BCE. A provisional legal resolution was only achieved with the passage of the *Lex Hortensia* in 287 BCE, although significant social inequalities continued to exist in practice.

The roots of the conflict lay in the profoundly imbalanced distribution of power. After the foundation of the Republic, all higher offices—most notably the consulship—remained exclusively reserved for patricians. Plebeians had no legal access to political decision-making, despite forming the majority of Rome's urban population and, more crucially, its military force. Furthermore, many plebeians suffered under severe economic pressure: small farmers often accrued debt during prolonged military campaigns, lost their land, and were driven into *nexum* —a form of debt bondage that exposed them to the authority of their creditors, who were frequently wealthy patricians.

In 494 BCE, the first organized plebeian revolt occurred—the *first secessio plebis*. The plebeian citizenry withdrew to the *Mons Sacer* ("Sacred Mount"), refused to perform military service, and threatened to found an independent city. Given Rome's external military threats and its reliance on plebeian manpower, the patrician leadership was compelled to make concessions. This led to the creation of the office of the *Tribunes of the Plebs* (*tribuni plebis*)—the first institutional response to the underlying social tensions. Initially two in number, these tribunes were granted the right to veto political decisions and to protect citizens from the arbitrariness of patrician magistrates. This office was later expanded to include ten tribunes.

However, these concessions did not resolve the underlying tensions. New crises repeatedly erupted, particularly around the issues of debt slavery and the absence of a codified legal framework. In 450 BCE, this led to the establishment of the *Decemvirate*, a ten-man commission tasked with drafting a written legal code. The result was the *Twelve Tables* (*duodecim tabulae*), which were publicly displayed in the Roman Forum. These laws addressed fundamental civil matters—from property rights to procedural regulations—and are considered the first codification of Roman law. While they did not achieve legal equality, they enabled plebeians to invoke known, written standards for the first time, thus significantly curtailing patrician arbitrariness.

Between 449 and 367 BCE, tensions remained high. Although

the Decemvirate collapsed due to its own abuse of power—most notoriously in the case of Appius Claudius and Verginia—political participation continued to be a contested domain. Repeated legislative initiatives sought to grant plebeians access to higher offices. A major turning point came in 367 BCE with the passage of the *Leges Liciniae Sextiae*, named after the tribunes Gaius Licinius Stolo and Lucius Sextius Lateranus. These laws stipulated, among other provisions, that one of the two consuls must henceforth be a plebeian, and attempted to reform land ownership by limiting private use of public land (*ager publicus*) to 500 *iugera*. The enforcement of these laws took several years and met with fierce resistance from the patrician elite—sometimes even involving violence. Nevertheless, in 366 BCE, Lucius Sextius Lateranus became the first plebeian to be elected consul—a landmark in the struggle of the orders.

Despite these advancements, the battle was far from over. For most plebeians, access to public office remained practically unattainable due to financial limitations, the lack of elite social networks, and educational barriers. The patricians continued to dominate key religious and political positions, such as the *Pontifex Maximus* (Chief Priest). Only in 300 BCE, through the *Lex Ogulnia*, were plebeians legally permitted to hold priestly offices. Likewise, the prestigious office of *Censor*—responsible for the census, citizen classification, and moral oversight—was opened to plebeians only in 339 BCE through the *Lex Publilia*.

Another central issue was legislative authority. For a long time, resolutions passed by the *Concilium Plebis* (Plebeian Assembly) were only binding upon plebeians. The *Lex Publilia Philonis* of 339 BCE marked progress by declaring that plebiscites could become binding for all citizens—though only with subsequent ratification by the Senate (*auctoritas patrum*). This condition effectively preserved a patrician veto. It was not until the enactment of the *Lex Hortensia* in 287 BCE—named after the dictator Quintus Hortensius—that this dependency was fully abolished. From that point on, plebiscites carried the same legal weight as laws passed by the *comitia centuriata* (Centuriate Assembly).

The third *secessio plebis* of 287 BCE is especially significant in this context. Once again, the plebeians withdrew—this time to the *Janiculum Hill*—to protest economic hardship, mounting debt, and continued political exclusion. Under pressure from the looming threat of civil war, the Roman leadership accepted the *Lex Hortensia*, thereby formally establishing legislative parity between the orders.

Nevertheless, legal equality did not automatically lead to equitable power distribution. Rather, a new elite emerged—the *nobilitas*—a social stratum composed of wealthy plebeian families that had allied themselves with patrician lineages. This new ruling class came to dominate both the Senate and the *cursus honorum* (the sequence of public offices). Thus, while access to power remained largely restricted, the rigid structure of the old order had been legally dismantled.

Beyond the legal and political dimensions, the Struggle of the Orders also had a pronounced cultural dimension. Plebeians increasingly developed a distinct political identity, which manifested in architectural patronage (e.g., temples dedicated to plebeian deities such as Ceres, Liber, and Libera on the Aventine Hill), in funerary rituals, unique festivals, and a growing infrastructure of political self-organization. The creation of the plebeian aedileship in 494 BCE, initially limited to the supervision of plebeian temples and religious festivals, later became a stepping stone within the political career ladder.

Another important aspect of the conflict concerned military service. Since the Roman army was composed of citizen-soldiers, the *suffragium* (voting right) also carried military implications. The centuriate organization, which classified citizens according to wealth, disadvantaged plebeians politically, despite their numerical dominance in the army. This structural inequality reinforced demands for political equity over the course of several decades.

In summary, the Struggle of the Orders cannot be reduced to a linear sequence of reforms. Rather, it was characterized by recurring crises, tactical alliances, threats of violence, economic hardship, and political innovation. Over the long term, the conflict not only led to a gradual opening of the Roman political system, but also to the development of institutional checks and balances that would underpin the stability of the Republic for centuries. The Roman Republic was not born from consensus, but was forged through constant struggle. This struggle—however intense and at times brutal—ultimately yielded a political system whose complexity and adaptability were unparalleled in the ancient world.

2.3 Expansion in Italy: The Allied System and Integration

Between 509 and 264 BCE, Rome transformed from a locally confined city-state into a territorial power controlling vast areas of central and southern Italy. At the heart of this transformation was not solely military superiority, but rather a highly developed form of political control: the so-called system of alliances (*foedus systema*), which converted conquest into a stable, long-term network of dominion. Rome consciously avoided integrating conquered territories into a uniform administrative structure. Instead, it developed a flexible, tiered system of alliances that allowed for local autonomy while securing political loyalty and centralized access to military resources.

This system was based on bilateral treaties with individual cities or tribal entities. These *foedera* set forth specific terms for each community's relationship with Rome. Unlike the provinces in the later empire, these allies retained self-governance: they regulated their internal affairs largely independently, retained their own legal systems, and elected their own officials. In return, Rome primarily demanded military support. This obligation to provide troops was no mere formality but a structural cornerstone of Rome's military strategy: by the 3rd century BCE, approximately two-thirds of the Roman army consisted of allied contingents.

The military benefits of this system were further reinforced through a graduated hierarchy of citizenship rights. Broadly speaking, three categories can be distinguished: Roman citizens with full rights (*cives optimo iure*), Latins with limited rights (*ius Latii*), and *socii*, the actual allies, who were generally denied Roman citizenship. This stratified participation was no accident—it was a deliberate mechanism of control. It prevented the multitude of subjected communities from acting uniformly against Roman authority. Each partner operated under different terms and thus had individual incentives to remain part of the system—or at least not to rebel against it.

A striking example of the consistent application of this strategy emerged after the Second Samnite War (326–304 BCE). The Samnites, a formidable and resilient people of the Apennines, had inflicted serious defeats upon Rome—most notably in the Caudine Forks in 321 BCE, where a Roman army was humiliated into surrender. Yet after the eventual subjugation of the Samnites, Rome did not impose a provincial administration. Instead, the region was integrated via a web of treaties, military roads—such as the Via Appia—and strategically placed colonies.

These colonies were not merely loose settlements but key instruments of Roman control. A distinction was made between *coloniae civium Romanorum* and *coloniae Latinae*. The former were founded by Roman citizens who retained full civic rights and were typically smaller and situated along the coast. The latter, although larger and often located inland, did not confer Roman citizenship but instead granted Latin rights, including privileges such as commercial and matrimonial rights with Romans. These Latin colonies were instrumental in controlling trade routes, border regions, and rebellious tribes. The founding of the colony of Venusia in 291 BCE following the Third Samnite War serves as a paradigmatic case: with over 20,000 settlers, it became the largest Latin colony of its time—clear evidence that Rome was prepared to enforce territorial control through demographic structuring.

Particularly noteworthy were cities granted Roman citizenship without the right to vote—so-called *civitas sine suffragio.* This legal status, prevalent especially in formerly hostile central Italian regions such as Capua after 338 BCE, created a legal intermediary class. These cities, like other allies, were required to contribute troops and retained their administrative autonomy but had no political influence in Rome. This was a sophisticated mechanism to enforce loyalty without granting political participation—and thus to prevent resistance over the long term.

Roman strategy also skillfully exploited existing hostilities and rivalries among the Italic peoples. Rather than fostering a unified identity among its allies, Rome capitalized on regional differences. In Etruria, for instance—where cities such as Veii, Caere, and Tarquinia had rivaled one another for centuries—Rome used selective treaties to prevent political unification. The destruction of Veii in 396 BCE by Marcus Furius Camillus was not only a military milestone but also marked the beginning of more direct Roman intervention in Etruscan politics. Meanwhile, other cities such as Caere were treated relatively favorably, receiving *hospitium publicum* (official guest-rights), which implied privileged status without the granting of citizenship and without punitive military action.

In southern Italy, where Rome encountered the Greek *poleis* and powerful tribes such as the Lucanians and Bruttians, the adaptability of the allied system was again evident. The Greeks in cities such as Neapolis, Tarentum, and Thurii maintained distinct languages and cultural traditions. Rome largely accepted these communal peculiarities, provided that military loyalty was assured. Neapolis, for example, was incorporated into the Roman system as an ally after 327 BCE but was allowed to preserve its Greek administrative structures and language. This cultural tolerance was not a sign of weakness but a calculated element of Roman integration policy: autonomy as a reward for cooperation.

By 264 BCE, Rome had constructed a deliberately maintained administrative heterogeneity. There was no unified system of governance. Instead, Rome exercised control over its Italian allies through a mosaic of differentiated relationships—each individually negotiated, each premised on loyalty, military obligations, and adherence to alliance terms. This lack of uniformity made it difficult for subject cities to coalesce into a unified resistance movement and allowed Rome to respond flexibly to local circumstances.

An often-overlooked but vital element of this system was infrastructure, particularly the construction of roads. Beginning in 312 BCE under the censor Appius Claudius Caecus, the Via Appia connected Rome with Capua, later extending to Beneventum and Tarentum. This land-based military and commercial artery was more than just a logistical asset—it symbolized the structural integration of Italian cities into Rome's sphere of influence. It facilitated troop movements, boosted trade and communication, and served as a constant physical reminder of Roman dominance.

The allied system was also ideologically and religiously underpinned. Shared festivals such as the *Feriae Latinae*, during which all Latin cities gathered on the Alban Mount, had both cultic and political significance. They reinforced the sense of a common order under Roman supremacy. The founding of new temples, such as that of Jupiter Latiaris, combined religious identity with political structure. Many newly founded colonies included central sanctuaries or replicated Roman temple architecture—a subtle form of cultural homogenization through religious symbolism.

Despite its many advantages, the system remained fragile. It was founded on control, not equality. The fact that allies were obligated to serve in the military for decades without receiving political representation created underlying tensions. That these tensions erupted in the Social War (*bellum sociale*) in 91 BCE demonstrates that the system ultimately could not resolve all of its inherent contradictions. Nevertheless, during the period up to 264 BCE, it functioned remarkably well: Roman expansion was secured not by the permanent stationing of troops, but through institutional cooperation—a model far ahead of its time.

2.4 Internal Political Tensions and the Beginning of Foreign Ambitions

Between 509 and 264 BCE, Rome developed not only militarily and territorially but also evolved into a politically stable republic, increasingly capable of channeling its internal tensions productively and cushioning them through institutional mechanisms. However, this period was by no means characterized by harmonious development; rather, it was marked by constant confrontation between the interests of the plebeian population, the socio-political elite, and the necessity to adapt internal structures to meet both growing external threats and Rome's own emerging ambitions. The result was a complex interplay of social conflict, legal reform, and the first tentative steps toward an active foreign policy.

The internal tensions of this period stemmed primarily from the social inequality between patricians and plebeians. The plebeians constituted the majority of Rome's population and, in particular, the core of the smallholding soldier-farmers who served as infantrymen in Rome's frequent military campaigns. Despite their vital contributions, they initially remained politically disenfranchised. The patrician elite monopolized all major offices, controlled the Senate, and—owing to their economic dominance—formed the principal creditor class. This situation led to severe social crises, especially during wartime, when many plebeians were forced to neglect their farms during military service and fell into debt bondage.

This structural injustice gave rise to repeated social tensions. One of the earliest manifest crises was the debt crisis of the 5th century BCE, during which numerous farmers became entangled in exploitative loan agreements with high interest rates, becoming dependent on their patrician creditors. This situation triggered several plebeian protests, most notably the first *secessio plebis* in 494 BCE, when the plebeians withdrew to the Mons Sacer and threatened to establish a separate political community. The patrician leadership responded not merely with pragmatism but initiated a series of institutional concessions: plebeians were granted the office of *tribunus plebis* (tribune of the people), an institution explicitly designed to protect them from the authority of patrician magistrates.

These developments were not linear but embedded in a protracted struggle for influence that would span centuries. This was particularly evident in the contest over eligibility for public office. A significant milestone was the legislation proposed by Gaius Licinius Stolo and Lucius Sextius Lateranus in 367 BCE. Their proposals called not only for plebeian access to the consulship but also for limitations on the excessive acquisition of public land by patricians. These so-called *Leges Liciniae Sextiae* were the product of a decade-long political deadlock: the two tribunes repeatedly vetoed the appointment of other magistrates over ten consecutive years to push through their agenda. Ultimately, they prevailed, and from 366 BCE onward, plebeians were formally eligible to hold the consulship.

Another significant step came with the *Lex Genucia* of 342 BCE, which included, among other things, a ban on holding two magistracies simultaneously or the same office in consecutive years. This legislation directly targeted the monopolization of public offices by powerful aristocratic families and aimed to distribute political power more broadly in both temporal and personal terms. Similarly, the enactment of laws prohibiting voter coercion reflected Rome's growing efforts to codify not only its constitutional order but also the ethical norms underpinning its political culture.

In parallel, a new political elite emerged: the *nobilitas*. Increasingly composed of patrician-plebeian mixed families, this new aristocracy was tightly interlinked through office-holding careers, intermarriages, and intricate social networks. As a result, Rome's political center of gravity shifted from a rigidly closed nobility to a more open yet oligarchic meritocracy. Access to the highest offices remained challenging for ordinary plebeians but was theoretically possible. In practice, a *cursus honorum*—a prescribed sequence of magistracies—was established, which had to be followed in order to become eligible for the consulship. This institutionalization of political careers intensified competition within the elite, serving as a catalyst for rhetorical prowess, public engagement, and military ambition.

While Rome thus matured internally through institutional reforms, its foreign policy horizons simultaneously began to expand. Initially, Rome's external policy was reactive in nature—aimed at defending the city's territory from hostile neighbors such as the Volsci, Aequi, or Sabines. However, by the late 5th century BCE and especially in the 4th century BCE, the character of these conflicts began to change. Roman expansion became not only a strategy of defense but increasingly an end in itself. This development was facilitated by several interrelated factors.

First, Roman society was deeply militarized. Military service was regarded as both a civic duty and a prerequisite for political advancement. Conquering new territories offered the prospect of land allotments—an especially attractive incentive for indebted plebeians. Second, the newly created political institutions allowed for increasingly coordinated warfare: with annual rotation of consuls and an increasingly professional military organization, war became a regular feature of Roman statecraft.

An early example of Rome's strategic foresight in foreign policy was its approach to the Latin League. After the successful conclusion of the Latin War (340–338 BCE), Rome dissolved the Latin League. Instead of annexing the Latin cities outright, Rome implemented a sophisticated blend of colonization, legal arrangements, and treaties. Cities such as Lanuvium and Aricia were granted full Roman citizenship, while others like Tibur and Praeneste became *socii* (allies). This principle of differentiated integration demonstrated that Roman hegemony did not require uniformity but could be secured through deliberate gradations of political inclusion.

As part of this expansionist foreign policy, Rome also began to undertake systematic military campaigns against more distant adversaries. The Samnite Wars (343–290 BCE) marked the first prolonged conflicts with an equally matched enemy within the Italian peninsula. Across three distinct phases of warfare, Rome proved not only its military effectiveness but also its adaptability: it reorganized its legions, adjusted its tactics to meet the challenges of mountainous terrain and guerrilla warfare, and employed diplomatic strategies to sow divisions among the Samnite tribes.

These wars had significant domestic consequences as well. Protracted conflict demanded constant military levies and placed heavy burdens on the agrarian foundation of the Republic. Simultaneously, it became increasingly evident that existing political mechanisms for distributing land and honors were insufficient. The settlement of newly conquered territories through colonies thus became a central pillar of Rome's expansion strategy. Domestically, new tensions emerged as military veterans began to demand more rights and patrician landowners sought to appropriate additional farmland—often at the expense of poorer citizens.

In addition to the Samnite region, Rome also turned its attention in the late 4th and early 3rd centuries BCE to Etruscan cities such as Volsinii, Perusia, and Clusium. These wars were of particular cultural and political significance, as the Etruscans, unlike many Italic tribes, had developed advanced urban civilizations. Victory over Etruscan cities also meant the adoption of numerous cultural elements—evident in temple architecture, religious rituals, and construction techniques.

Roman foreign policy acquired a new dimension around 280 BCE, when it confronted an internationally connected power: King Pyrrhus of Epirus, who had been invited by the Greek city of Tarentum to aid in its defense. During the so-called Pyrrhic Wars, Rome for the first time engaged a professional Hellenistic army on equal footing. The battles of Heraclea (280 BCE) and especially Asculum (279 BCE)—from which the famous phrase "Another such victory and I am lost" originates—revealed

Rome's remarkable resilience. Despite military setbacks, the Roman Senate refused to consider peace negotiations, signaling a newfound resolve in external affairs. The victory at Beneventum (275 BCE) and the subsequent withdrawal of Pyrrhus marked the end of the conflict in Rome's favor and signaled its definitive rise as the dominant power in Italy.

At the same time, these foreign policy successes had further repercussions on domestic politics. The integration of new territories required administrative reforms, fresh military conscription, and the forging of new alliances. Pressure mounted for broader political participation, social justice, and equitable land distribution. Early precursors of the populist politics of the later Republic emerged, as tribunes sought to win public favor through proposals for agrarian reform.

CHAPTER 3: ROME AS A GREAT POWER – PUNIC WARS AND MEDITERRANEAN DOMINANCE (264–133 BC)

3.1 The Punic Wars: Carthage as Rome's Principal Adversary

Between 264 and 133 BCE, Rome transformed from a regional power in Italy into the dominant hegemon of the western Mediterranean world. This transformation was inextricably linked to the so-called Punic Wars, particularly Rome's military successes in Spain, North Africa, and Sicily. The expansion of Roman influence in these territories was not merely a matter of conquest but had far-reaching political, economic, and cultural ramifications that profoundly shaped the development of the Roman Republic and later Empire. The period from 264 to 133 BCE represents a phase of intense military engagement and territorial annexation, during which Rome expanded its sphere of power through systematic warfare, strategic alliance-building, and administrative consolidation.

The first phase of this expansion began with the First Punic War, which erupted in 264 BCE between Rome and Carthage, a powerful maritime empire based in North Africa. The conflict was sparked by events in Sicily, a strategically vital island in the central Mediterranean that served as a bridgehead between Italy and Africa. When the city-state of Messana (modern Messina) was seized by a group of mercenaries known as the Mamertines, and subsequently drawn into a conflict with the Greek city of Syracuse, the Mamertines appealed to Rome for assistance. Carthage, which also had vested interests in Sicily, intervened militarily. The resulting contest for influence over Messana escalated into a full-scale war for supremacy on the island.

At the time, Rome had little naval experience, but it quickly recognized the strategic importance of maritime power. In 261 BCE, Rome initiated the construction of its own fleet, inspired by a captured Carthaginian warship that had washed ashore. Roman engineers developed the *corvus*, a boarding bridge that enabled Roman infantry tactics to be applied at sea. This innovation bore fruit in the Battle of Mylae in 260 BCE, where Roman forces under Consul Gaius Duilius achieved their first significant naval victory against the Carthaginian fleet.

The struggle for control over Sicily dragged on for more than two decades. Particularly fierce was the siege of Lilybaeum, the westernmost Carthaginian stronghold on the island, which lasted from 250 to 241 BCE. During this period, the Romans won several additional naval battles, culminating in the Battle of the Aegates Islands in 241 BCE, where Gaius Lutatius Catulus decisively defeated the Carthaginian navy. This victory compelled Carthage to seek peace.

The Treaty of Lutatius, signed in 241 BCE, brought the First Punic War to a close. Carthage was forced to cede Sicily to Rome, pay a substantial war indemnity, and renounce all claims to the island. Rome subsequently established Sicily as its first province outside the Italian mainland, administered by a *praetor*. In 238 BCE, taking advantage of internal unrest in Carthage, Rome also occupied Sardinia and Corsica, territories that Carthage had no choice but to relinquish with great reluctance.

After losing Sicily, Sardinia, and Corsica, Carthage—under the leadership of the Barcid family—redirected its expansionist efforts to Spain. In 237 BCE, the Carthaginian general Hamilcar Barca initiated the conquest of large portions of the Iberian Peninsula, aiming to secure new sources of revenue and military resources, particularly silver, in preparation for a potential future war with Rome. Hamilcar was killed in action in 229 BCE, but his son-in-law Hasdrubal the Fair continued the campaign and in 228 BCE founded the city of Carthago Nova (modern Cartagena), which soon became the main Carthaginian base in Spain.

Following Hasdrubal's assassination in 221 BCE, Hamilcar's son Hannibal Barca assumed command. According to later Roman sources, Hannibal had vowed eternal enmity against Rome as a child—a symbolic gesture reflecting his lifelong opposition to the Republic. He resumed expansion in Spain and, in 219 BCE, laid siege to the city of Saguntum, a Roman ally. Rome interpreted the fall of Saguntum as a casus belli, leading to the outbreak of the Second Punic War in 218 BCE.

The Second Punic War (218–201 BCE) ranks among the most dramatic and consequential conflicts of classical antiquity. Hannibal launched his legendary crossing of the Alps, bringing with him an army of approximately 50,000 infantry, 9,000 cavalry, and several dozen war elephants. In 218 BCE, he defeated Roman forces at the Battle of the Ticinus River, followed by another victory at the Trebia River. In 217 BCE, at the Battle of Lake Trasimene, Hannibal ambushed and annihilated a Roman army, killing Consul Gaius Flaminius. The most catastrophic Roman defeat came in 216 BCE at the Battle of Cannae, where Hannibal's forces encircled and destroyed a Roman army led by Lucius Aemilius Paullus and Gaius Terentius Varro, killing over 50,000 Roman soldiers—one of the most devastating losses in Roman military history.

Despite these victories, Hannibal was unable to capture Rome, which remained fortified and resilient. Roman diplomacy continued to secure allies, while Roman commanders shifted their focus to Spain, aiming to dismantle Carthage's power base there. From 218 BCE, Roman armies under Publius Cornelius Scipio and Gnaeus Cornelius Scipio Calvus were dispatched to Spain and achieved early successes. However, in 211 BCE, both were killed in a major Carthaginian counteroffensive led by Mago, Hasdrubal Barca, and Hasdrubal Gisco.

A turning point came with the rise of Publius Cornelius Scipio, son of the consul who had died in Spain. He arrived in 210 BCE and, in 209 BCE, captured Carthago Nova in a surprise assault. This city's fall dealt a severe blow to Carthage, as it housed key arsenals and treasuries. Scipio won further victories, including at Baecula in 208 BCE, where he defeated Hasdrubal Barca, who then attempted to march to Italy to support Hannibal. However, Hasdrubal was intercepted and killed at the Battle of the Metaurus River in 207 BCE by Roman consuls Claudius Nero and Marcus Livius Salinator. In a symbolic act of psychological warfare, Hasdrubal's severed head was thrown into Hannibal's camp.

With successive Roman victories, including the decisive Battle of Ilipa in 206 BCE, Carthaginian power in Spain was eradicated. The territory was gradually organized into two Roman provinces: Hispania Citerior and Hispania Ulterior. Scipio returned to Rome in 205 BCE, received the honorific "Africanus", and in 204 BCE launched a new campaign in North Africa. There, he allied with Massinissa, the Numidian prince and rival of the Carthaginian-aligned Syphax.

In 203 BCE, Scipio defeated the combined forces of Carthage and Syphax at the Great Plains (Campi Magni) and again at Cirta. Syphax was captured, and Massinissa was installed as king of Numidia. These defeats forced Carthage to recall Hannibal from Italy. The decisive battle took place in 202 BCE at Zama, where Scipio, leveraging Massinissa's cavalry and his own tactical superiority, defeated Hannibal. Though Hannibal's troops were seasoned, they were outnumbered and demoralized.

The Treaty of 201 BCE formally ended the Second Punic War. Carthage was compelled to surrender all its possessions outside Africa, limit its navy to ten ships, pay heavy indemnities, and obtain Rome's consent before engaging in any future wars. Rome had effectively secured hegemony over the western Mediterranean. Spain was absorbed into the Roman provincial system, and North Africa fell under Rome's influence, with Massinissa acting as a Roman client king.

In the subsequent decades up to 133 BCE, Rome continued to consolidate its hold over the western Mediterranean. In Spain, resistance persisted, especially among the Celtiberian and Lusitanian tribes, who sought to preserve their autonomy. One of the bloodiest uprisings was the Celtiberian War, which raged between 154 and 133 BCE. Its climax came with the siege and destruction of Numantia in 133 BCE by Scipio Aemilianus, adoptive grandson of Scipio Africanus. Rather than surrender, the Numantines chose mass suicide and razed their own city. With Numantia's fall, organized resistance in Iberia largely collapsed, and Roman dominion over Spain was consolidated.

Rome also maintained a significant presence in North Africa. Its close alliance with Massinissa led to Carthage's increasing weakness, as the city was forbidden from defending itself against Numidian incursions. This deepening humiliation was a major factor leading to the Third Punic War, although that conflict falls outside the chronological scope of this chapter.

In Sicily, following the First Punic War, Rome established a comprehensive provincial administration. The island became a critical grain supply hub for Rome and played a central role in feeding the capital's growing population. The Roman exploitation of Sicily, particularly through the creation of vast latifundia (large estates), significantly altered the island's social structure. This exploitation also led to repeated slave revolts, most notably the First Servile War (135–132 BCE), whose origins lay in the harsh conditions imposed by Rome's provincial policies.

In conclusion, between 264 and 133 BCE, Rome ascended to great power status in the western Mediterranean through a combination of military strength, strategic foresight, and economic exploitation. The conquest of Sicily, the expulsion of Carthage from Spain, and the imposition of effective control over North Africa were key milestones in this process. This transformative era laid the foundation for Rome's future expansion into the eastern Mediterranean and marked a critical stage in the Republic's path toward global supremacy.

3.2 Hannibal and Carthage

Hannibal Barca is regarded as one of the most fascinating and enigmatic figures of ancient history. His life is inextricably linked to the fate of Carthage, the powerful maritime and commercial empire that for centuries held a dominant position in the western Mediterranean. The story of Hannibal cannot be understood in isolation from the political, economic, and cultural development of Carthage—a Phoenician city-state that evolved from a trading colony into one of Rome's chief imperial rivals. To fully comprehend Hannibal's actions and significance, one must consider both his biography and the broader cultural and geographic context of Carthage.

Carthage was founded in the 9th century BCE by Phoenician settlers from the city of Tyre. According to Roman and Greek traditions, its foundation dates to around 814 BCE, although archaeological evidence suggests earlier habitation in some areas. The Tyrians, a seafaring people from what is now Lebanon, established numerous trading outposts along the Mediterranean coast. Carthage—originally called *Qart-ḥadašt* in Phoenician, meaning "new city"—was initially one such outpost. However, it quickly developed into an autonomous center with distinct political and economic power.

Carthage's geographic location on a peninsula along the North African coast, directly opposite Sicily, endowed it with crucial strategic importance. The city boasted a natural harbor, which was later expanded through artificial constructions. The renowned Carthaginian port complex consisted of an outer commercial harbor and an inner military harbor (*Cothon*), capable of housing over 200 ships. This facility was highly sophisticated, equipped with docks, workshops, and storage depots, and enabled Carthage to build one of the most formidable navies in the western Mediterranean.

Politically, Carthage functioned as an aristocracy dominated by wealthy mercantile families. Its principal institutions included the Council of 104—a tribunal responsible for overseeing military commanders—the Council of Elders (*Gerusia*), and two annually elected *suffetes*, akin to Roman consuls. Popular assemblies existed but wielded limited power. Carthage pursued influence through economic dominance and colonial expansion, establishing its power base in North Africa, the Balearic Islands, Sardinia, Corsica, Sicily, and eventually in Iberia. Its wealth was derived chiefly from trade, particularly in precious metals, Tyrian purple dye, ivory, slaves, and agricultural products.

Culturally, Carthage was deeply rooted in Phoenician traditions. Its religion was polytheistic, featuring a pantheon of deities, chief among them Baal Hammon and Tanit. Later Roman sources notoriously accused Carthaginians of practicing child sacrifice to Baal Hammon—a claim that remains hotly debated among modern historians. Archaeological discoveries such as the *Tophet*, a sanctuary containing urns with the cremated remains of children, suggest the possibility of ritual sacrifice, though the extent and interpretation of these practices are still contested.

The population of Carthage was ethnically diverse. In addition to the Punic inhabitants—descendants of the original Phoenician settlers—the city and its territories included Berbers, Iberians, Greeks, Libyans, and, in later periods, Celts. The Carthaginian realm was not a homogeneous state, but a complex system of tributary territories, colonies, and allies. Especially in the hinterlands of North Africa, various Numidian and Libyan tribes lived in a fluctuating relationship with Carthage, at times allied, at times hostile. This multicultural structure was reflected in Carthage's military forces, which were composed largely of mercenaries—Numidians served as cavalry, Iberians and Celts as infantry, and elephants from the Atlas Mountains were employed as psychological weapons on the battlefield.

It was within this political and cultural environment that Hannibal Barca was born, likely in 247 BCE, during the First Punic War. He was the son of the Carthaginian general Hamilcar Barca, a prominent commander in the struggle against Rome. Hamilcar had distinguished himself in Sicily and later spearheaded Carthaginian expansion in Spain. Hannibal grew up in an atmosphere marked by military conflict and deep-seated hostility toward Rome. According to tradition, Hamilcar famously made his son swear an oath at the altar of Baal Hammon never to become a friend of Rome—a symbolic act that highlights the ideological imprint on Hannibal and his lifelong enmity toward the Roman Republic.

Following Hamilcar's death in 229 BCE and the subsequent assassination of his son-in-law and successor Hasdrubal in 221

BCE, Hannibal—at approximately 26 years of age—assumed command of the Carthaginian forces in Spain. He soon demonstrated extraordinary strategic acumen, successfully campaigning against various Iberian tribes and consolidating Carthaginian control over southern and eastern Hispania. A key event in this phase was the siege and capture of Saguntum in 219 BCE, a city under Roman protection. Rome interpreted this attack as a violation of the peace treaty of 241 BCE, which triggered the outbreak of the Second Punic War.

In the spring of 218 BCE, Hannibal embarked on his legendary march toward Italy. He led an army of approximately 50,000 soldiers—including many Iberians, Libyans, and Celts—as well as a contingent of war elephants across the Pyrenees, through southern Gaul, and ultimately over the Alps. The precise route Hannibal took remains a subject of scholarly debate, but the crossing of the Alpine highlands is universally regarded as a logistical and military feat of the highest order. Despite severe losses from skirmishes with Gallic tribes, avalanches, and exhaustion, Hannibal managed to reach northern Italy with a battle-ready force.

Over the next few years, Hannibal inflicted several crushing defeats on Rome. In 218 BCE, he won the battles of the Ticinus River and the Trebia. In 217 BCE, he ambushed and annihilated a Roman army at Lake Trasimene. The pinnacle of his success came in 216 BCE at the Battle of Cannae, where he executed a masterful double envelopment tactic and destroyed a Roman force twice the size of his own. Cannae remains one of the most studied battles in military history and is frequently analyzed at military academies around the world.

Despite these triumphs, Hannibal failed to capture Rome itself. The city was heavily fortified, and the Romans shifted to a strategy of attrition and containment. Furthermore, Carthage's political leadership was indecisive and failed to dispatch the reinforcements Hannibal desperately needed. He remained in Italy for over 15 years, primarily operating in the south and forging alliances with cities such as Capua and Tarentum. Nevertheless, he was unable to deliver a decisive blow to Rome. In 211 BCE, the Romans launched a counteroffensive and captured Carthago Nova in Spain, thereby severing Hannibal's main supply base.

When Scipio Africanus landed in Africa in 204 BCE, Hannibal was recalled from Italy. The climactic confrontation took place in 202 BCE at the Battle of Zama, where the Carthaginian forces, exhausted by years of warfare and numerically inferior, were decisively defeated by the better-organized Roman army. Hannibal could not match Scipio's tactical ingenuity. After the peace settlement, Hannibal remained in Carthage and was elected *suffet*, initiating reforms to combat corruption and stabilize the state. However, his political enemies—particularly those aligned with Rome—denounced him to the Roman authorities, leading to his voluntary exile in 195 BCE.

Hannibal subsequently sought refuge at the court of the Seleucid king Antiochus III, then in Armenia, and finally in Bithynia. Rome repeatedly demanded his extradition, and when the threat of capture became imminent, Hannibal chose to end his life in 183 BCE in Libyssa, on the Sea of Marmara—reportedly by ingesting poison he always carried with him. According to the Roman historian Cornelius Nepos, his final words expressed a bitter lament on the ingratitude of mankind.

Hannibal's legacy far outlived him. Centuries later, he continued to be admired, feared, and respected by Roman historians such as Livy and Plutarch. His strategic brilliance, perseverance, and vision of a Punic-dominated Mediterranean secured his place among the greatest military commanders in world history.

Carthage, meanwhile, began a slow decline following the

Second Punic War. Though it retained economic strength, it was politically weakened and placed under Roman oversight. Persistent tensions between Carthage and its Roman-allied neighbor, Numidia, led to renewed hostilities in the following decades. The final demise of Carthage occurred in the Third Punic War, culminating in the city's total destruction in 146 BCE —a catastrophic event that Hannibal did not live to witness, but which marked the conclusive end of the long-standing rivalry between Rome and Carthage.

3.3 Rome's Transformation into an Imperial Power

Between 264 and 133 BCE, Rome underwent a fundamental transformation: from a regionally confined republic in central Italy, it evolved into an expansive great power whose political, military, and economic influence permeated the entire Mediterranean world. The period from the end of the First Punic War (241 BCE) to the conclusion of eastern expansion by 133 BCE was not merely a phase of external territorial gains but also an era of profound internal transformations. Rome became an imperial power—a development with dramatic consequences for its economy, society, politics, and culture. This transformation was not the result of a single plan or event but rather the cumulative outcome of a series of interconnected developments, decisions, and conflicts that profoundly reshaped the Roman state.

Following its victory over Carthage in the First Punic War (264–241 BCE), Rome for the first time brought an overseas province—Sicily—under its control. However, this was merely the beginning of a long period of uninterrupted expansion. Soon thereafter, Sardinia and Corsica were annexed (238 BCE), followed by the conquest of Spain beginning in 218 BCE and substantial portions of North Africa, especially after the Second Punic War (218–201 BCE). In the ensuing decades, the focus of Roman expansion shifted to the eastern Mediterranean. In Greece, Macedonia, Asia Minor, and the Syrian region, Rome increasingly asserted itself as a dominant power, though it initially operated formally through alliances and "protection treaties." The defeat of Seleucid King Antiochus III at the Battle of Magnesia (190 BCE), and the dismantling of the Macedonian kingdom over several wars—especially following the decisive Roman victory at Pydna in 168 BCE—made it clear that Rome had emerged as an imperial power with hegemonic ambitions.

This new imperial status necessitated profound structural adaptations, as the republican Roman system was originally not designed for the permanent governance of far-flung provinces. Roman administration, which had previously been confined to the city of Rome and the surrounding Italian territories, now had to extend across trans-Mediterranean regions. One of the most important institutional innovations was the establishment of the provincial system (*provinciae*). Each province was governed by an annually rotating magistrate—typically a former consul or praetor. These governors wielded near-absolute authority within their provinces, often leading to abuses of power, corruption, and the exploitation of local populations. While the Senate nominally supervised governors after their term ended, effective judicial oversight in the provinces was largely absent. Provinces became zones of economic exploitation, supplying Rome with tributes, grain, precious metals, and slaves.

A central instrument in maintaining order and securing power in the provinces was the standing army. Unlike earlier times when Rome's military consisted primarily of citizen-soldiers conscripted for short campaigns, it now became necessary to station troops permanently outside Italy. This imposed a heavy burden on the rural population, as many small farmers were absent for years serving in the military. Moreover, military service no longer guaranteed sufficient income, and the families of absent soldiers often fell into poverty or were forced to abandon their farms. This trend significantly contributed to increasing social inequality, as large landowners bought up abandoned plots and converted them into vast *latifundia*.

As the empire expanded, Rome's economy was fundamentally transformed. Rome was no longer primarily an agrarian regional power but had become the hub of a vast and intricate economic network spanning the entire Mediterranean. The influx of wealth—whether in the form of war booty, tributes, or customs revenues—led to a rapid accumulation of capital among the elite. The senatorial aristocracy and the rising equestrian order (*equites*) invested this capital in land acquisition, commerce, banking, and the slave economy. Slaves became the dominant labor force, especially on large agricultural estates. Entire cities and regions in Greece and Asia Minor were plundered, their populations enslaved and brought to Italy. Following the Third Macedonian War (171–168 BCE) alone, it is estimated that over 150,000 people were enslaved.

This massive influx of cheap labor led to a profound restructuring of Roman agriculture. Small family farms gave way to large agricultural estates focused on export goods such as wine and olive oil, with productivity maximized through slave labor. The impoverishment of the rural population, combined with the concentration of land in the hands of a few wealthy families, resulted in dramatic social polarization. Many displaced smallholders migrated to urban centers, particularly to Rome, where they lived as *proletarii*—propertyless citizens increasingly dependent on state-sponsored grain distributions (*alimenta*). This development created an urban underclass that was politically vulnerable and easily manipulated; their votes in the popular assemblies were often bought through gifts and promises.

The political structure of the Republic struggled to keep pace with these transformations. The senatorial aristocracy—comprised of ancient patrician families and successful *novi homines* (new men)—formally retained control over the state, but internal tensions within the ruling elite intensified. The pursuit of glory, power, and wealth led to growing rivalries among leading families, manifesting in an increasing number of legal battles, political intrigues, and violent confrontations. Simultaneously, new centers of power emerged in the form of wealthy equites, who collected provincial taxes on behalf of the state (via *publicani*) and amassed enormous profits as financiers. The economic power of the equestrian order increasingly competed with the political authority of the Senate, further destabilizing the republican system.

Rome's transformation into an imperial power also brought about profound cultural changes. Contact with the Greek-Hellenistic world introduced new ideas, lifestyles, and artistic expressions to Roman society. The Roman elite began to emulate Greek models: philosophy, literature, architecture, and sculpture experienced a renaissance, facilitated by Greek teachers, artists, and intellectuals who often came to Rome as war captives or immigrants. This led to a fundamental shift in Roman self-perception: traditional Roman austerity and discipline were increasingly supplemented—or, in the eyes of some traditionalists, supplanted—by an urban, luxurious lifestyle. Authors such as Cato the Elder (234–149 BCE) lamented this moral decline in their writings and called for a return to the *mos maiorum*—the customs of the ancestors.

A particularly striking example of this cultural transformation was Roman architecture. The city of Rome itself was adorned with monumental temples, triumphal arches, and basilicas, often financed by spoils of war. The triumph— a celebratory procession through the city to mark military victories—became the most important form of political legitimation. Generals such as Lucius Aemilius Paullus, victor at Pydna, commissioned splendid honorary monuments. At the same time, new forms of public entertainment emerged in Rome, such as gladiatorial games—originally of Etruscan origin—which became increasingly popular as mass spectacles.

Imperial expansion also led to a reorientation of foreign policy. Whereas Rome had originally focused on securing its interests through alliances and responding only to concrete threats, it evolved into an active hegemonic power, increasingly waging wars preemptively or for the sake of maintaining dominance. The term *imperium*, which had originally referred solely to a magistrate's legal authority, now acquired territorial and ideological connotations: Rome increasingly saw itself as the guarantor of an order founded on military superiority, cultural supremacy, and political control. This attitude was most clearly reflected in its policy toward the East: the dismantling of the Seleucid Empire, the division of Macedonia into dependent republics, and the establishment of Roman client kings in Pergamum, Bithynia, and Cappadocia were expressions of this new imperial mindset.

A key turning point came in 133 BCE, when King Attalus III of Pergamum bequeathed his kingdom to Rome in his will. This gift served both as a testament to the political allure of Roman protection and as a catalyst for new domestic tensions: the distribution of the Attalid treasury and the question of whether the territory should be organized as a province divided Roman politics. In the same year, the tribune of the people Tiberius Gracchus was assassinated after attempting to implement a sweeping agrarian reform—an event often seen as marking the beginning of the Late Republic's crisis. The connection between imperial expansion and internal social upheaval was becoming increasingly evident.

CHAPTER 4: CRISIS OF THE REPUBLIC AND CIVIL WARS (133–27 BC)

4.1 The Gracchi and the Agrarian Reform

Between 133 BCE and 27 BCE, the Roman Republic underwent one of the most profound crises in its history. At the heart of this period of upheaval stood the so-called Gracchan reform movement, named after the brothers Tiberius and Gaius Sempronius Gracchus. In the latter half of the 2nd century BCE, these two figures sought to address the growing social inequality of the Republic through a series of social and political reforms. Their actions mark the beginning of an escalating political crisis that ultimately culminated in the collapse of the Republican system.

The background of the Gracchan reform efforts lies in the deep structural changes that Rome had experienced in the preceding decades. Following the conclusion of the Second Punic War in 201 BCE and the subsequent expansion into the eastern and western Mediterranean, Rome had developed into a major imperial power. However, this economic and military success came at a significant social cost. The protracted wars had impoverished many smallholder farmers—traditionally the backbone of the Republican army—or forced them to neglect their farms. While they served on distant battlefields, large landowners—known as the *Optimates*—seized their lands, often illegally, and converted them into vast *latifundia*, large estates worked by slaves captured during Rome's many conquests.

This process led to an increasing concentration of land ownership in the hands of a few elite families and a corresponding rise in landlessness among the broader population. Many of the dispossessed rural citizens migrated to the city of Rome, where they lived as *proletarii*—propertyless citizens who lacked economic or political power but retained the right to vote in the popular assemblies, making them a significant potential political force. The growing divide between a wealthy aristocracy and an impoverished urban mass was perceived by many contemporaries as a threat to the stability of the Republic. These tensions were further exacerbated by the conflict between the Senate and popular politicians who appealed directly to the people, circumventing the traditional aristocratic pathways to power.

Within this context of social transformation, Tiberius Sempronius Gracchus emerged on the political stage. Born in 163 BCE, Tiberius came from one of the most distinguished families of the Republic. His father, Tiberius Sempronius Gracchus the Elder, had held the consulship twice and served as censor. His mother, Cornelia, was the daughter of Scipio Africanus, the celebrated conqueror of Hannibal. Despite his aristocratic lineage, Tiberius developed a strong social conscience, likely influenced by his military experiences. In 137 BCE, he served as quaestor during a campaign in Spain, where he witnessed firsthand the inadequate provisioning and harsh treatment of Roman soldiers—an experience that seems to have profoundly shaped his political convictions.

In 133 BCE, Tiberius was elected tribune of the plebs, an office endowed with considerable powers, including the ability to veto senatorial decrees and propose legislation directly to the popular assembly. Tiberius used his office to launch an ambitious reform program. At the core of this initiative stood the *Lex Sempronia Agraria*, which aimed to revive an old law from the 4th century BCE—the *Lex Licinia Sextia* of 367 BCE.

That law had limited the ownership of public land (*ager publicus*) to 500 *iugera* (approximately 125 hectares) per individual. Over the centuries, this regulation had been widely ignored, allowing many senators and wealthy equestrian families to amass enormous estates. Tiberius now sought to reclaim lands held in excess of this limit and redistribute them to landless citizens. To oversee the implementation of the reform, a new commission —the *triumviri agris iudicandis adsignandis*—was established. It initially comprised Tiberius himself, his brother Gaius, and the former consul Appius Claudius Pulcher, a political ally and father-in-law of Tiberius.

The agrarian reform met with fierce resistance in the Senate. The large landowners affected by the law perceived it as a threat to their economic interests. Tiberius attempted to circumvent this opposition by introducing the law directly to the popular assembly without prior consultation with the Senate—an unorthodox but legally permissible action. When his fellow tribune Marcus Octavius, a representative of the conservative senatorial faction, vetoed the proposal, Tiberius had him deposed by a vote in the popular assembly—an unprecedented and constitutionally questionable move. The law was subsequently enacted, but its implementation stalled due to a lack of funds for land redistribution.

In the same year, however, King Attalus III of Pergamum died and bequeathed his kingdom to the Roman people. Tiberius proposed using the royal treasury to fund the agrarian reforms, once again bypassing the Senate in the process—a move that deeply affronted the traditional ruling elite.

The political conflict escalated dramatically. Tiberius announced his candidacy for a second term as tribune—an act that, while not strictly illegal, violated Republican custom and was interpreted by his opponents as an attempt to establish a personal dictatorship. During a vote on the Capitoline Hill on

10 October 133 BCE, violence broke out. A group of senatorial supporters, led by the *Pontifex Maximus* and future consul Publius Cornelius Scipio Nasica, attacked Tiberius and his followers with clubs and broken furniture. Tiberius was killed, along with approximately 300 of his supporters. This marked the first time in centuries that a Roman politician had been slain in an internal political conflict. A fundamental taboo had been shattered: violence had now become an acceptable tool of political resolution.

Following Tiberius' violent death, the agrarian commission continued its work, albeit amid political strife. Only through the mediation of the consul Gaius Sempronius Tuditanus and the pro-Gracchan consul Publius Licinius Crassus Dives was a degree of stability restored. Yet the core conflict remained unresolved—merely postponed. About a decade later, Gaius Gracchus, Tiberius' younger brother, resumed the reform efforts.

Gaius Sempronius Gracchus, born in 154 BCE, had already distinguished himself as a gifted orator and skilled political organizer. In 126 BCE, he served as quaestor in Sardinia, but he soon returned to Rome and successfully ran for the office of tribune in 124 BCE, holding it again the following year. Unlike his brother, Gaius pursued a broader legislative agenda that aimed not only to address land reform but also to transform the political and economic structures of the Republic. Among his initiatives was legislation to curtail the Senate's power. One such law restructured the composition of the permanent courts (*quaestiones perpetuae*), mandating that they no longer be composed exclusively of senators but also include members of the equestrian order (*equites*). This measure was designed to alter the balance of power between the two dominant social classes and to combat judicial corruption.

Another significant measure was the *Lex Frumentaria*, which established a state-subsidized grain supply for the Roman populace—a pioneering example of social welfare legislation in antiquity. Gaius also sought to alleviate social pressures by founding colonies, including one on the site of ancient Carthage (*Colonia Junonia*), to provide settlement opportunities for surplus population. Furthermore, he proposed extending Roman citizenship to the allied Italian communities (*socii*), a policy that met with widespread opposition—both in the Senate and among the urban plebs, who were reluctant to share their privileges.

In 121 BCE, the confrontation reached a climax. Gaius lost the support of key segments of the populace and failed to secure election for a third term as tribune. In response, the Senate invoked a novel and controversial instrument: the *senatus consultum ultimum*—an emergency decree that granted the consul Lucius Opimius broad authority to suppress Gaius and his followers. On 10 December 121 BCE, violence erupted on the Aventine Hill. Gaius and his close ally, Fulvius Flaccus, attempted to organize resistance but were quickly overwhelmed. Gaius fled and ultimately ordered a slave to kill him to avoid capture. In the following days, up to 3,000 of his supporters were executed. His reform laws were largely reversed or rendered ineffective through various legal and administrative maneuvers.

Despite their violent end, the ideas of the Gracchi left a lasting legacy. For the first time in Republican history, a political movement had mobilized mass support and demonstrated that reform could be enacted through popular mechanisms independent of the Senate. At the same time, they introduced a perilous precedent of political polarization and violence—a pattern that would be repeatedly invoked in the decades to come. The Gracchan movement ushered in a new era—an age marked by social conflict, populist leaders, and institutional breakdown. Though their immediate reforms achieved only limited success, the Gracchi were the harbingers of a century of instability that would ultimately transform the Roman state.

4.2 Marius, Sulla, and the Militarization of Politics

Following the violent suppression of the Gracchan reform movement, the Roman Republic remained marked by deep social tensions, political polarization, and the gradual erosion of its institutions. In this transitional phase—spanning the 120s to the 80s BCE—two figures emerged who would fundamentally reshape the political culture of Rome: Gaius Marius and Lucius Cornelius Sulla. Their careers marked the beginning of the militarization of Roman politics, a development that would ultimately lead to civil war and the collapse of the republican order. The conflict between these two men and their respective factions introduced new and destabilizing elements into Roman political life: private armies, internal violence, the pursuit of power through military means, and a novel form of personal loyalty between general and soldier.

Gaius Marius was born around 157 BCE in Arpinum, a municipium located south of Rome. He came from a wealthy but non-senatorial family and thus belonged to the equestrian order (equites). His origins outside the aristocratic nobility significantly influenced both his political trajectory and his relationship with the traditional elite. Marius began his career in the military and gained a reputation for bravery and organizational skill. His first major political opportunity came in 107 BCE, when he was elected consul—despite having bypassed much of the traditional cursus honorum (sequence of public offices). His election was already indicative of a significant shift: a *homo novus*, a "new man" from outside the entrenched patrician families, had successfully challenged aristocratic dominance.

The immediate catalyst for his election was the deteriorating situation in North Africa, where the Numidian king Jugurtha had evaded Roman control. The Senate had initially entrusted the command to the patrician Quintus Caecilius Metellus, but the campaign dragged on. Marius, who had served under Metellus, returned to Rome and, promising a swift victory, gained popular support and was awarded command of the army—a highly unusual step that defied the Senate's authority. Subsequently, Marius undertook a fundamental reorganization of the army. As the pool of land-owning citizens—the traditional backbone of the republican legions—dwindled, he increasingly recruited landless citizens, the so-called *capite censi*. These men, lacking property and financial security, were deeply dependent on their general for pay and provisions. This development represented a profound paradigm shift: the general, rather than the state, now became the primary guarantor of a soldier's welfare. Marius' military reforms, carried out between 107 and 104 BCE, effectively created a professional standing army whose loyalty was primarily to its commander rather than to the Republic.

In 104 BCE, Marius returned to Rome as a victorious general, having captured Jugurtha—thanks in part to bribery and betrayal—and delivered him to the Senate. However, Marius' triumph was overshadowed by a new military emergency: the invasion of the Cimbri and Teutones. These Germanic tribes had been migrating southward since 113 BCE, defeating several Roman armies, most notably at the Battle of Noreia (113 BCE) and the catastrophic defeat at Arausio (105 BCE), where a Roman army was almost entirely annihilated. Faced with this existential threat, Marius was elected consul five consecutive times—from 104 to 100 BCE—a precedent-breaking series of terms in Roman republican history. During this period, he continued to reshape the army and achieved decisive victories:

in 102 BCE he defeated the Teutones at Aquae Sextiae (modern Aix-en-Provence), and in 101 BCE he vanquished the Cimbri at Vercellae in northern Italy.

These victories earned Marius immense acclaim as Rome's savior, but his increasing alignment with the radical elements of the popularis faction and his authoritarian tendencies provoked growing unease within the Senate. Tensions peaked in 100 BCE, when Marius, together with the populist tribune Lucius Appuleius Saturninus, attempted to pass a reform program including land distributions and grain laws. Saturninus even resorted to political assassinations. As violence escalated, Marius distanced himself from his ally and orchestrated the mass execution of Saturninus and his followers—a symbolic return to legality, but one that tarnished his reputation.

After a period of political withdrawal, Marius returned to public life during the Social War (Bellum Sociale), which lasted from 91 to 88 BCE. Rome's Italian allies, who had long fought in Roman wars without receiving citizenship, rose in a bloody rebellion demanding equal rights. The conflict was suppressed in part by Lucius Cornelius Sulla, a conservative aristocrat and former subordinate of Marius. In response to the crisis, the Senate passed the Lex Iulia in 90 BCE and the Lex Plautia Papiria in 89 BCE, granting citizenship to loyal allies and reintegrating most former rebels. This marked a significant transformation in Roman identity and the conceptualization of citizenship.

It was during this phase that Sulla's star began to rise. Born in 138 BCE into a once-noble but impoverished patrician family, Sulla had advanced through talent and ruthless ambition. He had distinguished himself in both the Jugurthine and Social Wars as a capable commander. In 88 BCE, Sulla was elected consul, and the Senate entrusted him with the command of a critical campaign against Mithridates VI Eupator, king of Pontus. Mithridates had overrun much of Asia Minor and, in the infamous "Asiatic Vespers" of 88 BCE, orchestrated the massacre of approximately 80,000 Roman and Italian settlers—an event of existential importance for Rome.

Despite his age and ill health, Marius contested Sulla's appointment. With the aid of the tribune Publius Sulpicius Rufus, Marius secured legislation transferring the command to himself. Sulla, already with his legions, responded with an unprecedented move: he marched on Rome with his army—a violation of the most sacred republican taboo. For the first time, a Roman army waged war on its own city. Sulla expelled Marius and his supporters, reversed their legislative reforms, and deposed political opponents. He then departed for Greece to prosecute the war against Mithridates.

In Sulla's absence, Marius and his allies staged a comeback. In 87 BCE, Marius allied with Consul Lucius Cornelius Cinna, who had also been deposed by Sulla. Together, they orchestrated a violent coup. Marius' return was marked by brutal retribution: in a wave of political purges known as the Marian Terror, numerous senators and opponents were executed. Marius assumed the consulship once again but died shortly thereafter, in January 86 BCE, just days into his seventh term.

Sulla returned to Italy in 83 BCE after concluding his campaign against Mithridates. The ensuing civil war lasted until 82 BCE, culminating in Sulla's decisive victory at the Battle of the Colline Gate. Thereafter, Sulla established an authoritarian regime. In 82 BCE, he had himself appointed dictator for an indefinite term (*dictator legibus faciendis et rei publicae constituendae causa*)—an office that had not been held for over a century. In this capacity, he implemented a wide-ranging program of reforms aimed at strengthening the Senate's authority and curbing the power of the tribunes. His rule, however, is most infamous for the proscriptions: public death lists of political enemies who could be killed without trial. Approximately 500 senators and more than 1,000 equites were executed, their properties confiscated and redistributed to Sulla's supporters.

Sulla's constitutional reforms were staunchly conservative. The powers of the tribunes of the plebs were severely curtailed; their right to propose legislation was virtually abolished. The number of quaestors was increased, enlarging the Senate to 600 members. Sulla also reorganized the administration of the provinces, seeking to limit the autonomy and influence of military commanders through clearer jurisdictional boundaries. Notably, in 79 BCE, Sulla voluntarily resigned his dictatorship and retired to his estate in Campania, where he died in 78 BCE. This voluntary abdication was unprecedented in Roman history, though it did not mitigate the brutal nature of his rule.

The careers of Marius and Sulla marked the beginning of a new era in Roman politics. The army had become the decisive instrument of power, and its loyalty was no longer tied to the state but to the personal fortunes and generosity of individual generals. Political conflicts were no longer resolved through debate and consensus but through violence, proscriptions, and civil war. The Republic had been irreversibly transformed—and the path to permanent rule through military might lay open.

4.3 Caesar vs. Pompey: Civil War and Dictatorship

Gaius Julius Caesar was born on either July 12 or 13 in 100 BCE into a patrician family that, although noble in origin, had by that time lost significant political influence. He belonged to the gens Julia, a lineage that claimed mythical descent from Iulus, the son of the Trojan hero Aeneas. While this ancestry conferred symbolic prestige, it offered little real power. His aunt Julia was married to Gaius Marius, aligning Caesar early on with the popularis faction—those advocating for the interests of the common people. This connection made him a target during the regime of Lucius Cornelius Sulla, who rose to power following a bloody civil war.

In 82 BCE, Sulla ordered Caesar to divorce his wife Cornelia, the daughter of Lucius Cornelius Cinna, a former ally of Marius. Caesar refused the command, risking his life, and went into hiding. He was later pardoned through the intercession of influential figures. This episode already revealed Caesar's political independence, personal courage, and a pronounced sense of loyalty and honor.

Caesar began his public career as a lawyer and orator. He refined his rhetorical skills under the renowned Apollonius Molon on the island of Rhodes. His first official post was as quaestor in Hispania (Spain) in 69 BCE. Quickly gaining popularity, he distinguished himself through generous public games and eloquent oratory. In 65 BCE, he was elected curule aedile, and in 63 BCE he became *Pontifex Maximus*, the chief priest of the Roman state religion—a prestigious office that provided both residence and significant religious authority in Rome. His election was a political milestone, reflecting his growing support among the populares.

The year 63 BCE also marked Marcus Tullius Cicero's consulship and the suppression of the so-called Catilinarian Conspiracy. Although Caesar was not directly involved, he controversially advocated for leniency towards the conspirators, a stance that won him favor among the lower classes but provoked the ire of the conservative senatorial elite. In the following years, Caesar systematically expanded his political influence. In 60 BCE, he entered into a private political alliance with Gnaeus Pompeius Magnus (Pompey the Great), the most celebrated general of the time, and Marcus Licinius Crassus, Rome's wealthiest citizen. This informal coalition became known as the First Triumvirate. It was based on mutual benefit: Caesar secured their backing for his bid for the consulship; Pompey obtained legal ratification for his veteran land settlements; Crassus gained favorable economic legislation.

Caesar was elected consul in 59 BCE. During his term, he passed a series of impactful laws, including the *Lex Julia Agraria*, which provided land for Pompey's veterans, and a law mandating the publication of Senate proceedings. To further solidify his political position, he married Calpurnia, the daughter of Lucius Calpurnius Piso Caesoninus, who was elected consul for the subsequent year—a strategic marital alliance.

Following his consulship, Caesar was granted proconsular command over Gallia Cisalpina, Gallia Narbonensis, and Illyricum in 58 BCE—a commission with significant military potential. The subsequent period, from 58 to 51 BCE, was dominated by Caesar's campaigns in the Gallic Wars, which he himself chronicled in the *Commentarii de Bello Gallico*. These accounts remain a principal source on the subject, though they are also unmistakably propagandistic. During these campaigns, Caesar subdued vast portions of Gaul, including tribes such as the Helvetii, Belgae, and Eburones. He even launched expeditions across the Rhine into Germania and across the Channel into Britannia in 55 and 54 BCE. These military successes greatly enhanced his fame and standing, but they also intensified senatorial fears regarding his expanding personal power base.

Meanwhile in Rome, the Triumvirate was beginning to fracture. Crassus was killed in 53 BCE at the Battle of Carrhae during a disastrous campaign against the Parthians. Pompey, growing increasingly wary of Caesar, began to align himself more closely with the Senate. In 52 BCE, after the violent death of the tribune Clodius and subsequent unrest in the city, Pompey was appointed sole consul—a move that solidified his authority and cast him as the protector of the republican order. At the same time, his distrust of Caesar deepened. The Senate, now dominated again by the optimates (the conservative faction), ordered Caesar to disband his army and return to Rome to stand for the consulship. Caesar insisted that he would do so only if Pompey did the same—a compromise the Senate rejected.

On January 10, 49 BCE, Caesar crossed the Rubicon River with the 13th Legion—an act that marked a point of no return. The Rubicon was the legal boundary between his provincial command and Italy proper. By crossing it under arms, Caesar effectively committed treason. The phrase attributed to him at the moment, *Alea iacta est* ("The die is cast"), has since become symbolic of irreversible decisions and defiance of authority. Pompey and the Senate, unprepared for immediate conflict, fled south to Brundisium and then eastward to Greece, hoping to draw on their provincial resources and conduct a prolonged war.

In the ensuing months, Caesar swiftly secured control over the Italian peninsula and then marched to Hispania, where he defeated the Pompeian forces under Marcus Petreius and Lucius Afranius at the Battle of Ilerda in the summer of 49 BCE. Having neutralized opposition in the West, Caesar turned his attention eastward. The decisive confrontation came on August 9, 48 BCE, at the Battle of Pharsalus in Thessaly. Though Pompey commanded superior numbers, Caesar's tactical brilliance yielded a resounding victory. Pompey fled to Egypt, where he was assassinated on September 28, 48 BCE, by order of the minister Pothinus—an apparent attempt to ingratiate Egypt with the triumphant Caesar.

Caesar followed Pompey to Alexandria and became entangled in the dynastic dispute of the Ptolemaic monarchy. He supported Cleopatra VII, with whom he established both a political and intimate relationship. In the Alexandrian War of 47 BCE, he defeated Cleopatra's brother and co-ruler, Ptolemy XIII, who drowned during the conflict. Caesar remained in Egypt for several months and fathered a son, Caesarion, with Cleopatra. His return to Rome was delayed by further campaigns, including a swift victory over Pharnaces II of Pontus, son of Mithridates VI, at the Battle of Zela in 47 BCE. Caesar famously summarized this triumph with the phrase *Veni, vidi, vici* ("I came, I saw, I conquered")—a propagandistic encapsulation of his rapid and decisive campaign.

By the time of his return to Rome, Caesar had replaced much of the Senate with his own loyalists and had been granted multiple dictatorial appointments. In 46 BCE, he defeated the remaining Pompeian forces at the Battle of Thapsus in North Africa, where key opponents such as Metellus Scipio and Cato the Younger perished—the latter by suicide. The final blow came in 45 BCE at the Battle of Munda in Hispania, where Caesar crushed Gnaeus Pompeius, the son of Pompey the Great. Caesar now stood as the unrivaled master of Rome.

In the final months of his rule, Caesar undertook a series of sweeping reforms: the reorganization of the calendar (introducing the Julian calendar), extension of Roman citizenship, social legislation for the settlement of colonies, expansion of the Senate to 900 members, and the creation of additional magistracies. Yet his concentration of power provoked growing resentment. His acceptance of the title *dictator perpetuo* ("dictator for life") in February 44 BCE deepened fears that he aspired to kingship. These anxieties culminated in a conspiracy involving around 60 senators, including Marcus Junius Brutus and Gaius Cassius Longinus—both former allies turned assassins.

On the Ides of March (March 15), 44 BCE, Caesar was stabbed to death with 23 blows during a Senate session held at the Theatre of Pompey. The assassination, intended to restore the Republic, instead plunged Rome into further turmoil. The conspirators had misjudged the popular support Caesar still commanded and the readiness of his followers to avenge his death.

The civil war between Caesar and Pompey marked a pivotal rupture in Roman history. It undermined the foundational principles of the Republic, entwining power with military command and rendering the Senate a nominal institution. Although the Republic nominally survived, it had become a hollow facade.

The events surrounding the Ides of March stand among the most dramatic and consequential turning points in Roman history. They not only marked the end of Gaius Julius Caesar's political life but also signaled the irrevocable collapse of the republican tradition—ironically, a tradition the conspirators sought to salvage by murdering him. The assassination was the culmination of long-standing tensions, immediate political conspiracies, and acute developments that converged within a matter of weeks into a singular act of political violence.

The term *"Ides"* originates from the ancient Roman calendar system and refers to the 15th day of March. It was traditionally a significant date in the Roman calendar, originally associated with religious significance, particularly dedicated to the god Mars, to whom the month of March was consecrated. In 44 BCE, this day fell on a Wednesday and became the stage for an unprecedented assassination.

The immediate weeks leading up to the murder were marked by an atmosphere of growing political insecurity, vanity, mistrust, and Caesar's increasing isolation from the aristocratic leadership of Rome. After his victory in the civil war against the remaining Pompeian forces and the Battle of Munda in March 45 BCE, Caesar returned to Rome, where he increasingly accumulated dictatorial powers. On January 26, 44 BCE, the Senate conferred upon him the office of *dictator perpetuo*—dictator for life—a move that deeply unsettled many of his opponents. Shortly before that, in February of the same year, he had himself styled as a kind of sacral monarch: statues depicted him with royal insignia, he allowed himself to be worshipped in temples like a god, and he demanded a seating arrangement in the Senate in which all senators stood while he alone remained seated.

A particularly explosive event occurred on February 15, 44 BCE, during the Lupercalia, an ancient Roman fertility festival. On that day, Marcus Antonius, Caesar's closest confidant and then consul, approached the dictator in public with a royal crown. In an obviously staged scene, he offered the crown to Caesar. Caesar demonstratively refused it—twice. The crowd cheered, but the incident remained ambiguous. The question of whether Caesar truly intended to become king remained unanswered, but the symbolic gesture suggested that he was at least considering it. For many Republicans, this was the final warning sign.

In this tense atmosphere, a circle of conspirators began to form around Marcus Junius Brutus and Gaius Cassius Longinus. Both had formerly supported Pompey, but Brutus had received Caesar's pardon after Pharsalus and had even been appointed praetor for the year 44 BCE. His inclusion in Caesar's inner circle of power, and his name—Brutus, like the legendary Lucius Junius Brutus, who had expelled King Tarquinius Superbus—lent the planned act symbolic weight. Cassius, on the other hand, bore deeper resentment toward Caesar and was ideologically as well as personally determined to end his sole rule. The group grew to around 60 individuals, including senators of all political factions—even former populares—demonstrating that opposition to Caesar was not rooted solely in conservative circles.

The precise timing of the assassination was deliberately chosen. Caesar had originally planned to depart for a military campaign against the Parthians on March 18, 44 BCE, during which he also intended to celebrate a triumph for his victories in Spain. Since he had convened a Senate session beforehand, the conspirators decided to strike during that meeting. The location was not the regular Senate house on the Forum, but rather the Theatre of Pompey on the Campus Martius, since the usual Senate building, the Curia Hostilia, was undergoing renovations. This detail turned out to be a cruel irony of fate: Caesar was destined to fall in a structure erected by his former rival, Pompey.

On the morning of March 15, various omens reportedly occurred that might have warned Caesar. Pliny the Elder reports that a sacrificial priest could not discern any favorable signs during the morning's animal offering. His wife, Calpurnia, begged him not to leave the house, having been plagued by nightmares. The soothsayer Spurinna, who had already warned him days earlier to beware the "Ides of March," was once again cited. Suetonius recounts that as Caesar passed Spurinna, he mocked: *"The Ides of March have come,"* to which the seer replied: *"Aye, they have come—but they have not yet gone."*

Despite these warnings, Caesar made his way to the Senate shortly before noon. He was accompanied by a small entourage, including Marcus Antonius, who, however, was distracted outside the building by a diversion orchestrated by the conspirators in order to keep him away from the scene. Inside the chamber, the senators surrounded Caesar under a pretext: they requested that he sign a decree permitting the return of exiled persons. When he refused, the assassination began. According to Plutarch, the first blow was struck by Servilius Casca, who stabbed Caesar in the neck from behind with a dagger. Caesar initially attempted to defend himself and cried out, "Casca, you scoundrel, what are you doing?" but then a cascade of blows followed. He is said to have received 23 stab wounds in total, of which, according to the autopsy, only one—a stab directly to the chest—was actually fatal.

At the end of the attack, multiple sources report that Caesar ceased resisting when he saw Marcus Brutus among the attackers. Whether he uttered the famous words *"Et tu, Brute?"* ("You too, Brutus?"), as later dramatized by Shakespeare, is historically doubtful. More likely is the account from Suetonius, who reports that Caesar silently pulled his toga over his head—a gesture symbolizing dignity in death.

His lifeless body remained lying on the steps of the Senate building, at the foot of the statue of Pompey. It was a deeply symbolic scene: Caesar died at the very location where political decision-making had been replaced by oratory, murdered by those who believed themselves to be saviors of the Republic—under the gaze of his old rival.

The immediate aftermath of the assassination was chaotic. The conspirators had hoped that the people and the Senate would greet them as liberators—*"liberatores."* But their plan for an immediate political overthrow failed. Marcus Antonius, although not designated as Caesar's successor in his will, swiftly emerged and outwardly maintained calm, even though he remained privately loyal to Caesar. Caesar's will, read publicly on March 18, revealed a strategic masterstroke: he bequeathed 300 sesterces to every Roman citizen and left his gardens beyond the Tiber as public parkland. Simultaneously, he adopted his great-nephew Gaius Octavius as his heir—the future Augustus.

The populace, initially uncertain, reacted with outrage and fury following the reading of the will and Antony's funeral oration, presumably delivered on March 20 on the Roman Forum. Caesar's body was not cremated outside the city, as tradition dictated, but rather on the Forum itself, on an improvised pyre. Public sentiment shifted dramatically: the mob looted the houses of the conspirators, and Brutus and Cassius were forced to flee Rome. The assassination had not saved the Republic—it had instead reignited the polarization of Roman society and paved the way for the next civil war, which would this time lead definitively to the establishment of autocratic rule.

In retrospect, March 15, 44 BCE, was not the end but rather the symbolic climax of the Republic's decline. The Ides of March became a historical *menetekel*—a moment in which personal motives, political illusions, and ideological delusion culminated in an act whose consequences extended far beyond Caesar's life. The Republic had not yet been officially abolished—but it had been mortally wounded beyond recovery.

4.4 The Triumvirates and Power Struggles until Augustus

Following the assassination of Gaius Julius Caesar on March 15, 44 BCE, the Roman Republic descended into a state of extreme instability. The conspirators' hope of restoring the old republican order by eliminating the dictator proved to be an illusion. Instead of a return to republican legality, a new and even more devastating phase of civil war ensued—one that would ultimately culminate in the establishment of the Principate under Octavian. At the heart of these developments was the struggle for Caesar's political legacy, primarily among Marcus Antonius, Octavian, and other key figures who formed what came to be known as the Triumvirates. The period from 44 to 27 BCE was marked by shifting alliances, massacres, propaganda campaigns, and bloody battles that laid the groundwork for the imperial era.

Immediately after Caesar's murder, the main conspirators fled

Rome. Marcus Junius Brutus and Gaius Cassius Longinus retreated to the eastern provinces. In Rome, Marcus Antonius —then serving as consul and a former confidant of Caesar— assumed a central role. Through deft political maneuvering, he managed to secure most of Caesar's estate, including his personal papers and official seal. However, the decisive turning point was Caesar's will, publicly announced on March 18, 44 BCE: it designated Gaius Octavius, Caesar's 18-year-old great-nephew, as his principal heir and adopted son. From that moment, Octavius adopted the name Gaius Julius Caesar Octavianus—commonly known as Octavian—and began asserting his claim as Caesar's rightful successor.

Octavian arrived in Rome in April 44 BCE. Although young and politically inexperienced, he quickly demonstrated tactical acumen. He appealed directly to Caesar's veterans, securing their loyalty through generous financial promises, raised his own troops independently, and positioned himself as the legitimate heir in opposition to Antonius, whom he portrayed as a usurper of Caesar's legacy. In an unprecedented act of self-empowerment, Octavian effectively assumed the role of imperator despite holding no official magistracies.

The conflict between Octavian and Antonius escalated as the latter sought to expand his influence through control of Gaul and Italy. A major point of contention arose over northern Gaul, which had been allocated to Decimus Junius Brutus. This dispute led to open hostilities. In the spring of 43 BCE, Antonius was defeated at the Battle of Mutina (modern Modena) by a senatorial army led by the consuls Aulus Hirtius and Gaius Vibius Pansa, in alliance with Octavian. Although the battle was a victory for Octavian, both consuls were killed in action. This development enabled Octavian to assert his military authority and gain political autonomy. He had himself proclaimed consul by his troops and marched on Rome, where he assumed the consulship on August 19, 43 BCE—an unprecedented event in

Roman history for someone so young.

During this period, the so-called Second Triumvirate was formed—an official pact among three men to restore order to the state. In November 43 BCE, Octavian, Antonius, and Marcus Aemilius Lepidus convened in Bononia (modern Bologna). Through the *lex Titia*, enacted on November 27, 43 BCE by the popular assembly, the Triumvirate was granted legislative and executive powers for a term of five years. This was not merely an alliance but a constitutionally enshrined form of emergency rule—a triumviral regime vested with dictatorial authority.

The Triumvirs' first joint act was ruthless: the Proscriptions. These were publicly posted death lists targeting political opponents, serving both to eliminate resistance and replenish the state treasury. Approximately 300 senators and 2,000 equestrians were executed. Among the most notable victims was Marcus Tullius Cicero, a fierce critic of Antonius, who was murdered in December 43 BCE—a symbolic execution of the Republican opposition.

With their rear secured, Antonius and Octavian marched eastward in 42 BCE to confront Brutus and Cassius, who had raised an army there. The decisive confrontations took place at the twin battles of Philippi in Macedonia, on October 3 and 23, 42 BCE. In the first engagement, Brutus managed to defeat Octavian, while Cassius, mistakenly believing all was lost, committed suicide. In the second battle, Antonius decisively defeated Brutus, who also took his own life. With the deaths of the leading assassins, the opposition was extinguished, and the Triumvirate solidified its grip on power.

A redistribution of provincial control followed: Lepidus received Africa, Octavian took Italy and the western provinces, while Antonius assumed control of the affluent East. Tensions between Octavian and Antonius, however, soon escalated.

In Italy, Octavian faced immense challenges, including the resettlement of veterans, land redistribution, and internal unrest. Particularly notable was the Perusine War (41–40 BCE), during which Lucius Antonius, brother of Marcus Antonius, and Fulvia, his wife, instigated an uprising against Octavian. The rebellion culminated in the siege of Perusia (modern Perugia), after which Octavian exacted brutal retribution on the city's elite.

A tenuous reconciliation was achieved in the Treaty of Brundisium in the autumn of 40 BCE. Antonius married Octavian's sister Octavia to cement the alliance, but underlying tensions remained. While Octavian consolidated power in Italy, Antonius returned to the East and established an independent sphere of influence, most notably through his alliance with the Egyptian queen Cleopatra VII. Their relationship was both political and personal. In 37 BCE, the Triumvirate was renewed for another five years by the *lex Tarpeia*, but the rivalry between Antonius and Octavian had become unmistakable.

Octavian launched an effective propaganda campaign in Rome against Antonius, portraying him as a traitor to Roman values who had subordinated himself to a foreign queen, fathered children with an Egyptian, and embraced the decadence of the East. Simultaneously, Octavian styled himself as the guardian of traditional Roman morals. In 36 BCE, he managed to politically neutralize Lepidus, who had compromised himself through an unsuccessful power play in Sicily. Although Lepidus retained his formal titles as *pontifex maximus* and Triumvir, he was, in practice, politically irrelevant. The power dynamic had thus been reduced to a rivalry between two figures: Antonius and Octavian.

The final escalation occurred in 32 BCE, when, at Octavian's urging, the Senate stripped Antonius of his offices and formally declared war—not on Antonius himself, but on Cleopatra.

This maneuver allowed Octavian to present the conflict as a defense of Rome against a foreign threat. The decisive military engagement was the naval Battle of Actium on September 2, 31 BCE, off the western coast of Greece. Octavian's fleet, commanded by Marcus Vipsanius Agrippa, secured a decisive victory. Antonius and Cleopatra fled to Egypt, where, in August 30 BCE, they both committed suicide following Octavian's entry into Alexandria.

With the deaths of his last political rivals, Octavian emerged as the sole ruler of the Roman world. In January 27 BCE, he formally relinquished his extraordinary powers to the Senate—a political gesture that earned him the honorific title Augustus. This marked the official end of the Roman Republic and the beginning of the Principate: a new political system that operated under republican terminology but was, in reality, monarchical in nature.

Between 44 and 27 BCE, the Roman world was transformed—not through legal reform, but through the violent struggle of competing powerbrokers. The Triumvirates did not represent a revival of republican collegiality but rather were desperate, violent alliances forged in a civil war for legitimacy, resources, and ideological supremacy. Octavian's victory was not merely personal—it signaled the triumph of a new political order, forged through bloodshed, annihilation, and relentless propaganda.

CHAPTER 5: THE PRINCIPATE – AUGUSTUS AND THE GOLDEN AGE (27 BC–68 AD)

5.1 Augustus' Rise to Power and State Reform

Following the bloody end of the Roman Republic and the turbulent period of civil wars—culminating in the assassination of Gaius Julius Caesar in 44 BCE—a new era commenced with the rise to power of his grand-nephew and adopted son, Gaius Octavius, better known as Augustus. This epoch, later referred to as the *Principate*, not only signified a profound reorganization of the Roman state constitution but also ushered in a phase of relative stability, during which the Roman polity transitioned into a monarchy in all but name—without formally abolishing the traditional republican institutions. The years between 44 and 27 BCE marked the ascendancy of Octavian, culminating in his establishment as the first Roman emperor—although the title "emperor" (*imperator*) was never officially used in this context during his lifetime.

After Caesar's death, Octavian skillfully seized the political initiative by claiming the inheritance left to him in Caesar's will (in which he had been posthumously adopted and designated as chief heir). He returned to Rome in the summer of 44 BCE, despite being initially disregarded by the Senate. Nevertheless, he began methodically gathering Caesar's former supporters, asserting his claim to the legacy of his adoptive father, and forging strategic alliances with influential political actors. One of his first decisive actions was the use of private funds to distribute the monetary bequests promised to the Roman people in Caesar's will—an act that earned him immense popular acclaim.

At this juncture, the political atmosphere in Rome was tense. The Senate was under the sway of Marcus Tullius Cicero, while Marcus Antonius (Mark Antony), a close associate of Caesar, sought to fill the resulting power vacuum. Tensions between Octavian and Antony escalated in 43 BCE when the Senate formally commissioned Octavian to act against Antony, and he joined forces with the consuls Hirtius and Pansa in military engagements near Mutina (modern Modena). Following the deaths of both consuls, Octavian assumed command of their legions, marched on Rome, and compelled the Senate to appoint him consul—a dramatic act of political coercion, achieved at the young age of twenty.

In the subsequent months, Octavian entered into a pragmatic alliance with Mark Antony and Marcus Aemilius Lepidus. This so-called Second Triumvirate, legally established by the *lex Titia* on November 27, 43 BCE, granted the trio nearly dictatorial authority over the Roman state. Over the following years, systematic proscriptions against political opponents commenced, during which Cicero was assassinated in December 43 BCE. The Triumvirs also directed their efforts against Caesar's assassins. At the Battle of Philippi in October 42 BCE, the leading conspirators, Marcus Junius Brutus and Gaius Cassius Longinus, were decisively defeated and committed suicide.

Tensions soon arose among the Triumvirs. In 36 BCE, Lepidus was sidelined after an unsuccessful coup attempt and was relegated to political irrelevance. The true power struggle emerged between Octavian and Antony, who became increasingly reliant on the eastern provinces and Egypt—particularly due to his intimate alliance with Cleopatra VII, the reigning queen of Egypt. The situation deteriorated irreversibly after the so-called "Donations of Alexandria" in 34 BCE, wherein Antony granted extensive territorial rights to Cleopatra and their children, including Caesarion, the alleged son of Caesar, thereby implying dynastic claims to Rome's eastern territories.

Octavian masterfully portrayed this act as evidence of Antony's betrayal of Roman values. In a groundbreaking instance of political propaganda, he arranged for Antony's will to be publicly read aloud in 32 BCE, revealing its controversial contents and painting Antony as a traitor manipulated by a foreign queen. The ensuing war was officially framed not as a civil conflict, but as a war against Egypt. The decisive confrontation occurred at the naval Battle of Actium, on September 2, 31 BCE, off the western coast of Greece. Octavian's fleet, under the capable command of Admiral Marcus Vipsanius Agrippa, decisively defeated the combined forces of Antony and Cleopatra. The victory was total, and Octavian's military and moral supremacy was indisputable.

Antony and Cleopatra fled to Egypt, where, following Octavian's capture of Alexandria in 30 BCE, they both committed suicide. Egypt was annexed as a Roman province and designated as the personal domain of Octavian, directly governed by him as *Princeps*. This acquisition afforded him immense control over the Empire's grain supply and the wealth of one of the richest regions of the ancient world.

Having vanquished all rivals, Octavian now stood as the unchallenged master of the Roman world. However, rather than proclaiming himself king or dictator—titles that had become politically toxic since Caesar's assassination—he pursued a subtler course. On January 13, 27 BCE, he ceremonially returned his extraordinary powers to the Senate and the Roman people, an act presented as the *res publica restituta* (restoration of the Republic). This gesture, however, was purely symbolic, for only days later, on January 16, the Senate bestowed upon him the honorific title *Augustus*, meaning "the Revered One." This title carried religious connotations, marking him as a quasi-divine figure, without invoking the monarchical terminology that would alienate traditionalist sensibilities. He simultaneously retained the title *Princeps Senatus* ("First among the Senate") and the *tribunicia potestas* (tribunician power), granting him legislative initiative and personal inviolability.

The post-27 BCE period was characterized by a constant balancing act between republican façade and monarchical reality. Augustus maintained the external structure of republican governance but exercised effective control through a sophisticated concentration of powers and personal authority. He held both consular and tribunician powers concurrently and was granted the *imperium maius* in 23 BCE—superior military authority over all provincial governors. In practical terms, this made Augustus the supreme commander of the Empire's armed forces and allowed him direct control over provinces where legions were stationed. These so-called "imperial provinces" were personally administered by him, while the more tranquil "senatorial provinces" remained under the nominal oversight of the Senate.

A major institutional reform undertaken by Augustus was the reorganization of the military. He reduced the number of legions from approximately 60 to about 28, deploying them primarily along frontier regions such as Germania, Pannonia, and Syria. Soldiers were discharged after twenty years of service with a one-time payment, financed through the *aerarium militare* (military treasury), which Augustus established specifically for this purpose. Veterans were settled in colonies, serving both as instruments of Romanization and as stabilizing forces in the provinces.

To ensure loyalty and consolidate his rule, Augustus implemented a system of personal allegiance. The oath of *fides* (loyalty) to the *Princeps* became a standard practice throughout the Empire. Augustus also demonstrated exceptional skill in the symbolic communication of power. Through monumental construction projects—such as the Forum of Augustus and the Temple of Mars Ultor (dedicated in 2 BCE)—he physically manifested his political and religious role. The *Ara Pacis Augustae* (Altar of Augustan Peace), constructed between 13 and 9 BCE, glorified his image as a bringer of peace after decades of civil strife. His religious authority was further solidified in 12 BCE, when he assumed the position of *Pontifex Maximus*, the highest priestly office.

Augustus also pursued a deliberate program of moral legislation. Through the *Leges Iuliae*—including the *Lex Iulia de maritandis ordinibus* (Marriage Law) of 18 BCE and the *Lex Iulia de adulteriis coercendis* (Law on the Punishment of Adultery)—he aimed to realign Roman society with conservative, traditional values. These laws were designed to restore the *mos maiorum* (ancestral customs) and encourage marital fertility among the elite. Ultimately, these efforts served to morally legitimize his regime and reinforce societal stability.

Social control was maintained through a vast network of loyal administrators, predominantly drawn from the equestrian order (*Equites*). Augustus favored a hybrid administrative model that combined republican officeholding with personal dependency on his authority. The Praetorian Guard, which he reorganized and stationed in the *Castra Praetoria* in Rome, functioned as both an elite military unit and a central instrument of his power. Its commander, the *Praefectus Praetorio*, became one of the most influential positions in the Empire.

By 2 BCE, Augustus had reached the zenith of his public esteem. The Senate awarded him the honorific title *Pater Patriae* ("Father of the Fatherland"). That same year, the Forum of Augustus was officially inaugurated. Augustus presented himself as the guardian of peace, Roman virtue, and institutional continuity. Nevertheless, dynastic succession remained a contentious issue: his intended heir, Marcus Agrippa, had died in 12 BCE, and both of his grandsons, Gaius and Lucius Caesar, died prematurely in 4 and 2 CE respectively. In response, Augustus formally adopted his stepson Tiberius in 4 CE, thereby securing the dynastic transmission of power.

Augustus died on August 19, 14 CE, in Nola, Campania. His death did not signal the end of the order he had established. On the contrary, the *Principate* he had constructed endured as a stable form of autocracy adopted by his successors. The Senate decreed his deification—he became *Divus Augustus*, the deified emperor. His ashes were interred in the Mausoleum he had commissioned in 28 BCE.

Augustus' rise to power and subsequent reforms marked the beginning of a new epoch. His rule was a masterful blend of tradition and innovation, balancing republican rhetoric with monarchical substance. Through his calculated statecraft, Augustus not only laid the foundation for two centuries of relative imperial stability, but also ushered Rome into a new historical era—the age of the Roman Empire.

5.2 The Pax Romana and Economic Prosperity

Following the protracted civil wars that had shaken Rome from the mid-1st century BCE until the definitive consolidation of autocratic rule under Augustus, the Roman Empire entered a new era in 27 BCE. This period was characterized by relative internal stability, secure foreign relations, and substantial economic growth. Historians refer to this phase as the *Pax Romana*—the "Roman Peace"—a term denoting a roughly two-century-long era that commenced with Augustus and extended until the death of Emperor Marcus Aurelius in 180 CE. During this time, the Roman leadership not only succeeded in consolidating its territorial acquisitions but also, through targeted policies concerning the economy, infrastructure, and provincial administration, steered the Empire to an economic zenith unmatched in antiquity.

Shortly after the conclusion of the final military conflicts in the eastern provinces—most notably following the annexation of Egypt in 30 BCE—a period of increasing economic stability commenced. Egypt was placed under the direct control of the emperor rather than the Senate, owing to its strategic importance for grain supplies to Rome and its immense fiscal resources. At times, shipments of Egyptian grain fulfilled up to 30% of the annual grain requirement of the city of Rome, which already had a population exceeding one million under Augustus.

The economic foundations of the Pax Romana rested on secure frontiers maintained by a standing army, an effective communications network, and orderly administration. The provinces, which accounted for approximately 90% of the Empire's total territory, were systematically integrated into the broader economic framework. By the turn of the millennium, the Roman Empire had a population exceeding 60 million people—of which about 6 to 7 million lived in Italy, with the remainder spread across more than 40 provinces. According to the historian Cassius Dio, around 600 Roman cities existed in 14 CE—a number that had increased to well over 1,200 by the 2nd century. This urbanization significantly contributed to economic connectivity and prosperity.

A cornerstone of this development was the extensive road network, which was greatly expanded under Augustus and his successors. The *Via Augusta* in Hispania alone extended over 1,500 kilometers of paved roads, while the renowned *Via Appia* led all the way to Brundisium (modern Brindisi), serving as a critical trade route to Greece and Asia Minor. Current estimates suggest that the Roman Empire possessed between 80,000 and 100,000 kilometers of paved roads, including roughly 30,000 kilometers in Italy. This infrastructure facilitated not only rapid military deployment but also the efficient distribution of goods, people, and information. The *Cursus Publicus*, a state-organized courier and transport system, ensured the delivery of correspondence and couriers at average speeds of 80 to 120 kilometers per day.

The security of these routes was ensured by stationed legions and auxiliary troops. Between 27 BCE and 68 CE, the number of military installations in the frontier provinces increased significantly. Fortified camps such as Vindobona (Vienna), Mogontiacum (Mainz), and Antioch were established in Germania, the Danube region, and the East. The military presence generated a steady demand for food, clothing, weapons, and construction materials, thereby stimulating local economies. According to modern estimates, the legions consumed approximately 200,000 tons of grain and 300 million liters of water annually. Numerous local producers benefited from these large-scale state contracts.

The period of peace also allowed for the development of a robust domestic market and the massive expansion of long-distance trade. In Gaul, new administrative structures were implemented under Augustus, including the creation of the three provinces Gallia Narbonensis, Gallia Lugdunensis, and Gallia Belgica. Cities such as Lugdunum (Lyon), Colonia Claudia Ara Agrippinensium (Cologne), and Augustodunum (Autun) evolved into regional trade hubs. In Germania, territorial ambitions were scaled back after the disaster of the Battle of the Teutoburg Forest in 9 CE, yet commercial activity along the Rhine remained robust.

Maritime trade in the Mediterranean flourished particularly. The harbor of Ostia was significantly expanded under Emperor Claudius (r. 41–54 CE). With the construction of an artificial basin, the *Portus Claudii*, larger ships could now be unloaded efficiently. By the mid-1st century CE, annual grain imports through Ostia had reached around 300,000 tons. Luxury goods such as silk from China, spices from India, and ivory from Africa arrived in Rome via ports like Alexandria, Antioch, and Leptis Magna.

The economic prosperity was also reflected in the monetary system. In 23 BCE, Augustus initiated a comprehensive monetary reform. The resulting coinage system was based on the *Aureus* (gold coin, approx. 7.8 grams), the *Denarius* (silver coin, approx. 3.9 grams), as well as the *Sestertius* (brass coin) and the *As* (copper coin). This stable currency system enabled regional price comparisons and fostered trust in the Roman market. Up to the reign of Nero, the exchange ratio between silver and gold remained relatively stable at approximately 12:1. Taxes were levied regularly—usually every five years in the provinces—and included both in-kind and monetary contributions. The Empire's annual revenue under Augustus is estimated to have been around one billion *sestertii*, with approximately half allocated to military expenditures.

Agriculture remained the dominant economic sector. Italy continued to be the heartland of latifundia-based production. In Campania, Etruria, and Apulia, large estates produced primarily grain, olive oil, and wine. Wine exports peaked under Emperor Tiberius (14–37 CE). Amphorae filled with Roman wine were exported to Gaul, Britain, and along the Rhine. In Gaul, viticulture expanded under Augustus, particularly around Massilia (Marseille), as well as in Hispania Tarraconensis.

Mining was also systematically promoted. In Hispania—especially around Asturia and Carthago Nova—extensive gold and silver mining operations were conducted, producing enormous yields. Pliny the Elder mentions up to 20,000 slaves working in the gold mines of Las Médulas. The annual output of these mines is estimated at around 6,000 kilograms of gold. In Noricum (modern Austria and Slovenia), high-quality iron was extracted and exported primarily for the manufacture of weapons and tools.

In the field of manufacturing, pottery developed into a major export industry. *Terra Sigillata*, a glossy red fineware, was initially produced in Arezzo, Etruria, and later in Gaul and the Rhineland (e.g., Trier, Rheinzabern). These products reached both the British Isles and the Eastern Mediterranean through trade. Glass production in Syria and Egypt also deserves mention: mass-produced glassware became increasingly common and was exported widely—a novelty in ancient consumer culture.

Economic prosperity was further evidenced by demographic trends. According to estimates by modern historians, the Empire's annual population growth ranged from 0.1% to 0.3%. Cities such as Alexandria (approx. 300,000–500,000 inhabitants), Carthage (approx. 200,000), and Antioch (over 250,000) served not only as economic hubs but also as multicultural crossroads. The economic integration of the provinces fostered cultural exchange. Roman law, the Latin language, and Roman building techniques spread across the Empire. Cities were outfitted with forums, baths, aqueducts, and amphitheaters, which not only enhanced urban life but also provided substantial employment opportunities.

The construction sector particularly benefited from the Pax Romana. Public works projects—including roads, bridges, temples, and bath complexes—employed thousands of laborers. In Rome itself, numerous major building programs were undertaken in the decades following Augustus's death under the emperors Claudius and Nero. These included the *Aqua Claudia* (completed in 52 CE), the Colosseum (begun under Vespasian but planned under Nero), and the *Domus Transitoria*, a new urban district.

The Pax Romana also marked a period of relative social stability. Although significant disparities between rich and poor persisted, unrest in Rome was relatively well contained through grain distributions (*frumentationes*), public entertainments, and infrastructural investment. Between 150,000 and 200,000 grain rations were distributed annually to needy citizens in Rome —sometimes free of charge—providing a basic level of social security.

In summary, the Pax Romana between 27 BCE and 68 CE constituted one of the most economically stable and productive epochs in Roman history. It was founded on the political centralization of the Principate, the military securing of borders, and the economic integration of the provinces. Trade flourished, cities expanded, infrastructure was modernized, and agriculture intensified. During these decades, the Roman Empire attained an economic standard that would not be matched in many regions until the High Middle Ages or even the modern period. The Pax Romana was thus not merely a military and political success but also an economic and civilizational model of lasting historical significance.

5.3 Social Structure and Urban Life

The social order of the Roman Empire during the early Principate, particularly under the Julio-Claudian emperors from Augustus (r. 27 BCE–14 CE) to Nero (r. 54–68 CE), was characterized by a complex and multilayered hierarchy that rested both on traditional aristocratic norms and new socioeconomic realities. The transition from Republic to Principate brought profound changes to the organization of Roman society, especially in urban environments, which expanded significantly and experienced intense cultural development during this period.

At the top of the social hierarchy stood the *senatores* of Rome. This elite group, comprising around 600 men, held office either by birthright or by imperial appointment. A minimum property requirement of one million sesterces was necessary for entry into the senatorial order. Senators occupied the highest offices in both civil administration and the military and enjoyed considerable legal and social privileges. Although their political power had diminished in comparison to the Republican era, their social prestige remained largely intact. Many senatorial families resided in opulent townhouses (*domus*) on the Palatine Hill or near the Roman Forum.

Immediately below them were the *equites*, a wealthy upper class originally derived from the cavalry order. Under Augustus and his successors, their significance increased markedly, as they were frequently employed in the imperial administration, tax collection, and provincial governance. The minimum wealth threshold for membership in the *ordo equester* was set at 400,000 sesterces. Many *equites* were simultaneously entrepreneurs, lessees of state monopolies, or directors of imperial financial offices (*procuratores*). Although the exact number of equestrians is difficult to determine, they likely numbered several thousand in the capital alone.

Below these two leading orders was the broad class of Roman citizens (*cives Romani*), encompassing a wide spectrum of social strata—from affluent merchants and skilled artisans to day laborers and small-scale farmers. A crucial distinction existed between full citizens, who enjoyed political rights and legal protections, and groups such as the *Latini* and *peregrini*, who possessed limited or no citizenship rights. In 14 CE, the number of Roman citizens was estimated at approximately 4 to 5 million, a minority within the total imperial population. However, this figure steadily increased due to the ongoing integration of provincial populations.

A significant portion of the urban population, however, was legally unfree. Slaves constituted a pervasive demographic within Roman cities. In Rome itself, the slave population during the 1st century CE is estimated at around 300,000 to 400,000 individuals—roughly one-third of the city's total population, which numbered close to one million. Slaves fulfilled diverse roles: they worked as domestic servants, craftsmen, scribes, teachers, physicians, and agricultural laborers on the large estates (*latifundia*). Under Emperor Claudius, certain legal positions of slaves were improved, notably their access to manumission (*manumissio*). Freedmen (*liberti*) formed an ascending social group that often found success in business and could accumulate considerable wealth, although they remained barred from holding certain public offices. Tacitus, with a tone of criticism, remarked on the influence of wealthy freedmen at the imperial court—such as Pallas and Narcissus, favorites of Claudius, who wielded significant political power.

Urban life in the Roman Empire was marked by pronounced social differentiation. The city of Rome, due to its unique structure and scale, stood as an exceptional case among the cities of the empire. In contrast to the Greek *poleis* or smaller Italic towns, Rome was a colossal urban agglomeration where elites and the masses coexisted in physical proximity yet remained socially distinct. The majority of urban inhabitants lived in multi-storey apartment buildings (*insulae*), typically constructed of stone on the lower levels and wood on the upper floors. These structures were prone to fire and collapse—as exemplified by the Great Fire of Rome in 64 CE during Nero's reign, which destroyed large portions of the inner city.

Living conditions varied dramatically depending on wealth. Patrician families inhabited luxurious *domus* complete with atria, peristyles, fountains, and private baths. By contrast, the urban poor lived in cramped one-room apartments without running water or sanitary facilities. Rome's water supply was ensured by a sophisticated network of aqueducts—nine were in operation by Nero's time—delivering approximately one million cubic meters of water per day. Public fountains, latrines, and bathhouses provided access to basic hygiene for the broader population.

A central feature of urban life was the *fora*—public squares that functioned as marketplaces, political arenas, and social gathering points. The Forum Romanum remained the heart of the city, complemented by Augustus' Forum Augustum, which included the Temple of Mars Ultor. In the provinces, similar fora were established following Roman models, for example in Emerita Augusta (modern Mérida), Thugga, and Timgad, which often served simultaneously as administrative and commercial hubs. Activities in these spaces included trade, legal proceedings, political speeches, and religious ceremonies.

The culture of public bathing was another defining aspect of urban life. Roman bathhouses (*thermae*) were not only places for personal hygiene but also venues for social interaction, relaxation, and political discourse. Long before the grand imperial baths of the 2nd and 3rd centuries CE, major facilities like the Thermae Agrippae (constructed around 25 BCE) and the Thermae Neronianae (around 60 CE) had already been established. Entrance was usually free or cost very little, with funding provided by wealthy patrons or the emperor himself. Visits to the baths followed a structured routine: changing clothes, physical exercise, sweating in the *sudatorium*, bathing in the *caldarium*, and cooling down in the *frigidarium*.

Culturally, urban life in the Roman Empire was vibrant

and multifaceted. Public spectacles, theatrical performances, chariot races, and gladiatorial contests were among the most popular forms of entertainment. The Circus Maximus could accommodate up to 150,000 spectators during chariot races. The *ludi*, organized in honor of deities or the emperor, were overseen by aediles or by the emperor himself and could last for several days. Gladiatorial combats, such as those held in the *Amphitheatrum Neronis*, were highly ritualized and immensely popular. The frequency of public games increased under the early emperors—for instance, Nero organized a ten-day festival in 57 CE in honor of his mother Agrippina.

Religiously, urban life was deeply interwoven with ritual practices, cultic institutions, and processions. Household deities (*Lares* and *Penates*) were worshipped daily, while public festivals such as the Saturnalia and Lupercalia mobilized large segments of the population. The imperial cult gained substantial prominence during this period, with altars and temples for the *Divi* (deified emperors) being erected in numerous cities—for example, the *Ara Pacis Augustae* in Rome, completed in 9 BCE. The emperor increasingly served as the sacred center of the political order, particularly in the eastern provinces such as Asia and Egypt.

Another central element of urban life was the phenomenon of associations (*collegia*). These organizations, founded for religious, professional, or social purposes, provided their members with social security, political representation, and a sense of community. There were *collegia fabrum* (guilds of craftsmen), *collegia funeraticia* (funerary associations), and *collegia iuvenum*, which prepared young men for civic responsibilities. The state increasingly sought to regulate these associations—especially under Tiberius and Claudius—due to concerns over their potential for political subversion.

In the provincial world, Roman social structures were mirrored in modified forms. Cities such as Lugdunum, Caesarea Mauretaniae, and Antioch saw the emergence of local elites who combined Roman and indigenous elements. These *notabiles* held municipal offices (e.g., *duumviri, aediles, quaestores*), financed public buildings and games, and acted as intermediaries between Rome and local populations. Provincial urbanization served not only as a means of control but also as a mechanism of cultural and administrative integration.

The fabric of Roman urban society was strongly influenced by patronage. The relationship between a *patronus* and his *clientes* structured political careers, economic transactions, and opportunities for social mobility. The daily *salutatio*, in which clients greeted their patron each morning, was a cornerstone of Roman social life. Patrons supported their clients through financial aid, influence, or legal assistance, while clients, in turn, accompanied their patron in public, voted for them when elections were held, and publicly praised their achievements.

In sum, the social structure of the early Principate was defined by the interplay between traditional Roman values such as *dignitas, virtus,* and *fides,* and the new realities of imperial governance: the emperor as a focal point of loyalty, the rising influence of freedmen and provincials, the ongoing urbanization and increasing anonymity of city life, and the pervasive presence of social inequality. The cities of the Roman Empire—from Rome to Ephesus, Lyon, Carthage, and Alexandria—mirrored this complex and dynamic society, whose tensions and accomplishments laid the groundwork for the Roman culture.

5.4 Culture, Literature, and Architecture

The Augustan period, along with the subsequent Julio-Claudian era, marks a pivotal cultural turning point in the history of Rome. Its impact was not only visible in the ideologically charged literature of the time but also in the monumental architectural reshaping of the city of Rome and a flourishing of artistic self-awareness. The years between 27 BCE and 68 CE formed the cultural framework for a deliberate staging of the new imperial order — the *res publica restituta* under the rule of *princeps* Augustus and his successors. This cultural upswing was by no means incidental; rather, it was systematically employed as a tool of political legitimation.

A defining feature of this epoch was the state-sponsored production of literature, which reached a remarkable zenith under Augustus. Augustus clearly recognized that literature could serve as a powerful medium for disseminating his political vision and securing his rule within a historical and mythological framework. His patronage of poets such as Virgil, Horace, and Ovid was therefore not purely driven by aesthetic considerations, but fulfilled a deep ideological function.

Virgil (70–19 BCE), whose epic *Aeneid* was composed between 29 and 19 BCE, provided a mythological and patriotic foundation for the legitimacy of the Roman state. The *Aeneid*, comprising twelve books, casts the Trojan refugee Aeneas — ancestor of the Romans — as a precursor to Augustus. His journey to Latium symbolizes order, *pietas*, and the divine destiny of Rome. Particularly significant is Book VI, in which Aeneas descends into the Underworld and beholds the souls of future Roman heroes — among them Augustus himself. Although Augustus did not officially commission the work, Virgil operated under the protection of his friend and political patron Maecenas, widely regarded as the foremost *patronus* of Augustan arts.

Another key figure in Augustan literature was Quintus Horatius Flaccus (65–8 BCE), known commonly as Horace. His *Odes* and *Satires* reflect the new moral ideals of Augustan society:

moderation, a sense of duty, idealization of rural life, and rejection of luxury. The famous ode *Exegi monumentum aere perennius* (*Odes* III, 30) asserts the literary immortality of the poet, proclaiming the superiority of intellectual creation over material architecture. This motif of literary *immortalitas* was closely intertwined with the Augustan self-portrayal as a restorer of the Golden Age (*saeculum aureum*).

Less aligned with the official line was Publius Ovidius Naso (43 BCE – after 17 CE), whose oeuvre oscillated between artistic virtuosity and social provocation. His *Metamorphoses*, a fifteen-book epic completed around 8 CE, interweaves over 250 myths and offers a mythological-humanist perspective on transformation and identity. In contrast, Ovid's *Ars Amatoria* (*The Art of Love*) — a handbook on the techniques of love — clashed with Augustus' moral reforms and likely contributed to the poet's exile to Tomis on the Black Sea in 8 CE. The exact cause of his banishment remains uncertain; Ovid enigmatically referred to a "poem and a mistake" (*carmen et error*). What is clear, however, is that culture was political — and literature that deviated from the official moral program was marginalized.

In the field of historiography, new voices emerged under the reigns of Tiberius, Caligula, Claudius, and Nero. Titus Livius (*Livy*), who died in 17 CE, had by then completed a comprehensive history of Rome, *Ab urbe condita*, originally planned in 142 books, of which only 35 survive. In the subsequent generation, works began to appear that adopted a more critical stance toward the Principate. Velleius Paterculus, writing under Tiberius, and Seneca the Elder, who explored issues of justice and tyranny in his *Controversiae*, are notable examples. Under Nero, Lucan's *De Bello Civili* (*On the Civil War*) introduced a tragic-pessimistic tone: the civil war was no longer portrayed as a necessary transition toward a new order, but rather as a catastrophic rupture.

Parallel to this literary flourishing, architecture evolved into a monumental and visually impactful aesthetic, aimed at expressing permanence, Roman grandeur, and imperial order. Augustus not only restored countless temples — reportedly over 82, according to the *Res Gestae Divi Augusti* — but also reshaped the image of the capital through ambitious new constructions. The Temple of Mars Ultor (*Mars the Avenger*), dedicated in 2 BCE, symbolized vengeance for the assassination of Caesar and simultaneously affirmed the divine legitimization of the new regime. That same year saw the completion of the Forum Augustum, a symmetrically axial complex with colonnades, statues of Roman heroes, and a central square that united tradition with the present.

Of particular importance is the *Ara Pacis Augustae* (*Altar of Augustan Peace*), dedicated in 9 BCE, a work of art and politics that stands as a key expression of Augustan ideology. Its reliefs depict mythological scenes alongside a realistic procession of the imperial family — an unprecedented motif in Roman art, promoting dynastic continuity and peace. The synthesis of sculptural art, mythological allegory, and state symbolism in this monument represents an early imperial ideal.

Roman architecture reached new heights under Augustus' successors. Tiberius (r. 14–37 CE) completed many of Augustus' unfinished projects, including a pantomime theater in the Campus Martius. Caligula (r. 37–41 CE) expanded the Palatine complex and initiated the construction of a new aqueduct, the *Aqua Claudia*, which was completed under Claudius (r. 41–54 CE). Stretching 69 kilometers, it supplied hundreds of thousands of people daily — a milestone in urban infrastructure and architectural engineering.

Claudius also expanded the port of Ostia to secure Rome's grain supply. This resulted in the creation of the *Portus Claudii*, a man-made harbor with a lighthouse modeled after that of Alexandria. The project was both technically ambitious and costly, underscoring the tight interconnection between architecture, administration, and logistical policy.

Under Nero (r. 54–68 CE), imperial self-representation entered a new phase. The Great Fire of Rome in 64 CE, which devastated much of the city center, provided Nero with the opportunity to pursue a radical urban redesign. At the heart of this vision was the *Domus Aurea* (*Golden House*), a luxurious palace complex featuring an artificial lake, a rotunda with a revolving dome, and extensive gardens. Designed by the architects Severus and Celer, the *Domus Aurea* marked the first time in Roman architecture that an integrated artistic concept — combining space, light, and material — was systematically realized.

Roman painting and mosaic art also experienced a flourishing during this period. In Pompeii and Herculaneum — both later buried under the eruption of Mount Vesuvius in 79 CE — wall paintings of the so-called Third and Fourth Pompeian Styles exhibit a sophisticated interplay of illusionistic architecture, mythological narratives, and stylized ornamentation. These artworks formed part of bourgeois self-representation and mirrored a desire for cultural participation in the imperial aesthetic.

The synthesis of art, literature, and architecture into a coherent cultural program was a hallmark of the early imperial era. These forms of expression served not merely as vehicles of aesthetic affirmation but were integral components of the political system. Augustus had deliberately initiated this integration, and his successors each continued it in their own way. What remained evident throughout was this: culture was never neutral. It was an instrument of power, a medium of collective memory, and an expression of imperial identity — immortalized in word, stone, and image.

5.5 Successors: Tiberius, Caligula, Claudius, Nero

Following the death of Augustus on August 19, AD 14, power was transferred to his stepson Tiberius. Adopted in AD 4, Tiberius had already been granted a series of authoritative powers as co-princeps, including the *imperium maius* and tribunician power. Although the Senate formally confirmed his accession, the transition in reality marked a dynastic succession, transforming the Principate into a quasi-hereditary institution for the first time. Tiberius ruled until his death in AD 37, leaving behind a deeply ambivalent legacy.

Tiberius (r. AD 14–37) was an experienced general who had distinguished himself especially during the German campaigns between AD 4 and 6. Upon ascending the throne, he abandoned expansionist military policies and instead pursued a defensive foreign policy. In Germania, he stabilized the Rhine frontier and delegated most military operations to his nephew and adopted son Germanicus, who between AD 14 and 16 led several punitive expeditions against Germanic tribes, particularly the Cherusci under Arminius. The Battle of the "Long Bridges" in AD 16 was the last major Roman attempt to regain the territory lost in the disastrous Battle of the Teutoburg Forest in AD 9, yet it ultimately failed to produce lasting territorial gains.

Domestically, Tiberius emphasized strict fiscal discipline. He refrained from imposing new taxes and accumulated substantial reserves in the *aerarium* (state treasury). At the time of his death, he is said to have left approximately 2.7 billion sesterces. Simultaneously, he tightened control over the Senate and increasingly relied on a repressive system of *maiestas* trials

—charges of treason frequently used to eliminate critics and political rivals. This led to a climate of fear, denunciations, and judicial arbitrariness in the capital.

After the mysterious death of Germanicus in AD 19 and the death of his own son Drusus in AD 23, Tiberius withdrew permanently to the island of Capri in AD 26. From that point on, real power in Rome was exercised by the Praetorian Prefect Lucius Aelius Sejanus, who initiated a brutal purge of the senatorial class. In AD 31, Sejanus himself was overthrown and executed—a turning point that effectively ended Tiberius' influence over the capital. Tiberius died on March 16, AD 37, in Misenum, possibly as the result of a violent death at the hands of the Praetorian Prefect Macro, who had already shifted his support to Gaius Caesar, known to posterity as Caligula.

Caligula (r. AD 37–41), son of Germanicus and grandson of Augustus through his daughter Agrippina the Elder, ascended to the throne amid widespread public enthusiasm. Initially, he presented himself as a benevolent ruler: he repealed burdensome taxes, released political prisoners, and sponsored lavish games and grain distributions. However, this initial euphoria quickly gave way to disappointment. A severe illness in October AD 37 may have marked the turning point toward an increasingly autocratic and erratic style of rule.

Caligula promoted a personality cult of unprecedented intensity. He demanded divine honors, erected statues of himself in temples, and required acknowledgment of his divinity in official contexts. One of the most notorious, though historically disputed, anecdotes is his alleged appointment of his horse, Incitatus, as consul. Much of this account derives from the polemical narratives of Suetonius and Cassius Dio. Nevertheless, Caligula's actions increasingly provoked opposition from both the Senate and the Praetorian Guard.

In foreign affairs, he led no significant military campaigns. A planned invasion of Britain in AD 40 devolved into a bizarre episode on the Gallic coast, where Caligula allegedly ordered his troops to collect seashells—interpreted as "spoils of the sea"—further reinforcing his reputation for megalomania. In the East, he appointed Herod Agrippa I as ruler over large parts of Palestine, which caused tensions in Judea. In Egypt, he curtailed the autonomy of the priesthoods and emphasized the emperor's role as both Pharaoh and divine figure.

His increasingly despotic rule culminated in his assassination on January 24, AD 41, in a conspiracy involving the Praetorian Prefect Cassius Chaerea. Caligula was the first Roman emperor to be assassinated. In the political vacuum that followed, his uncle Claudius was unexpectedly proclaimed emperor by the Praetorian Guard.

Claudius (r. AD 41–54) had long been considered an unlikely candidate for the throne. Afflicted by various health conditions and dismissed by his family as intellectually inferior, he had played no prominent political role prior to his accession. Nonetheless, his reign marked a remarkable period of administrative efficiency and imperial expansion. In AD 43, he personally oversaw a large-scale invasion of Britain, during which Camulodunum (modern Colchester) was captured and established as the first Roman colony on British soil. In subsequent years, the tribes of the Iceni and Trinovantes were subdued, and the province of Britannia was formally established.

Claudius undertook a consistent policy of administrative centralization. He relied heavily on a new elite composed of equestrians and imperial freedmen, to whom he entrusted key administrative posts. Figures such as Narcissus (chief of the imperial secretariat) and Pallas (finance minister) wielded immense influence—an affront to senatorial tradition that generated considerable resentment. Claudius also enacted numerous legal reforms, including measures against provincial corruption and the establishment of standardized procedures for granting Roman citizenship to non-Italians.

One of the milestones of his reign was the extension of Roman citizenship. Claudius elevated several Gallic cities to *colonia* status, including Lugdunum (modern Lyon). In a famous speech before the Senate in AD 48—preserved on bronze tablets known as the *Tabula Claudiana*—he advocated for the inclusion of Gallic elites into the Roman Senate, a revolutionary step in the integration of the provinces.

Domestically, Claudius was plagued by familial intrigue. After the poisoning of his third wife, Messalina, he married Agrippina the Younger, who used her influence to promote her son Lucius Domitius Ahenobarbus—later known as Emperor Nero—as heir to the throne. Claudius adopted Nero in AD 50 and arranged his marriage to his own daughter, Octavia. On October 13, AD 54, Claudius died—likely poisoned at Agrippina's behest—and Nero ascended the throne.

Nero (r. AD 54–68), the last emperor of the Julio-Claudian dynasty, came to power at the age of 16. The early years of his reign (AD 54–59) were largely guided by his tutor Seneca and the Praetorian Prefect Burrus. This period was characterized by moderation and prudent governance. However, following the assassination of his mother Agrippina on March 23, AD 59, Nero's style of rule began to change markedly.

Nero did not pursue military glory; rather, he sought artistic fulfillment. He publicly performed as a singer, poet, and charioteer—actions that elicited ridicule and disdain among the Roman aristocracy. Despite this, he did implement significant reforms: in AD 62, new judicial laws were enacted, including harsher penalties for extortion in the provinces and relief measures for small debtors.

The situation deteriorated dramatically with the Great Fire of Rome in July AD 64, which devastated ten of the city's fourteen districts. Nero initiated extensive relief efforts and commenced a comprehensive rebuilding program under new fire safety regulations. However, he also seized the opportunity to construct his vast palace complex, the *Domus Aurea*, which attracted public criticism. To deflect blame, he accused the Christians, initiating the first documented persecution of Christians in Rome.

In foreign affairs, unrest erupted in Judea in AD 66, marking the beginning of the First Jewish–Roman War. Simultaneously, rebellions flared in Gaul and Hispania. The governor Gaius Julius Vindex proclaimed rebellion in Gaul in AD 68 and found support from Servius Sulpicius Galba in Hispania. The Praetorian Guard eventually abandoned Nero. Declared a *hostis* (public enemy) by the Senate, he committed suicide on June 9, AD 68.

With Nero's death, the Julio-Claudian dynasty came to an end. The four emperors who succeeded Augustus shaped the foundations of the Principate through a complex interplay of dynastic legitimacy, political reform, autocracy, military expansion, and personal rule. The system they developed would be tested and transformed in the ensuing decades through civil wars and the emergence of new dynasties.

CHAPTER 6: THE ROMAN EMPIRE UNDER THE FLAVIANS AND ADOPTIVE EMPERORS (69–192 AD)

6.1 Vespasian and the Stabilization of the Empire

With the death of Emperor Nero in AD 68, the Julio-Claudian dynasty came to an end, plunging the Roman Empire into a period of severe internal turmoil. This interregnum, historically known as the "Year of the Four Emperors" (AD 69), was marked by rapid successions and violent power struggles. Within a single year, four claimants—Galba, Otho, Vitellius, and finally Vespasian—vied for control of the imperial throne. Vespasian's rise was particularly noteworthy, as he hailed not from the ancient Roman aristocracy but from a plebeian family of Sabine origin in central Italy. His career in the military and civil administration had developed steadily under the reigns of Claudius and Nero. Notably, he served as legate in Germania and Britannia, before being appointed supreme commander of Roman forces in the Jewish War in the province of Judaea in AD 66.

While Vespasian conducted military operations in Palestine, Rome descended into chaos following Nero's suicide. Galba, the initial claimant to the throne, was murdered in January AD 69 by supporters of Otho. Yet Otho's rule was short-lived, as he was defeated in April of the same year by Vitellius, who relied on the loyalty of legions stationed in Germania. Meanwhile, Vespasian secured the allegiance of the eastern legions, particularly those in Egypt and Syria. In July AD 69, he was proclaimed emperor by his troops in Alexandria—a crucial development, given Egypt's strategic importance in supplying grain to Rome. By December, forces loyal to Vespasian, under the command of Marcus Antonius Primus, entered Rome, defeated Vitellius' supporters, and installed Vespasian as sole ruler. Thus began the Flavian dynasty, which would govern until AD 96.

From the outset, Vespasian's reign was marked by a concerted effort toward stabilization and consolidation. One of his first priorities was the reestablishment of state order and the restoration of imperial authority, both of which had been severely compromised during the upheavals of the previous year. Vespasian placed a strong emphasis on discipline within the army and on the meticulous governance of the provinces. He reformed the recruitment process for the legions, promoted the integration of provincial elites into the Roman governing class, and sought a balanced distribution of power among the Senate, the equestrian order, and the military. Although of non-senatorial background himself, Vespasian endeavored to maintain a cooperative relationship with the Senate—though without relinquishing imperial control over the core instruments of power: the military, finances, and bureaucracy.

The financial condition of the empire upon Vespasian's accession was precarious. Years of civil war, Nero's extravagance, and the sack of Rome by Vitellian forces had nearly depleted the imperial treasury. Vespasian responded with strict fiscal policies. He raised existing taxes and introduced new levies—including the infamous *vectigal urinae*, or urine tax, on the use of public latrines. Additionally, he implemented rigorous oversight of state expenditures. These measures significantly contributed to the long-term stabilization of imperial finances. The provinces, too, were more heavily taxed. Tax collection became more efficient, and the oversight of provincial governors was intensified to curb corruption.

Vespasian's administrative reforms had profound and lasting implications for the structure of the Roman state. He increased the number of equestrians (*equites*) employed in bureaucratic functions and increasingly relied on them—rather than senators—for key provincial appointments. This shift facilitated greater control by the imperial center and reduced the likelihood of senators establishing independent power bases in the provinces. Vespasian also founded numerous colonies, particularly for military veterans. Examples include *Colonia Claudia Ara Agrippinensium* (modern-day Cologne) and various settlements in Hispania. These colonies functioned not only as rewards for loyal service but also as instruments of Romanization, promoting cultural and administrative integration in the provinces.

In the cultural and urban spheres, Vespasian played a crucial role in the revitalization of Rome. The Great Fire of AD 64 and the subsequent political instability had left large portions of the city in ruins. Vespasian launched an ambitious reconstruction program. The most iconic project initiated during his reign was the Flavian Amphitheatre—better known as the Colosseum—whose construction began around AD 72. It was built on the site of the artificial lake that had been part of Nero's extravagant *Domus Aurea* (Golden House). The replacement of such private luxury with a public monument was a deliberate political statement: the new dynasty sought to portray itself as modest, fiscally responsible, and devoted to the public good.

Although the Colosseum was officially inaugurated only in AD 80 under his son and successor Titus, Vespasian had laid the symbolic and architectural foundations for a return to traditional Roman values in imperial representation. Other notable building projects included the Temple of Peace (*Templum*

Pacis), dedicated in AD 75, the restoration of the Capitoline Temple, and numerous infrastructural works such as roads, aqueducts, and granaries (*horrea*). These efforts were not merely displays of imperial power but served practical purposes: improving supply logistics, administrative efficiency, and public morale.

In foreign policy, Vespasian's reign was characterized by consolidation rather than expansion. Following the suppression of the Jewish Revolt in AD 70—achieved through the capture of Jerusalem and destruction of the Second Temple by Titus—the eastern provinces were pacified. The wealth acquired through the sack of Jerusalem and the accompanying triumphal processions in Rome further reinforced Flavian authority and financed additional construction and administrative initiatives. Judaea was transformed into a militarized imperial province directly administered by the emperor, reflecting both strategic interests and punitive measures.

In Germania, which had received relatively little attention under Claudius and Nero, Vespasian undertook measures to reinforce the frontier. Although he did not pursue large-scale expansion, he laid the groundwork for the long-term fortification of the Rhine frontier (*limes*), constructing fortresses, roads, and settlements. Naval deployments were also strengthened to enhance control over the North Sea coastline. In Britannia, Roman authority was further consolidated under the governorships of Quintus Petillius Cerialis (AD 71–74) and Gnaeus Julius Agricola (from AD 77 onward). Agricola—Tacitus' father-in-law—extended Roman influence as far as modern-day Scotland, although these achievements belong more to the post-Vespasian period.

Vespasian also paid particular attention to the provinces of Hispania and Africa. In Hispania, he promoted the establishment of new *municipia* and granted many cities the *ius*

Latii, a legal status between full Roman citizenship and local autonomy. This policy facilitated the integration of provincial elites into Roman political culture. In *Africa Proconsularis*, one of the empire's wealthiest provinces, grain production was expanded and subjected to tighter imperial control to secure Rome's food supply. Construction activity in North Africa also intensified, leaving behind a legacy still visible in numerous inscriptions and public buildings.

Vespasian skillfully cultivated an image of legitimate and effective rulership. He was the first emperor to consciously develop a ruler cult centered on himself and his dynasty. Like his predecessors, he was deified posthumously (*divus Vespasianus*), but even during his lifetime he promoted a public persona that emphasized humility, wit, and resolute leadership. His famously ironic last words—*"Vae, puto deus fio"* ("Alas, I think I'm becoming a god")—reveal a skeptical attitude toward the deification process, even as he made strategic use of imperial ideology. Despite his cultivated modesty, Vespasian was not devoid of personal ambition or dynastic intent. He promoted his sons Titus and Domitian to high offices early on and prepared them for succession.

Vespasian died on June 23, AD 79, in Aquae Cutiliae, in his native Sabine homeland. His death concluded a decade-long reign that had steered the Roman Empire through one of its most severe crises, reestablished administrative order, stabilized finances, and rejuvenated public life. His succession by his elder son Titus marked the first peaceful and dynastically legitimate transfer of imperial power since Augustus. The Flavian dynasty was thereby firmly entrenched, and Vespasian entered Roman history as one of its most capable and pragmatic rulers.

Contemporary and later historians such as Tacitus, Suetonius, and Cassius Dio generally assessed his reign with respect and recognition. They emphasized his energy, military experience, administrative acumen, and ability to restore order in the wake of near collapse. While not an intellectual like Augustus or a visionary like Caesar, Vespasian proved to be an exceptionally effective statesman, laying the foundation for another century of relatively stable rule. His legacy extended beyond monumental architecture to the institutional consolidation of the Principate, which had now become the definitive model of Roman imperial governance.

6.2 The Construction of the Colosseum and Flavian Infrastructure Policy

Following the consolidation of imperial authority, the Flavian dynasty inaugurated a new phase of Roman building policy, characterized by both pragmatic infrastructural measures and symbolically charged monumental architecture. Among the most prominent achievements stands the Flavian Amphitheatre —known worldwide today as the Colosseum—which was initiated during the reign of Vespasian and completed under his son Titus. This structure, however, was not an isolated undertaking; it formed part of a comprehensive urbanistic program through which the Flavians sought to reshape the appearance of Rome and public life across the Empire. Their aim was twofold: to reinforce the legitimacy of the new dynasty through architectural representations of imperial power, and to tangibly improve the daily lives of the population through functional infrastructure.

Construction of the Flavian Amphitheatre commenced in AD 72, as evidenced by inscriptions, including one found on a bronze plaque originally located at the building's entrance (CIL VI 32094). The decision to erect the amphitheatre on the site of the artificial lake that had been part of Nero's

Domus Aurea was highly symbolic. It represented a political act of *damnatio memoriae*—a condemnation of Nero's self-aggrandizing excesses. In place of a luxurious private palace, a public venue accessible to the entire populace was established. A large portion of the funding for this vast construction project derived from the spoils of the Jewish War (AD 66–70), particularly following the sack of Jerusalem in AD 70. These resources enabled the realization of one of the largest amphitheatres in the Roman world.

The Colosseum measured approximately 188 × 156 meters in ground plan and rose to a height of around 48 meters. It could accommodate an estimated 50,000 to 70,000 spectators arranged in a hierarchically structured seating plan that reflected the stratification of Roman society. Constructed of travertine, tuff, and concrete, the amphitheatre featured a complex architectural design consisting of four stories, each with its own distinctive order: Tuscan, Ionic, Corinthian, and an attic story. An advanced system of 80 entrances—including the *Porta Triumphalis* and the *Porta Libitinensis*—ensured efficient ingress and egress. Beneath the arena floor, which was covered with wood and sand, lay the *hypogeum*, an underground network of tunnels, chambers, and lifts used for the preparation of animals, scenery, and gladiators. This subterranean structure, however, was only completed under Domitian (r. AD 81–96).

The Colosseum was inaugurated in AD 80 by Titus with a hundred-day festival, according to the accounts of Suetonius (*Titus* 7.3) and Cassius Dio (66.25–26). These festivities featured an immense display of gladiatorial combat, beast hunts (*venationes*), and *naumachiae*—staged naval battles. The latter required the temporary flooding of the arena, a feat of engineering that underscored Roman technical prowess. The significance of the Colosseum extended beyond its practical functions; ideologically, it embodied the emperor's *liberalitas*—his generosity toward the people—and served as a symbol of the restoration of traditional Roman virtues: discipline, courage, and order.

Concurrent with the construction of the Colosseum, Vespasian also commissioned the building of the *Templum Pacis* (Temple of Peace), dedicated in AD 75. This temple complex, located to the east of the Roman Forum, functioned as a locus of political and cultural identity for the Flavian regime. It housed, among other treasures, artworks looted from Jerusalem, including—according to some sources—the Menorah from the Jewish Temple. The complex functioned not only as a sacred space but also as a kind of public museum celebrating the *pax Romana* in architectural form.

Beyond monumental projects in Rome itself, the Flavian emperors pursued a systematic infrastructure policy throughout the Empire. Their objective was the integration of remote provinces, the stabilization of trade routes, and the facilitation of military control. Vespasian and his successors invested heavily in the expansion of the road network. In Italy, existing long-distance roads such as the *Via Appia*, *Via Aurelia*, and *Via Flaminia* were repaired and maintained, while in the provinces, new routes were developed. In Britain, for instance, the so-called *Fosse Way* between Exeter and Lincoln was expanded, easing military logistics and civilian administration alike.

Water supply infrastructure was also a priority under the Flavians. Particularly noteworthy is the restoration of the *Aqua Claudia* and *Anio Novus*—two aqueducts originally begun under Emperor Claudius but neglected during the years of crisis. Domitian, Vespasian's youngest son, completed the works in AD 81. These aqueducts enabled the supply of fresh water to Rome's rapidly growing population, estimated at between 800,000 and 1 million inhabitants. The reliable availability of water was crucial not only for drinking but also for the functioning of public baths, fountains, and latrines.

Another vital area was the construction of storage facilities for grain, oil, and wine. The so-called *horrea*—large warehouses—were erected not only in Rome but also in strategically important provincial cities. In Ostia, Rome's seaport, extensive storage facilities were constructed during the Flavian period, including the renowned *Horrea Galbae*, with more than 140 rooms, making it one of the largest storage complexes in the ancient world. These facilities ensured the capital's food supply while also allowing for tighter control of commerce and price regulation. The secure importation of grain from Egypt, Africa Proconsularis, and Sicily remained a core element of domestic policy, since the grain distribution (*annona*) was an essential aspect of imperial legitimacy.

The Flavian building program also extended into the religious sphere. The reconstruction of the Capitoline Hill, which had been devastated during the conflict against Vitellius in AD 69, was pursued with urgency. The Temple of Jupiter Optimus Maximus atop the Capitoline was not only the central sanctuary of Rome but also a symbol of the continuity of both the Republic and the Empire. Reconstruction began in AD 70 and was completed by AD 75. This act represented a reconnection with Roman tradition and the divine order, intended to confer religious legitimacy upon the Flavian house.

In Rome's urban fabric, attention was also given to improving residential conditions. The Great Fire of AD 64 under Nero had devastated large swaths of densely populated areas, especially the Subura. The Flavians began constructing more durable housing, with *opus latericium* (brickwork) increasingly replacing the older *opus caementicium*. New regulations on maximum building height were implemented to prevent collapses, and fire protection measures were institutionalized. In various districts of the city, new *insulae*—apartment blocks—were erected by equestrian entrepreneurs under state oversight.

On a cultural level, the Flavian administration promoted the establishment of public amenities. Libraries, baths, and basilicas were constructed not only in Rome but also throughout the provinces. The emperors actively supported the creation of cultural edifices to affirm Rome's self-perception as a civilizing force. In Hispania, Gaul, and North Africa, theaters, forums, and temples were built, many bearing Flavian dedicatory inscriptions. These buildings facilitated Roman acculturation and underscored the emperor's beneficence (*beneficium principis*).

A particularly striking example of Flavian urban renewal is the reconstruction of Pompeii after the earthquake of AD 62. Although the city was destroyed by the eruption of Mount Vesuvius in AD 79, significant resources had been allocated by the Flavian administration in the preceding years for its restoration. Numerous inscriptions, statues, and altars found in the excavated ruins reference Vespasian or Titus. In nearby Herculaneum, similar evidence of Flavian urban planning is found, especially in the restoration of public bathhouses and aqueducts.

The building policy of the Flavians, therefore, went far beyond mere representation. It constituted a far-reaching program aimed at the integration, stabilization, and self-assertion of the Roman Empire following the crises of the first century. The expansion of roads, aqueducts, harbors, and administrative buildings served not only practical but also ideological purposes. The Flavians successfully employed architectural projects to inscribe their political message—order, peace, authority, and closeness to the people—into the very stone of the Empire.

6.3 The "Five Good Emperors": Trajan,

Hadrian, Marcus Aurelius

Following the assassination of Emperor Domitian in 96 CE and the consequent end of the Flavian dynasty, the Roman Empire entered a period often referred to in historiography as the "Golden Age of the Principate." This era, known among historians as the age of the "Five Good Emperors," spanned nearly a century (96–180 CE) and encompassed the reigns of Nerva (96–98), Trajan (98–117), Hadrian (117–138), Antoninus Pius (138–161), and Marcus Aurelius (161–180). The term "good emperors" originates from the Renaissance political thinker Niccolò Machiavelli, who, in the 16th century, praised these rulers as paragons of virtuous and rational governance—a perspective that continues to find resonance in modern scholarship, albeit with more nuanced interpretations.

The transfer of power following Domitian's death marked a critical transition. The new emperor, Marcus Cocceius Nerva, was not appointed by hereditary succession but through a senatorial decree—a constitutional novelty since the time of Augustus. Nerva, already advanced in age and with a distinguished senatorial career, ruled for a brief period from 96 to 98 CE. His tenure was characterized primarily by efforts to mend the fractured relationship between the Senate and the imperial office, which had suffered under Domitian's autocratic rule. Nerva issued numerous political amnesties, restored confiscated property, and attempted to rebuild public trust through measures such as repealing the inheritance tax on orphans (the *vicesima hereditatium*), thereby alleviating the financial burden on lower social strata.

A pivotal act of Nerva's brief rule was the adoption of the popular general Marcus Ulpius Traianus in 97 CE, establishing a clear and stable succession. Trajan, born on 18 September 53 CE in Italica near Hispalis (modern-day Seville), was the first emperor of non-Italian origin. A seasoned military commander and loyal supporter of the Flavian regime, Trajan had distinguished himself in the provinces of Germania and Pannonia and was widely regarded as a guarantor of military prowess and internal stability.

Upon Nerva's death on 27 January 98 CE, Trajan ascended to the throne without opposition. His reign marked the zenith of Roman territorial expansion and is noted for exceptional military efficiency, administrative reform, and a strong commitment to the welfare of provincial populations. The early years of his reign were spent largely outside Rome, particularly in Germania, where he focused on securing the Rhine frontier and reinforcing the region's military infrastructure. Numerous forts, including those at Oberaden and the legionary base at Vetera (near modern Xanten), were modernized and fortified under his command.

Trajan's most significant foreign policy achievement was the Dacian Wars (101–102 and 105–106 CE), during which the kingdom of Dacia, ruled by King Decebalus, was decisively conquered. Following the second campaign, the province of Dacia was established, a territory of considerable strategic and economic importance. Its vast gold and silver mines, particularly near Alburnus Maior (Roșia Montană) and Apulum (Alba Iulia), rendered the region one of the wealthiest in the empire. These victories were celebrated with a grand triumph in Rome, and Trajan commissioned the construction of the renowned Trajan's Column, inaugurated in 113 CE in the newly built Forum of Trajan. The column, adorned with a spiraling relief frieze, vividly depicts the Dacian campaigns and is hailed as a masterpiece of Roman relief sculpture and imperial iconography.

Domestically, Trajan implemented substantial administrative reforms aimed at improving governance. A hallmark of his social policy was the *alimenta* program—a state-sponsored initiative providing financial support to impoverished children. This system was funded through state loans to large landowners, with the interest payments directed toward child welfare in Italy, representing an early form of state-managed social assistance. Architecturally, Trajan was equally ambitious. In addition to the monumental Forum of Trajan, designed by Apollodorus of Damascus, he commissioned the construction of new roads, including the *Via Traiana* (109 CE), which offered a more direct route between Beneventum and Brundisium.

Trajan died in 117 CE, likely in Selinus (modern Gazipaşa, Turkey) during his return from a campaign against the Parthians. He was succeeded by his adoptive son, Publius Aelius Hadrianus. Although Hadrian enjoyed military backing, his accession was not uncontested; several senators were executed, likely in connection with conspiracies against him.

Hadrian's approach to governance stood in marked contrast to that of his predecessor. While Trajan had pursued aggressive territorial expansion, Hadrian adopted a policy of consolidation. He voluntarily relinquished several of Trajan's eastern conquests, including Mesopotamia, and focused instead on securing and stabilizing the empire's existing borders.

Hadrian is perhaps best known for the construction of the defensive fortification that bears his name—the *Hadrian's Wall* in Britannia—initiated in 122 CE. Spanning approximately 117 kilometers from the mouth of the River Tyne to the Solway Firth, the wall served both as a military defense structure and a potent symbol of Roman authority and presence. Hadrian traveled extensively across the empire, more than any of his predecessors, to inspect local conditions and address provincial concerns directly. Between 121 and 125 CE, he visited Gaul, Germania, Britannia, Hispania, North Africa, Greece, and Asia Minor, initiating numerous building projects.

In Athens, he oversaw a significant urban renovation, including the construction of Hadrian's Arch and the completion of the Temple of Olympian Zeus.

A passionate admirer of Greek culture, Hadrian was a dedicated philhellene who championed humanism and philosophy. Under his rule, classical education experienced a revival, marked by the establishment of new libraries and rhetoric schools, particularly in the eastern provinces. His reign was also notable for significant legal reforms. Hadrian commissioned the jurist Salvius Julianus to codify the *Edictum perpetuum* —a consolidated version of the Praetorian Edict—which significantly influenced the evolution of Roman law.

Upon Hadrian's death in 138 CE at Baiae, his adoptive son Antoninus Pius assumed power. His reign (138–161 CE) is regarded as one of the most peaceful and stable in Roman history. Unlike Hadrian, Antoninus remained in Rome for the entirety of his rule, dedicating his attention to internal administration, fiscal policy, and judicial affairs. He continued Hadrian's legal policies and was lauded as a just and conscientious adjudicator, often involving himself in individual cases. Through various edicts, he mitigated harsh penalties, improved the legal standing of slaves, and strengthened property rights for the lower classes.

Despite the general tranquility, Antoninus Pius was not entirely inactive militarily. In Britannia, the frontier was temporarily extended northward through the construction of the Antonine Wall, approximately 160 kilometers beyond Hadrian's Wall. Minor uprisings in Mauretania, Egypt, and Dacia were swiftly suppressed. Through skillful diplomacy and limited military interventions, Antoninus reinforced Rome's position along its frontiers. He also undertook extensive building and restoration projects both in Rome and the provinces. Notable among these were the reconstruction of the *Pons Aelius*, the renovation of the

Cloaca Maxima, and the consecration of a temple to the deified Hadrian on the Campus Martius.

Following Antoninus' death in 161 CE, his adoptive sons Marcus Aurelius and Lucius Verus assumed joint rule —an unprecedented arrangement aimed at managing the complexities of the vast empire through collegial governance. While Lucius Verus, a man of indulgent temperament and limited political ambition, focused primarily on military matters, Marcus Aurelius (r. 161–180 CE) undertook the majority of administrative and legislative responsibilities. Trained in Stoic philosophy from a young age—particularly under the guidance of Junius Rusticus—Marcus embodied the rare ideal of the philosopher-king.

Marcus Aurelius' reign was marked by a succession of severe crises. Between 161 and 166 CE, Lucius Verus led a successful campaign against the Parthian Empire, which had invaded Armenia. However, returning soldiers brought with them the so-called Antonine Plague—likely smallpox—which ravaged the empire, claiming the lives of an estimated 5 to 10 million people. The epidemic had devastating effects on the economy, agriculture, and military. Marcus responded with emergency measures, including wage increases for soldiers, the establishment of new recruitment districts, and grain distributions to support the impoverished.

From 166 to 180 CE, the Danube frontier came under heavy pressure from Germanic tribes, notably the Marcomanni, Quadi, and Iazyges. The Marcomannic Wars, fought in several campaigns, saw Marcus Aurelius personally take to the battlefield—an unusual move for an emperor of his philosophical disposition. During these campaigns, he composed portions of his *Meditations* (*Meditationes*), a seminal work of ancient philosophy. Despite achieving key victories, such as the reconquest of Pannonia and the re-stabilization of the Danube border, the conflict remained unresolved at his death.

Marcus Aurelius died on 17 March 180 CE in Vindobona (modern Vienna) or possibly in Sirmium. His death marked the end of the era of the Five Good Emperors. He was succeeded by his son Commodus, whose accession inaugurated a new phase in Roman history—one increasingly defined by internal corruption, autocratic excess, and political instability.

6.4 Expansion into Dacia, Parthia, and Germania

Following the consolidation of internal stability under the Flavian emperors, the 2nd century CE—particularly during the reigns of the Adoptive Emperors—ushered in a phase of intense foreign policy activity. This period witnessed significant territorial expansion as well as profound strategic challenges. Three regions of critical geopolitical importance came into focus: the Kingdom of Dacia in the Carpathian Basin, the Parthian Empire in the East, and the Germanic territories beyond the Rhine and Danube rivers. These areas represented key zones of Roman economic and military interest, though the motivations for and structures of expansion varied considerably in each case.

The Roman expansion into Dacia constituted one of the first large-scale conquest campaigns of the 2nd century. Already under Emperor Domitian (r. 81–96), military conflicts with King Decebalus of the Dacians had occurred between 85 and 89 CE, although these had yielded no lasting territorial gains. The hostilities began in 85 CE, when the Dacians under Decebalus invaded Moesia and inflicted a significant defeat on Roman forces near Tapae (in present-day Romania). Following a series of fluctuating engagements, a peace treaty was signed in 89 CE, which formally recognized Decebalus as a client king but in effect allowed him considerable autonomy.

This precarious arrangement persisted until the accession of Emperor Trajan (r. 98–117), who sought to revitalize the military ethos of the Principate. He launched two major campaigns against Dacia. The First Dacian War began in the spring of 101 CE, when Trajan crossed the Danube with an estimated 60,000 soldiers. The army advanced via the newly constructed Trajan's Bridge at Drobeta, engineered under the supervision of the Syrian architect Apollodorus of Damascus. In the decisive Battle of Tapae (autumn 101), Roman forces defeated the Dacians and advanced to the Dacian capital, Sarmizegetusa Regia. Due to attacks by other tribes on Roman territory, however, a temporary armistice was concluded, once again recognizing Decebalus as a client king.

The Second Dacian War commenced in 105 CE after Decebalus violated the terms of the earlier agreement. This time, Rome aimed at full annexation. In 106 CE, after fierce battles, Sarmizegetusa Regia was captured, and Decebalus committed suicide. The territory was subsequently incorporated as the Roman province of *Dacia*, officially titled *Dacia Felix*. Rich in mineral resources—particularly gold, silver, and iron—Dacia was swiftly integrated into the Roman infrastructure through the establishment of a dense network of colonies and military camps (e.g., Apulum, Porolissum, Napoca). The economic exploitation of Dacia became central to the financing of the imperial state during the first half of the 2nd century. However, due to its exposed location, the province remained a hotspot of military conflict and necessitated a permanent and substantial garrison presence, notably of *Legio XIII Gemina* and *Legio V Macedonica*.

Parallel to the Dacian campaigns, Trajan also pursued an offensive eastern policy against the Parthian Empire, which had been Rome's most formidable rival in the East since the 1st century BCE. Tensions flared anew in 113 CE when Parthian King Osroes I installed an unauthorized client ruler as king of Armenia—an act that contravened the Treaty of Rhandeia negotiated during Nero's reign in 63 CE. Trajan regarded this as a casus belli and launched a full-scale military campaign in 114 CE. His objectives included bringing Armenia under direct Roman control and extending the Roman sphere of influence deep into Mesopotamia.

In 114 CE, Roman forces crossed the Euphrates and swiftly captured Artaxata and Tigranocerta. Armenia was declared a Roman province, and a Roman governor was installed. In 115 CE, Trajan turned toward Mesopotamia, capturing Nisibis and Edessa, and by 116 CE advanced as far as Babylon, Ctesiphon, and Susa—an extraordinary military feat that gave Rome nominal control over the entire region. Trajan appointed a client king for the Parthian realm, Parthamaspates, and established the provinces of *Mesopotamia* and *Assyria*. However, this zenith of Roman expansion was short-lived. By 117 CE, widespread revolts had erupted in Mesopotamia, Judaea, and North Africa. Combined with logistical overstretch and local resistance, these uprisings forced Rome to relinquish most of the territories east of the Euphrates.

Trajan's successor Hadrian (r. 117–138) renounced further expansion in the East and largely abandoned the newly acquired provinces. It was not until the reigns of Lucius Verus (r. 161–169) and Marcus Aurelius (r. 161–180) that hostilities with the Parthians resumed. Following a Parthian incursion into Armenia in 161 CE, Rome initiated a new Parthian War in 162 CE. Lucius Verus assumed supreme command of the army, while Marcus Aurelius remained in Rome. Between 163 and 165 CE, Roman forces under Avidius Cassius achieved significant victories, recapturing Seleucia, Ctesiphon, and Babylon. Yet again, these conquests did not result in long-term annexation, as Rome withdrew to its traditional boundaries following the campaign. The war, however, had a disastrous side effect: returning soldiers brought with them a deadly epidemic later known as the Antonine Plague.

Another key theater of Roman expansion and military activity was the Germanic frontier. While the Rhine had long served as a stable border, the Danube frontier became a focal point of imperial defense and expansion during the 2nd century. From the Roman perspective, the term "Germania" was broadly applied to various tribes beyond the Rhine and Danube, including the Chatti, Marcomanni, Quadi, Hermunduri, and later the Alamanni.

Under Domitian, the so-called Chatti War occurred in 83 CE, during which Roman forces under Gnaeus Julius Agricola—and later Domitian himself—advanced against the Chatti in the region of present-day Wetterau. This campaign aimed to safeguard the Roman provinces of *Germania Superior* and *Germania Inferior*. To secure the newly gained territories, the *Upper Germanic-Rhaetian Limes* was constructed over the ensuing decades. This frontier system of watchtowers, palisades, and forts extended over 550 kilometers from Rheinbrohl on the Rhine to Eining on the Danube.

While the Rhine-Danube border remained largely stable during Trajan's reign, massive incursions by Germanic tribes took place between 166 and 180 CE under Marcus Aurelius, in what became known as the Marcomannic Wars. These invasions were triggered by a combination of climatic shifts, inter-tribal conflicts, and the westward pressure of the migrating Sarmatians and Iazyges. Numerous tribes crossed the Danube and ravaged Roman territories in Pannonia, Noricum, and Northern Italy. The cities of Carnuntum, Vindobona, and

Aquileia suffered significant damage, and vast rural areas were depopulated.

Marcus Aurelius responded with comprehensive military mobilization. In several campaigns between 168 and 175 CE, Roman forces managed—under severe conditions—to repel the invasions. In 172 CE, Marcus penetrated deep into Quadi territory and won a decisive victory near modern-day Hradisko near Olomouc. A year later, a colony of Roman veterans was established in Germanic territory—an unprecedented event that suggests preparations for founding a new province. A Roman presence north of the Danube also seemed imminent, as fortifications were constructed in what is now Moravia and Slovakia, such as at Mušov.

However, internal crises—especially the rebellion of Avidius Cassius in Syria in 175 CE—prevented the full realization of these expansion plans. The proposed provinces of *Marcomannia* and *Sarmatia* were abandoned following the death of Marcus Aurelius in 180 CE. His son and successor, Commodus, concluded a disadvantageous peace with the Germanic tribes and relinquished plans for a permanent Roman presence north of the Danube.

Despite this strategic withdrawal, the Marcomannic Wars left a lasting legacy. The military infrastructure along the frontier was significantly enhanced, particularly in Pannonia, Noricum, and Raetia. Cities such as Carnuntum, Lauriacum, and Castra Regina (modern Regensburg) received new fortifications. Simultaneously, the gradual Romanization of frontier regions began to take hold, as Roman culture, law, and economic practices increasingly permeated these areas.

In conclusion, the expansion into Dacia, Parthia, and Germania during the 2nd century CE marked the apex of imperial ambition. Roman strategy during this period was far from uniform: whereas direct annexation was pursued in Dacia and Mesopotamia, the approach in Germania combined military pressure, border fortification, and diplomatic engagement. These varying methods reflect the geopolitical challenges and strategic priorities of an empire whose frontiers under the Adoptive Emperors were not only expanded but also rationally fortified.

6.5 Administration and Integration of the Provinces

The period of the Flavian emperors and the so-called adoptive emperors (69–192 CE) represents not only an era of territorial expansion but also a pivotal transformation in the administration and integration of the Roman provinces. This development was essential for maintaining imperial stability within an empire that, by this time, stretched from Britain to the Sahara and from the Atlantic Ocean to the Tigris River. The administrative policies of this era aimed not merely at military security but at a comprehensive political, legal, economic, and cultural integration of the provinces. The Roman state pursued a strategy combining centralized control with local autonomy, shaped significantly by the experiences of the civil wars and the institutional reforms initiated by the Flavian and Antonine emperors.

A fundamental element of provincial administration was the distinction between imperial provinces (*provinciae Caesaris*) and senatorial provinces (*provinciae senatus*). This division, established by Augustus during his reorganization of 27 BCE, remained in effect and was further refined under the Flavians. Imperial provinces were typically located along the empire's frontiers and were under the direct control of the emperor, who appointed his own legates (*legati Augusti pro praetore*) to govern them. These officials possessed both civil and military authority. In contrast, senatorial provinces were considered pacified and were governed by proconsuls appointed by the Senate, who, however, were not allowed to command troops.

During the reign of Vespasian (69–79 CE), particular attention was given to reorganizing the eastern provinces. In the wake of the instability following the Year of the Four Emperors in 69 CE, Vespasian recognized that effective control could only be achieved through close ties between provincial administration and the imperial court. For instance, Egypt—which already held a unique status as the personal possession of the emperor—was governed by a *praefectus Aegypti*, typically drawn from the equestrian order (*ordo equester*). This administrative model was gradually extended under the Flavians and adoptive emperors to other provinces. Mauretania, which had been divided into two provinces under Claudius, was brought under tighter military supervision during Flavian rule.

A crucial aspect of provincial administration was the stationing of legions. Between 28 and 30 legions were active during the second century CE, mainly stationed in frontier provinces. Their presence served not only military purposes but also fulfilled administrative functions. Legionaries acted as road builders, surveyors, engineers, and often as magistrates. In Syria, the *Legio III Gallica* was responsible for numerous infrastructure projects, while in Britain, *Legio XX Valeria Victrix* contributed not only to the construction of Hadrian's Wall but also to the development of cities such as Deva (modern Chester).

Provincial administration increasingly relied on a standardized bureaucracy. Under Domitian and later under Hadrian, a state postal system (*cursus publicus*) was established, enabling the rapid transport of official communications, magistrates, and goods. This infrastructure extended far beyond Italy and permeated the entire empire. A notable example is the road from Antioch to Palmyra, which was paved in sections and equipped with waystations during the second century. Similarly, the archiving of administrative documents was professionalized. In provinces such as Gallia Narbonensis or Asia, public record offices (*tabularia*) were established to house tax registers, edicts, and census data.

Economic integration was pursued with particular intensity. All provinces were systematically incorporated into the Roman tax system. The most important tax was the *tributum soli* (land tax), supplemented by the *tributum capitis* (poll tax) levied on non-citizens. Regular censuses, typically held every five years, were conducted to ensure accurate tax assessments. Under the reigns of Trajan and Hadrian, tax administration was reformed to rely more heavily on local notables and city councils (*decuriones*), who were tasked with maintaining tax registers and ensuring the fiscal obligations of their municipalities were met under the framework of local self-governance.

Urbanization was another critical tool for integration. The Flavian and adoptive emperors recognized that Roman cities functioned not only as administrative centers but also as conduits of Roman culture, language, and religion. In the provinces, new colonies (*coloniae*) and municipalities (*municipia*) were deliberately established or existing settlements elevated to the status of Roman towns. In Hispania, for instance, Emerita Augusta (modern Mérida) had been founded under Augustus, but cities such as Tarraco (Tarragona) and Caesaraugusta (Zaragoza) experienced a flourishing period under the adoptive emperors due to extensive construction projects, including baths, theatres, aqueducts, and temples.

Urbanization efforts were especially pronounced in North Africa. Under Hadrian, Lambaesis in Numidia was developed into a legionary base and simultaneously transformed into a thriving urban center. Leptis Magna in Tripolitania, the hometown of Septimius Severus, saw the construction of numerous monumental buildings during his reign, including a forum, basilica, and commercial exchange. These cities served not only as administrative hubs but also as vital nodes in the empire's trade network.

Another important mechanism of integration was *Romanization*, the gradual adoption of Roman lifestyle, language, clothing, architecture, and religion by the local elites. This process was generally voluntary and motivated by the tangible advantages associated with Roman citizenship. The *civitas Romana* was increasingly awarded in the second century CE as a reward for loyal service, often granted to local leaders, military veterans, or affluent merchants. Numerous inscriptions attest to this phenomenon. In Lugdunum (modern Lyon), a Latin honorific epitaph commemorates a Gallic merchant who received citizenship under Antoninus Pius and was later elected as *duumvir* of the city.

Culturally, Roman temples and theatres played a significant role in the assimilation process. In cities such as Timgad (Numidia), Philippopolis (Thrace), and Ephesus (Asia), forums, basilicas, and triumphal arches were constructed according to Roman architectural models. This led to a synthesis of local and Roman traditions. In Egypt, for instance, the imperial cult was merged with the worship of Isis, while in Syria, local deities such as Baal were equated with Roman gods like Jupiter.

Legal harmonization also played a central role in integration. Under Hadrian, the *praetorian edicts* were revised and codified into the *Edictum Perpetuum*, a standardized legal reference used by provincial governors. In towns with *ius Latii* (Latin rights), inhabitants could acquire Roman citizenship upon assuming a municipal office. This legal permeability encouraged loyalty among the local elites. A prominent example is the city of Italica in Hispania, where numerous members of the local aristocracy attained Roman magistracies under Hadrian.

Military control remained a foundational pillar of provincial integration. Legionary camps often evolved into permanent settlements, around which civilian communities (*canabae*) developed. This process gave rise to important urban centers such as Vindobona (Vienna), Mogontiacum (Mainz), and Augusta Treverorum (Trier). Soldiers contributed to the dissemination of Latin, Roman culinary habits, and the urban lifestyle. Upon discharge, veterans frequently settled near their former garrisons, thereby promoting regional stability.

Administrative communication was also systematically organized. Imperial rescripts, edicts, and mandates were disseminated to all provinces via the *cursus publicus*. To manage the complex administrative structure, the empire relied on imperial correspondence, with governors sending regular reports to the emperor. Numerous papyri from Egypt—especially from Oxyrhynchus and Elephantine—reveal the level of detail in these administrative records, including instructions concerning grain distributions, judicial procedures, border disputes, and construction matters.

Finally, the role of local elites must be emphasized. The so-called *municipal aristocracy* formed the backbone of local administration. Its members actively participated in city councils (*ordo decurionum*), held offices such as *aedilis*, *duumvir*, or *quaestor*, and often financed public buildings and games (*munera*) from their own resources. This sense of civic pride and ambition was deliberately encouraged by Rome. Titles such as *patronus civitatis* were highly prestigious, as was entry into the equestrian order or eventually the Senate. Numerous statues and inscriptions from cities like Thamugadi or Gerasa bear witness to the prominence of these local benefactors.

CHAPTER 7: CULTURE, RELIGION AND EVERYDAY LIFE IN THE ROMAN EMPIRE

7.1 Roman Religion: Pantheon, Cults, and Temples

At the heart of Roman culture from the earliest days of the Republic lay a complex and multilayered religious world, which was not merely a spiritual expression but deeply embedded in the social, political, and institutional structures of Roman life. Roman religion, characterized by its pantheon of gods, a wide range of public and private cults, and the monumental significance of temple architecture, evolved over the centuries from an archaic form of polytheistic devotion into an increasingly integrative system. This system absorbed foreign deities and blended ritualized forms of worship with imperial representation and state ideology.

The origins of Roman religion reach back to the period of the monarchy, between the legendary founding of Rome in 753 BCE and the abolition of kingship in 509 BCE. In this archaic phase, Roman religion was closely tied to the agrarian lifestyle. The deities worshipped were personifications of natural forces: Janus, the god of doors and transitions; Vesta, the goddess of the hearth; and Saturn, associated with sowing and harvest. There were no anthropomorphic representations of the gods in this period. Instead, worship was conducted through altars or symbolic objects. This early stage was shaped by a belief in the numinous—the idea that divine forces (numina) were present in all aspects of the natural and human world. Consequently, countless small rituals and sacrificial acts were performed to maintain the equilibrium between humanity and divine order.

With the transition to the Republic in 509 BCE, Roman religion underwent a process of institutionalization and formalization. The Roman state assumed responsibility for organizing public cults, and religious offices became increasingly entwined with political functions. At an early stage, the *Collegium Pontificum* (College of Pontiffs) was established, with the *Pontifex Maximus* as the highest-ranking priest—an office that would later be assumed by the emperors themselves. Another key religious institution was the *Collegium Augurum* (College of Augurs), whose members interpreted the will of the gods through the observation of bird flights (*auspicia*). The practice of *auspicium* became a crucial component of nearly all political and military decisions of the Republic: without favorable omens, a popular assembly's resolutions were invalid, and a military campaign lacked divine legitimacy.

A fundamental trait of Roman religion was its pronounced ritual orientation. Rather than belief in the modern sense, the focus lay on the correct performance of rites and sacrifices, following the principle *do ut des* ("I give so that you may give"). This highly ritualized relationship with the gods defined both public and private life. During the Republic, annual religious festivals were celebrated, drawing partly from pre-urban Latin traditions and partly from distinctively Roman developments. Among the oldest festivals were the Lupercalia, held on February 15 in honor of the god Faunus and associated with fertility, and the Saturnalia on December 17, celebrating the god Saturn. The Saturnalia, with their temporary reversal of social roles—slaves were permitted to mock their masters—demonstrated a unique social dynamism within the rigid Roman hierarchy.

During the 4th and 3rd centuries BCE, Roman religion underwent a significant transformation, tied to Rome's expansion throughout Italy and later beyond the Italian Peninsula. Contact with Etruscan and Greek cultures brought about a profound reconfiguration of the Roman pantheon. Numerous Greek deities were either equated with Roman counterparts or adopted outright. The Greek Zeus became the Roman Jupiter; Hera became Juno; Athena became Minerva. Together, these three formed the so-called Capitoline Triad, whose temple on the Capitoline Hill became one of the central religious sites of the Roman state. Although the first great temple to Jupiter—*Templum Iovis Optimi Maximi*—was allegedly dedicated as early as 509 BCE, its symbolic importance grew especially in the 3rd and 2nd centuries BCE, as Rome emerged as a dominant Mediterranean power.

Encounters with foreign powers repeatedly led to the incorporation of new deities. A striking example is the introduction of the cult of Magna Mater (Cybele) from Phrygia during the Second Punic War in 204 BCE. According to an oracle of the Delphic Apollo, Rome could only defeat Hannibal with the help of the "Great Mother Goddess of Pessinus." Consequently, her cult was established in Rome. Likewise, the cult of the healing god Asclepius (Roman Aesculapius) was introduced in 293 BCE following a devastating plague. A statue of the deity was brought from Epidaurus, and a sanctuary was established on the Tiber Island, which became a center for the sick and for religious pilgrims.

A further decisive development occurred during the Late Republic. The increasing individualization of society and the erosion of traditional values—particularly against the backdrop of civil wars from 133 BCE onward—fueled the popularity of mystery cults and eastern religions. The cult of the Egyptian god Serapis, the worship of Isis, and the Dionysian cult gained many followers, despite being viewed by the Senate as subversive or dangerous. The so-called Bacchanalian Scandal of 186 BCE serves as a notable example of the Senate's attempt to curtail uncontrolled and orgiastic cult practices via a restrictive decree. Nevertheless, many of these movements persisted, offering a more personal and emotionally resonant form of religious experience, increasingly absent from the rigid and state-regulated Roman cults.

During the Imperial period, beginning with Augustus' rise to power in 27 BCE, religion became more than ever a political instrument. Augustus not only restored numerous decaying temples—over 80 by his own account—but also orchestrated a deliberate revival of traditional values (*mos maiorum*), portraying himself as the supreme priest (*Pontifex Maximus*). The construction of the *Ara Pacis Augustae* (Altar of Augustan Peace) in 13 BCE is a vivid expression of this sacral-political ideology. The altar features mythological scenes alongside realistic depictions of the imperial family, symbolizing the *Pax Romana* as a divinely sanctioned order of peace. Simultaneously, Augustus institutionalized the imperial cult, which rapidly gained traction in the provinces. The veneration of the emperor's *genius* alongside *Roma*, the personification of the empire, became a standardized form of civic loyalty—those who made public sacrifices demonstrated allegiance to the state.

As the Empire expanded, the religious landscape became increasingly pluralistic. New temples arose in the provinces, often combining local and Roman traditions. In Gaul, the Lenus Mars cult emerged, merging the Celtic war god Lenus with the Roman Mars. In North Africa, the Punic goddess Tanit was identified with Juno. This practice of *interpretatio Romana*—equating foreign gods with Roman counterparts—enabled the religious integration of conquered peoples without completely eradicating their cultural identities.

Temples in the Roman world were not merely places of worship but also political and cultural centers. Their architecture evolved over the centuries, influenced by Etruscan, Greek, and later Hellenistic models. A typical Roman temple stood on a raised podium, with a columned front and a central sanctuary (*cella*). The Temple of Portunus in Rome (circa 100 BCE) is a well-preserved example of Roman adaptation of Greek architectural forms. One of the most impressive temples was the Pantheon, rebuilt under Emperor Hadrian around 125 CE. This revolutionary structure featured a massive dome with a diameter of 43.3 meters—still among the largest in the world. Although dedicated to all gods (*pan-theon*), the Pantheon's architectural perfection and monumental scale symbolized the idea of a universal empire under divine protection.

During the High and Late Empire (2nd–3rd centuries CE), many cults experienced a resurgence. Particularly noteworthy was the rise of the Mithras cult, which originated in Persia and was practiced in closed male communities, especially among soldiers. The so-called *Mithraea*, subterranean temples featuring depictions of a bull sacrifice, have been found in nearly all frontier provinces of the empire. The cult involved initiation rites, esoteric teachings, and a dualistic worldview, appealing to Romans in search of spiritual certainty in an increasingly unstable world.

At the same time, the Roman state made efforts to secure religious unity. In 250 CE, Emperor Decius mandated a universal obligation to perform sacrifices to the Roman gods in an attempt to placate the "will of the ancient gods" and stabilize the empire. This edict led to the first systematic persecutions of Christians—not merely on religious grounds but also political ones: refusal to perform the sacrifices was interpreted as a refusal of loyalty to the state.

Roman religion was, for centuries, a dynamic system based on expansion, adaptation, and integration. From the archaic *numina* to the worship of Jupiter and the introduction of oriental cults, the Roman pantheon reflected the history of an empire in constant flux—one which simultaneously strove to establish lasting order through the veneration of its gods. Even in the 4th century CE, when the Roman emperors under Constantine and his successors began to favor Christianity, many of these ancient cults still endured—whether in temples, household altars, or public rituals—before being definitively banned by Theodosius I between 391 and 394 CE. Until that point, however, the gods of Rome had for nearly a millennium formed the backbone of one of the most influential civilizations of antiquity.

In addition to the structural embedding of religion into the political and social framework of the Roman Empire, the pantheon—that is, the entirety of the gods—constituted a system of religious ideas that was both mutable and surprisingly stable. The Roman pantheon was by no means static or uniform; rather, it reflected centuries of accumulation, syncretization, and localization. The gods were not merely worshipped as omnipresent forces but were each assigned highly specific spheres of influence that were deeply interwoven into the daily lives of individuals. The following aims to introduce the most important deities of Roman religion, illustrating in detail their respective cultic, mythological, and social significance.

At the center of the Roman state cult stood Jupiter Optimus Maximus, the supreme deity, regarded as the ruler of the sky, the god of thunder and weather, and the guarantor of law and order. His counterpart in the Greek pantheon was Zeus, yet in Rome, Jupiter developed a distinct character: as the god of the state and protector first of the Republic and later of the Empire. His most important place of worship was the Temple of Jupiter on the Capitoline Hill, which, according to tradition, was consecrated as early as 509 BCE. Here, major state sacrifices were offered, Senate sessions were announced, and military triumphal processions concluded. Jupiter was typically depicted holding a bundle of lightning bolts and was associated not only with weather but also with oaths—as *Dius Fidius*, no oath was valid unless sworn in his presence.

The second major figure of the Capitoline Triad was Juno, Jupiter's consort and simultaneously one of the most complex goddesses in the Roman pantheon. Juno was worshipped in multiple aspects: as Juno Regina (Heavenly Queen), Juno Lucina (Protector of Childbirth), Juno Moneta (the Admonisher), and Juno Sospita (the Helper, especially in warfare). Her cult was widespread across Italy and particularly central in Latium. As Juno Moneta, she was associated with the Capitoline Hill, where the Roman mint was also located—hence the term "monetary." The goddess was frequently depicted with a spear, shield, or goat, especially in her role as Juno Sospita of Lanuvium.

Minerva, the third member of the Triad, was originally an Etruscan goddess but was early on equated with the Greek Athena. She was regarded as the goddess of wisdom, strategy, the arts, craftsmanship, and commerce. Artisans and teachers in particular venerated Minerva. Her principal festival was the *Quinquatria*, celebrated from March 19 to 23. These were school-free days, during which students offered small gifts to the goddess. In visual representation, Minerva often appeared armed with helmet, spear, and shield, as well as the *aegis*, a breastplate adorned with the head of the Gorgon Medusa.

In addition to these three central deities, there existed a multitude of other gods who personified various aspects of life, professions, and conditions. Mars, originally an Italic deity of vegetation and fertility, became primarily known in Rome as the god of war. During the early Republic, Mars was the second most important god after Jupiter, as Rome's expansion was always believed to be under divine protection. His temple on the *Campus Martius* (the Field of Mars) was not only a site of worship but also the scene of military levies and mustering. Traditionally, Roman military campaigns began in March—a month named after Mars. The priesthood of the *Salii*, who paraded through the streets of Rome in March performing ritual dances and chants, was dedicated to him.

Venus, the goddess of love, beauty, and fertility, was originally a local Roman deity but was quickly identified with the Greek Aphrodite. Among the Julii—the family to which Gaius Julius Caesar belonged—Venus was elevated to the status of an ancestral goddess (*Venus Genetrix*). In 46 BCE, Caesar built a magnificent temple to Venus Genetrix in the Forum Julium, further enhancing her cultic importance. Augustus, who saw himself as Caesar's adoptive son, continued to promote the cult of Venus. She was associated not only with love and sensuality but also with the founding of Rome, for according to myth, Aeneas—son of Venus—was the progenitor of the Roman people.

Neptune, the god of the sea, was initially worshipped only in his capacity as a god of freshwater. However, with the expansion of the Roman navy during and after the Punic Wars, he gained increasing importance as god of the sea. His festival, the *Neptunalia*, was held on July 23, in the midst of the hot and dry season when water was scarce—a reflection of his older function as a spring and water deity. The god was depicted with a trident and sea horses, in clear imitation of Hellenistic models.

Vesta, the goddess of the hearth fire, was among the oldest and most revered deities of the Roman state. Her cult was exclusively performed by the Vestal Virgins, a priestly order of celibate women. The round Temple of Vesta on the Roman Forum housed the sacred hearth fire, which was never allowed to go out. The Vestals enjoyed numerous privileges but were also subject to strict discipline—neglect of duty could result in the cruel punishment of being buried alive. The cult of Vesta was a central symbol of Rome's wellbeing and was only abolished in the late 4th century CE with the final triumph of Christianity.

Ceres, goddess of agriculture and fertility, was worshipped alongside Liber and Libera in a temple on the Aventine Hill, erected in 493 BCE. This cult was especially supported by the plebeians. Her main festival, the *Cerialia*, was celebrated from April 12 to 19, coinciding with sowing and preparation for harvest. The cult of Ceres had a strongly agrarian character and exemplified the integration of Roman religion into the cycle of the agricultural year.

Apollo, originally a Greek deity, was only officially incorporated into Roman religion at a relatively late stage. A temple to Apollo was built in 431 BCE outside the *pomerium* (the sacred boundary of the city)—an exception reflecting his foreign origin. Under Augustus, however, Apollo became one of the most important gods: the Temple of Apollo Palatinus, inaugurated in 28 BCE, stood directly beside Augustus' residence on the Palatine Hill. Apollo came to symbolize Roman virtues such as moderation, reason, and harmony. As god of poetry and music, he was closely linked to the literary flourishing of the Augustan age and its propaganda.

Diana, Apollo's sister and goddess of the hunt, animals, and chastity, was especially venerated in rural parts of Italy. Her most famous temple was located in Aricia, a town in the Alban Hills southeast of Rome. There, she was worshipped under the title *Diana Nemorensis*. Her cult often incorporated elements of nature mysticism and traces of matriarchal tradition, which led some conservative Romans to view it as unorthodox.

Mercury, the god of commerce, thieves, and travelers, corresponded to the Greek Hermes. His cult was especially popular among merchants. He was often depicted with a winged helmet, winged sandals, and the *caduceus* (herald's staff). His festival, the *Mercuralia*, was celebrated on May 15—on this day, traders sprinkled their goods with water from a sacred spring near the Porta Capena to invoke divine protection and profit.

Numerous other gods enriched the Roman pantheon: Pluto as god of the underworld, Janus as god of doors, beginnings, and transitions (especially prominent at the beginning of the year in the month of January), Bacchus as god of wine and ecstasy, *Genius* as the personal guardian spirit of every man, and the *Lares* and *Penates* as household deities venerated at small domestic altars. The *Lares Compitales*, gods of crossroads, were honored during the *Compitalia* festivals (usually in January) with offerings to ensure divine protection of neighborhoods and street crossings.

This abundance of gods, demigods, spirits, and nature beings made Roman religion a highly complex system that functioned both through centralized state mechanisms and localized pluralism. The Roman conception of religion was deeply pragmatic and integrative: new gods were not suppressed but incorporated—provided they were compatible with public order. Worship of the gods was a civic duty, not a matter of personal faith, and the religious pluralism of the Roman pantheon mirrored the cultural breadth and administrative sophistication of the Empire.

Up until the late 4th century CE, many of these gods remained central points of reference in Roman culture. Only with the edicts of Emperor Theodosius I—especially those of 391 and 392 CE—was the public cult of the traditional gods officially prohibited, their temples closed, and their priesthoods dissolved. Yet in art, language, literature, and architecture, Jupiter, Juno, Mars, Venus, and all the others continued to live on—as eternal symbols of a vanished, though never entirely forgotten, world.

7.2 Family Life, Education, and Social Hierarchies

Family life, education, and the structure of social hierarchies formed the foundation of societal functioning and the continuity of the Roman state. Unlike in many modern societies, the Roman family was not merely a private matter but a social, legal, and even religious institution of profound significance to both the state and its citizens. The rigid social hierarchy, in which every individual occupied a clearly defined place, was closely intertwined with family organization and educational practices. These structures evolved over centuries, shaped by cultural, political, and economic factors alike.

At the heart of Roman domestic life stood the *familia*, a term that encompassed more than the nuclear family of father, mother, and children. It included all individuals living under one roof: slaves, freed clients (*liberti*), adopted children, and often members of older generations. The head of the household was the *pater familias*, a male figure who held nearly absolute legal authority over all family members, including the ancient right of life and death (*vitae necisque potestas*). This patriarchal principle was deeply embedded in Roman culture and constituted a cornerstone of Roman identity. The *pater familias* also served as the religious representative of his *gens* (clan), responsible for domestic rituals and the veneration of ancestral spirits (*Lares* and *Manes*).

Marriage (*matrimonium*) in Rome was primarily a social and political alliance. Among the upper classes, it served to cement alliances and secure inheritance claims. Roman marriage was not necessarily intended to be permanent—divorce was socially accepted and could be initiated mutually or unilaterally. As early as the late Republic, it was not uncommon for elite Roman women, such as Clodia, the sister of the politician Clodius, to have multiple marriages. Marriages could be contracted in three principal forms: *confarreatio* (a traditional, quasi-priestly ceremony used primarily among patricians), *coemptio* (a symbolic purchase), and *usus* (cohabitation without formal ceremony). Upon marriage, women either remained under the legal authority of their father (*manus libera*) or passed into the control of their husband (*manus mariti*), although the latter became increasingly rare by the end of the Republic.

Children held considerable symbolic and economic importance for the continuation of the family line. Shortly after birth, the *dies lustricus*—the naming day—was celebrated on the eighth day for girls and the ninth for boys. The father would lift the newborn from the ground, a symbolic act signifying acceptance into the family. A concept of "childhood" in the modern sense did not exist. Children were quickly integrated into public life and exposed early on to ideals of duty, virtue (*virtus*), and honor. Boys in particular were prepared from a young age for their future roles as citizens and soldiers.

Education in Roman society was strongly influenced by class and origin. In the early periods of the Republic, instruction typically took place at home, especially in wealthy families, and was conducted by private tutors. Later, public schools emerged, although they were often run by slaves or freedmen and catered primarily to boys from the urban elite. Girls received formal education less frequently, although exceptions existed— Cornelia, mother of the Gracchi brothers, was considered highly educated and was renowned for her letters.

The Roman educational path typically began at the school of the *litterator*, where children learned reading, writing, and basic arithmetic. Schooling generally commenced around the age of seven. More advanced students would then attend the *grammaticus*, where they were introduced to classical literature, particularly the works of Homer, Vergil, and other canonical poets. For especially talented or status-conscious youths, the final stage was training with a *rhetor*, a teacher of rhetoric. Here, students learned argumentation, legal oratory, and public presentation—skills essential for a career in politics or law. The renowned orator Cicero, for example, received extensive training in Rome and Athens and honed his rhetorical abilities in Asia Minor.

Social hierarchies were visibly reflected in daily life. Roman society was rigidly divided into distinct social orders. At the top stood the *ordo senatorius* (senatorial order) and the *ordo equester* (equestrian order), followed by the *plebeians*, free citizens of non-noble origin, and the *liberti*, freed slaves with limited rights. At the bottom of the hierarchy were the *servi*, slaves who were legally considered property rather than persons. This social structure was strictly codified through clothing, names, rights, and obligations.

One illustrative example of such differentiation was the toga, the traditional Roman male garment. Only citizens were permitted to wear the toga, and the version with a purple border (*toga praetexta*) was reserved for magistrates and certain priests. Boys wore the *toga praetexta* until reaching adulthood (around age 14 or 15), after which they donned the *toga virilis*. Slaves wore simple tunics and were forbidden from displaying any symbols of civic identity. Members of the equestrian order were distinguished by a narrow purple stripe (*angustus clavus*) on their tunics, whereas senators wore a broader stripe (*latus clavus*).

The *patronus-clientes* relationship formed another vital pillar of Roman social structure. A *patronus*—typically a wealthy senator or equestrian—provided social, legal, and often financial support to his *clientes*. These clients would accompany their patron to the Forum, assist him in elections, and offer loyal service. In return, they could expect protection, monetary aid, or legal representation. Such patron-client ties were critical not only in urban centers but also in rural areas and the provinces, where large landowners acted as regional power brokers.

The role of women in Roman society was complex and multifaceted. On the one hand, a woman remained legally subordinate to her father or husband. On the other, particularly during the Imperial period, elite women could attain significant levels of autonomy and influence. Wealthy Roman women such as Livia Drusilla, wife of Augustus, and Agrippina the Younger, mother of Nero, wielded substantial political power through family networks. Women could own property, conduct business, employ freed slaves, and participate in temple colleges. The *matrona Romana* was the idealized image of a virtuous Roman wife—chaste, domestic, and devoted to family values.

The inculcation of Roman virtues (*virtus*, *pietas*, *gravitas*) was a core component of both familial and societal life. Boys were introduced to military ideals at an early age; many aristocrats began their public careers as *tribuni militum* (military tribunes) during adolescence. Training as a soldier was part of the socialization process, as was accompanying one's father to court, the Forum, or political assemblies.

Social hierarchy was also prominently displayed in funerary practices. Wealthy citizens were interred in elaborate tombs, often located along major roads such as the Via Appia. These burial monuments served not only as final resting places but as public declarations of wealth, ancestry, and status. The *Via Scipionum*, the burial ground of the ancient Scipio family, offers a striking example of this tradition. Poorer citizens were buried in communal columbaria, and slaves were often buried anonymously.

In the provinces, social structures tended to be hybrid in nature. On one hand, local elites adopted Roman customs, such as wearing Roman dress or constructing Roman-style baths and forums. On the other hand, many indigenous family structures persisted, particularly in rural areas. The *ius Latii* (Latin right), which granted limited legal privileges to many provincial inhabitants, gradually led to a degree of social convergence. The *Constitutio Antoniniana* issued by Emperor Caracalla in AD 212, which extended Roman citizenship to all free inhabitants of the Empire, further contributed to the formal leveling of social distinctions—at least in legal terms.

In urban centers—especially large cities such as Rome, Ostia, Carthage, and Alexandria—a multitude of social groups coexisted in close quarters. Living conditions ranged from luxurious urban villas (*domus*) to multi-story apartment buildings (*insulae*), where several families often lived under precarious conditions. Among the lower classes, child labor, illiteracy, and cramped housing were common. The classical ideal of Roman education was largely unattainable for these segments of society.

7.3 Gladiators, Baths, and Leisure

Leisure held a remarkably central position in both public and private life within the Roman Empire. Although the daily lives of many citizens—especially those in the lower social strata— were marked by hard labor and deprivation, the Roman state systematically created spaces for relaxation, physical exercise, public spectacle, and social interaction. This multifaceted culture of recreation found its most vivid expression in gladiatorial combat, the elaborate bath complexes, and a wide array of games and festivals. Leisure in ancient Rome was not merely a private need; it was a public and political tool—serving integration, distraction, and demonstrations of power.

Gladiatorial games, a quintessential form of Roman popular entertainment, may have originated in Etruscan funerary rites in which armed combat symbolized a ritual contest with death. The earliest recorded Roman gladiatorial combat took place in 264 BCE at the Forum Boarium in Rome, when Decimus Junius Brutus Pera organized a match with three pairs of fighters to honor his deceased father. In the following centuries, this custom evolved into a form of mass entertainment, increasingly staged with elaborate pomp and grandeur. During the late Republic, the *munus gladiatorium*—originally a funerary offering—became a public spectacle, often financed by wealthy citizens or politicians seeking to curry favor with the populace.

Under Julius Caesar and Augustus, the scale of these spectacles reached unprecedented levels. In 46 BCE, Caesar celebrated his quadruple triumph with games involving 320 pairs of gladiators. Augustus subsequently introduced regulations: he imposed limits on the number of fighters, curtailed excessive luxury in the games' presentation, and instituted state oversight. The amphitheaters—purpose-built venues for these combats—spread from Rome to all provinces of the empire. The first stone amphitheater in Rome was built in 29 BCE by Statilius Taurus. The most famous, the Colosseum (*Amphitheatrum Flavium*), was begun under Vespasian in 72 CE and inaugurated by Titus in 80 CE with hundred-day-long games. These spectacles featured not only gladiatorial duels but also wild beast hunts (*venationes*), staged naval battles (*naumachiae*), and public executions.

Gladiators were typically slaves, prisoners of war, or condemned criminals, though some were *auctorati*—volunteers who, driven by poverty or the pursuit of fame, pledged themselves to the arena. They trained in specialized schools (*ludi*), such as the *Ludus Magnus* in Rome, which was connected to the Colosseum by an underground passage. Gladiators were classified according to their equipment: for example, the *murmillo* fought with helmet, gladius, and large shield; the *retiarius* wielded a net and trident; and the *secutor* was trained specifically to combat the *retiarius*. Despite their low social status, successful gladiators could achieve immense popularity—their names appeared in graffiti, were stamped onto oil lamps, and depicted in mosaics. Some, such as the legendary Spartacus, became iconic. Spartacus led the infamous slave revolt from 73 to 71 BCE, a major upheaval that shook the Roman world and remains emblematic to this day.

In addition to spectacular combat, the Roman bath culture (*thermae*) represented another central facet of leisure in the empire. The first public baths (*balnea*) appeared in Rome as early as the 2nd century BCE. These were often modest, privately run establishments with limited facilities. With the advent of the imperial period, bath complexes evolved into monumental structures, known as *thermae*, which became integral elements of urban life. Baths were far more than places for hygiene—they were hubs of social gathering, relaxation, education, and even political dialogue.

Under Agrippa, a close associate of Augustus, the first grand-scale bath complexes—the *Thermae Agrippae*—were constructed around 19 BCE. These were followed by the *Thermae Neronianae* (ca. 62 CE) and, under the Flavian and Severan dynasties, the great imperial baths: the Baths of Titus, the Baths of Trajan (ca. 109 CE), and the Baths of Caracalla, built between 211 and 216 CE. These featured not only the classic bathing sections —*frigidarium* (cold room), *tepidarium* (warm room), *caldarium* (hot room), and *natatio* (swimming pool)—but also libraries, gardens, colonnaded halls (*porticus*), gymnasia, dining rooms, and even theaters.

Access to the baths was generally open to all free citizens, regardless of social rank or wealth. Admission fees were low or sometimes waived altogether, particularly when emperors or wealthy benefactors covered operational costs. For many Romans, visiting the baths was a fixed part of the daily routine: in the afternoon, typically after the ninth hour (approximately 3 PM), citizens flocked to these establishments. There they bathed, received massages, exercised, engaged in philosophical conversations, and discussed current affairs. During the imperial era, the bath culture became a hallmark of urban civilization. In numerous provincial cities—such as Trier, Lepcis Magna, Ephesus, and Londinium—local elites constructed bathhouses modeled on Roman examples, equipped with heating systems (*hypocausts*) and running water supplied by aqueducts.

Another key component of Roman leisure was the *circus* games, most notably the chariot races in the Circus Maximus. Originally laid out during the monarchy in the 6th century BCE, the Circus Maximus was massively expanded during the imperial era and is estimated to have held up to 250,000 spectators. Celebrated charioteers—such as Gaius Appuleius Diocles, a Hispano-Roman said to have earned over 35 million sesterces in prize money—achieved fame akin to modern-day sports superstars. The racing teams (*factiones*) were distinguished by color: blue, green, red, and white. Rivalries between factions occasionally erupted into violent unrest, as exemplified by the Nika Riots in Constantinople in 532 CE, although that incident belongs to the Eastern Roman Empire.

Theater also played a vital role in Roman recreational life. Especially under Augustus, who actively promoted the arts, dramatic performance flourished. Plays, pantomimes, and recitations were staged in venues such as the Theatre of Pompey (built in 55 BCE), the Theatre of Marcellus (completed in 13 BCE), and numerous provincial theaters in cities like Lyon, Orange, and Mérida. Comedies inspired by Greek models—especially those by Plautus and Terence—were particularly popular. Unlike the more elitist sphere of literature, the theater was a site of popular entertainment and satire. Performances frequently included political allegories, eliciting cheers or boos from the audience.

Festivals and holidays rounded out the Roman leisure calendar. The Roman year was replete with *feriae*—public holidays in honor of the gods. Major festivals such as the *Ludi Romani* (established in the 4th century BCE) and the *Ludi Megalenses* (from 204 BCE) combined religious ceremonies with public entertainment. By 354 CE, the Roman festival calendar already listed 175 holidays—a number that increased under the emperors. The *Saturnalia*, a seven-day December festival dedicated to Saturn, featured a near-anarchic reversal of social roles: slaves dined like their masters, gifts were exchanged, and public revelry abounded.

The synthesis of entertainment, ritual, hygiene, and social interaction rendered Roman leisure culture a mirror of the society itself. Here, rich and poor, slave and freedman, senator and merchant converged. The emperors quickly recognized the political utility of public spectacles: *bread and circuses* (*panem et circenses*), as the poet Juvenal observed, became a strategic instrument of mass control. Emperors such as Trajan, Hadrian, or Commodus—who notoriously entered the arena himself—leveraged games to stage their power and curry public favor.

Thus, leisure in the Roman Empire was far from mere diversion. It was a culturally embedded institution that spanned religious significance, state organization, and personal ambition. It created collective identities, fostered provincial integration, and —through its splendor, cruelty, and vitality—revealed the face of a world power held together not only by legions and roads, but also by spectacle, thermal waters, and athleticism.

7.4 Cultural Exchange in the Provinces

Cultural exchange in the provinces of the Roman Empire was a complex and multifaceted phenomenon, encompassing both the dissemination of Roman lifestyles and the reciprocal influence of local cultures on Roman society. Contrary to the notion of a one-sided "Romanization process" in which Rome simply imposed its culture upon the conquered peoples, this exchange was, in truth, a dynamic and often asymmetrical interaction between center and periphery. The provinces were not mere recipients of Roman culture; rather, they were co-creators of a cultural network that stretched from Britannia to Egypt, from Hispania to Armenia. The diversity of the Empire was simultaneously a source of strength and an expression of an imperial identity that prioritized integration over homogeneity.

As early as the initial stages of expansion, Roman practices began to blend with local customs. In Hispania, which had been progressively Romanized following its conquest during the Second Punic War (from 218 BCE onwards), early forms of cultural symbiosis emerged. Cities such as Emerita Augusta (founded in 25 BCE) and Tarraco (modern Tarragona) combined Roman urban planning with Iberian elements. In Emerita, for instance, temples were erected in the typical Roman architectural style, while local deities such as Endovelicus and Ataecina continued to be venerated—now, however, within cult spaces inspired by Roman design. Latin inscriptions were used extensively, albeit often interspersed with local idioms. Many Spanish elites adopted Roman names, wore the toga, and sent their sons to Roman schools. At the same time, Spanish products—particularly *garum*, a concentrated fish sauce, and olive oil from Baetica—were exported to Rome in significant quantities and became everyday staples in the capital.

In Gaul, which had been conquered militarily under Julius Caesar between 58 and 50 BCE, cultural exchange unfolded in similarly intricate ways. The so-called "Gallo-Roman culture" represented a fusion of Celtic traditions and Roman forms. Settlements such as Lugdunum (modern Lyon), established as a Roman colony in 43 BCE, developed into cultural melting pots. Here, Gallic druidic sanctuaries stood alongside Roman temples, and in local healing baths, Celtic water deities were equated with Roman nymphs. One particularly striking aspect of this cultural amalgamation was the incorporation of Celtic gods into the Roman pantheon—for example, Jupiter Poeninus or Lenus Mars, a Gallo-Roman war deity embodying traits from both traditions. Roman architecture was adopted in Gaul, yet often retained regional characteristics: the *Maison Carrée* in Nîmes, one of the best-preserved Roman temples, demonstrates such hybridity with its ornate local elements in decoration and construction.

Similarly rich were the cultural interactions in the Eastern Mediterranean, particularly in the Greek provinces and Roman Egypt. Unlike in the western provinces, the aim here was not to introduce urban culture, which had already been firmly established for centuries through cities, theaters, gymnasia, and literacy. Rather, cultural exchange in this context often meant that Rome itself drew heavily on Hellenistic traditions. In Alexandria, the cultural center of Egypt, scholarship flourished under Roman rule. Libraries, philosophical schools, and religious centers—such as the Serapeum temple—were not only preserved but actively integrated into imperial representation. The god Serapis, a syncretic figure combining aspects of the Greek Zeus and the Egyptian Osiris, was readily embraced by the Romans and honored with temples in western provinces such as Rome, Ostia, and Puteoli.

In the province of Asia—western Asia Minor—Roman law and administration were intertwined with the traditions of the Greek *polis*. Cities such as Ephesus, Pergamon, and Smyrna received grand Roman-style buildings, including aqueducts, baths, stadiums, and theaters, yet retained their native languages, deities, and many of their political institutions. The imperial cult, initially controversial in Rome itself, found especially fertile ground in this region. In Pergamon, the first provincial temple dedicated to Emperor Augustus was erected in 29 BCE—a fusion of Roman imperial symbolism and Eastern sacral architecture. Such temples were often financed by local elites, who sought prestige and proximity to the imperial court. The resulting cultic landscape in Asia Minor is a prime example of cultural hybridization.

In frontier provinces such as Dacia (modern-day Romania, conquered in 106 CE under Trajan) or Germania, the Roman presence was often more militarized. Nevertheless, significant cultural exchanges occurred even here. In the *canabae* (civilian settlements adjacent to military camps) and *vici* (villages surrounding Roman forts), merchants, artisans, soldiers' wives, and indigenous service providers cohabitated and interacted. In places like Colonia Claudia Ara Agrippinensium (modern Cologne) or Mogontiacum (Mainz), one finds both Roman statuary and votive inscriptions dedicated to local Celtic deities. Particularly noteworthy is the cult of the *Matronae*—protective goddesses of fertility and family—depicted in Roman form (wearing the toga and accompanied by altars) but unmistakably rooted in pre-Roman traditions.

In North Africa, cultural exchange was closely tied to urban development. The cities of Africa Proconsularis (modern-day Tunisia), Numidia, and Mauretania—such as Carthage, Thugga, and Leptis Magna—developed into thriving centers of Roman culture. The famous North African mosaics, for instance from the "Villa of Theseus" in Neapolis (modern Nabeul) or the House of Venus in Carthage, featured classical Roman motifs, including scenes from the *Iliad*, while also reflecting local nature themes, animal depictions, and distinctive African stylistic traits. North

African elites adopted the Roman educational system, funded amphitheaters, and supported public construction projects. The renowned Christian Church Father Augustine of Hippo himself emerged from this cultural environment: an African provincial citizen, trained in Latin rhetoric, yet shaped by local traditions and realities.

In the eastern frontier regions, such as Syria and Palestine, cultural exchange was particularly intense—though often marked by conflict. Cities like Antioch and Damascus served as cultural hubs where Greco-Roman, Semitic, and Persian influences coexisted. Archaeological findings in Palestine indicate that Roman-style villas often featured distinctly Jewish elements, such as *mikva'ot* (ritual immersion baths). Conversely, Roman architectural forms—such as aqueducts, roads, and triumphal arches—were adapted to local building styles. Following the Jewish War (66–73 CE) and the Bar Kokhba revolt (132–136 CE), Rome established the colony of Aelia Capitolina in Jerusalem, a Roman veterans' settlement built according to classical urban principles—on a site with centuries of sacred tradition. These efforts were part of a deliberate strategy of cultural overwriting, which elicited both acceptance and resistance.

One must not underestimate the role of Roman soldiers as agents of cultural transmission. Legionaries who served twenty or more years in distant provinces disseminated language, architecture, clothing, and customs. Upon discharge, they were often granted land in the provinces, where they settled permanently, forming a cultural bridge between Rome and the periphery. Entire veteran colonies emerged where Roman lifestyles fused with local traditions—for instance in Timgad (Algeria) or Viminacium (Serbia).

In conclusion, cultural exchange in the Roman provinces was not a uniform or linear process but rather a mosaic of regional interactions. It was a "glocal" culture—local appropriation of global Roman forms—that held the Empire together not through cultural uniformity but through functional diversity. Roman identity was thus defined not in spite of its plurality, but because of it. A Roman citizen in Trier, Alexandria, or Ephesus might speak a different language, worship different gods, and live in a different kind of house—but the Roman world remained legible and coherent in its streets, its games, its legal system, its coinage, and its shared vision of belonging to a world order that not only tolerated diversity, but made it productive.

7.5 Language, Writing, and Legal System

The domains of language, writing, and jurisprudence were foundational pillars of Roman culture and profoundly shaped the Roman Empire—not only as instruments of governance but also as carriers of cultural identity. Amid the vast diversity of ethnic groups, languages, and traditions that coexisted within the provinces of the Roman Empire, Latin and Roman law in particular emerged as shared cultural cornerstones. Their influence extended well beyond the fall of the Western Roman Empire and continued to shape Europe into the modern era. This chapter seeks to trace the historical trajectory of linguistic and legal developments in the empire in a detailed manner, taking into account their dissemination, institutionalization, relevance to daily life, and their mutual interconnection.

The Roman language—Latin—originated from the linguistic region of Latium and was initially the dialect spoken in the city of Rome and its surroundings. As early as the 5th century BCE, so-called Old Latin began to assert itself as the language of administration and religious practice, as evidenced in the Twelve Tables (*Leges Duodecim Tabularum*) around 450 BCE, regarded as the earliest codification of Roman law. These tablets, which were displayed in the Roman Forum, represented not only a legal milestone but also the first instance of publicly accessible Latin literacy. They included provisions concerning inheritance law, obligations, penalties for theft, and civil procedures—composed in an archaic form of Latin that differed markedly from the later Classical Latin.

With Rome's expansion from the 3rd century BCE onward, the Latin language spread first throughout Italy and then gradually across the Mediterranean basin. A decisive factor in this dissemination was the establishment of veteran colonies and Roman municipia, in which Latin became the language of governance and education. This phenomenon is especially apparent in the western provinces, such as Gaul, where Latin inscriptions are attested already under Caesar, and in Hispania, where a wide array of Latin graffiti, funerary inscriptions, and votive texts have been preserved. A notable example is the bronze plaque of Botorrita (c. 70 BCE), which illustrates how Latin was used alongside Iberian languages in public inscriptions.

However, the spread of Latin was by no means uniform. In the eastern regions of the empire—particularly in Greece, Egypt, and Asia Minor—Greek remained the dominant language of high culture, education, and administration. Imperial decrees in these areas were frequently issued bilingually, such as the *Edict on Maximum Prices* by Diocletian in 301 CE, which survives in both Latin and Greek. This coexistence led to a bilingual culture in many eastern provinces of the empire.

Writing was not restricted to the realm of administration but was deeply embedded in everyday life. In Pompeii, preserved by the eruption of Mount Vesuvius in 79 CE, thousands of wall inscriptions—known as *dipinti* and graffiti—have been found, including political slogans ("Vote for Lucius Popidius!"), commercial price lists, declarations of love, business contracts, and casual scribbles. These examples demonstrate that literacy had moved beyond elite circles and had increasingly permeated lower social strata. Writing tablets, ink pots, and styluses have also been discovered in remote garrison towns such as Vindolanda near Hadrian's Wall (in modern-day northern England), where numerous wooden tablet letters from the 1st and 2nd centuries CE have been preserved—including birthday invitations and shopping lists.

The shift from spoken to written language was also an expression of growing societal professionalization. Administrative officials, jurists, and military commanders increasingly required trained scribes (*scribae*) who were familiar with legal forms and terminology. The education of these scribes often took place in rhetorical and grammatical schools, where classical Latin literacy was first taught, followed by legal vocabulary, stylistic conventions, and the logic of legal organization. Renowned authors such as Quintilian (c. 35–100 CE), who operated the first systematic school of rhetoric in Rome, emphasized in their works the importance of linguistic precision for public and legal life.

Closely linked to language and writing was the Roman legal system, which became one of Rome's most enduring contributions to European cultural history. It evolved from early religiously influenced legal forms during the Republic to a complex, secular, and systematic legal corpus under the Principate and in Late Antiquity. Already in the Twelve Tables, a distinction was made between divine and human law (*fas* vs. *ius*), a dichotomy that would be elaborated upon over the centuries.

During the 2nd and 1st centuries BCE, a professional class of legal scholars emerged—the *iuris prudentes* (jurists). Prominent figures such as Gaius, Papinian, Ulpian, and Paulus shaped legal interpretation in the Imperial era. Gaius' *Institutiones*, composed around 160 CE, offered a comprehensive introduction to civil law in four parts: the law of persons, the law of things, the law of obligations, and procedural law. This work later served as the model for the *Institutiones Iustiniani* and was incorporated into the *Corpus Iuris Civilis* under Emperor Justinian I.

Roman law was based on various sources: *leges* (laws) passed by popular assemblies or, under the Principate, decreed by the emperor; *senatus consulta* (senatorial resolutions); *edicta* of the praetors; and interpretative legal writings by jurists. Under Emperor Hadrian (r. 117–138 CE), the *Edictum Perpetuum* was codified—a standard legal text that had previously been renewed annually by the praetor. This codification of procedural law was a crucial step toward legal consistency and transparency in judicial practice.

A particularly significant aspect of Roman law was its role in the integration of the provinces. Through the *civitas* system, Roman citizenship—and thus access to Roman legal protection—was gradually extended. The most pivotal development came with the *Constitutio Antoniniana* issued by Emperor Caracalla in 212 CE, which granted Roman citizenship to all free inhabitants of the empire. This act instantly transformed millions of people into legal subjects within the Roman legal framework, significantly facilitating the spread of Latin legal terminology and practice.

Roman law permeated not only courtrooms but also the fabric of everyday life: from marriage law (e.g., *manus* marriage versus free marriage), inheritance, obligations, and property law. A common example is *manumissio*—the formal emancipation of slaves—which required legal acts such as testamentary declarations or symbolic manumission before a magistrate. Rental agreements, commercial transactions, guarantees, and loans were governed by written contracts, numerous examples of which survive in papyri, especially from Egypt.

Last but not least, Roman law functioned as a central element of Roman cultural self-identity. The term *civitas* denoted not only the legal status of a citizen but also a sense of belonging to the Roman order—a *res publica* organized through law and writing. This order transcended not only geographic borders but also social hierarchies: in theory, the courts of the empire allowed ordinary citizens, former slaves, and provincial inhabitants to bring legal actions against persons of higher social standing—even if success in practice was not always guaranteed.

The longevity and systematic elaboration of Roman law explain its enduring influence on later European legal systems. Particularly in Late Antiquity, under Emperor Justinian I (r. 527–565), Roman law was comprehensively codified in the *Corpus Iuris Civilis*, which consisted of four parts: the *Institutiones*, the *Digest*, the *Codex*, and the *Novellae*, encompassing the entire body of valid Roman law. This compilation formed the foundation of the medieval and early modern *ius commune* and had a lasting impact on national legal codes such as the French *Code civil* (1804) and the German *Bürgerliches Gesetzbuch* (1900).

CHAPTER 8: CHRISTIANIZATION AND RELIGIOUS TRANSFORMATION (1ST–5TH CENTURY AD)

8.1 Early Christianity: Persecution and Expansion

Early Christianity emerged within a complex religious and political environment shaped by the Roman Empire during the 1st century CE. The origins of this new religion coincided with a period of profound social transformation, religious pluralism, and increasing tensions within the Jewish population of Judaea, a Roman province since 6 CE. Under Emperor Augustus (27 BCE–14 CE), the region was governed through a sophisticated system of client kings and Roman administration, with Jerusalem serving as its religious epicenter. It was within this historical and geopolitical context that Jesus of Nazareth began his activity—his life, ministry, and crucifixion, dated approximately between 30 and 33 CE, mark the inception of the Christian movement.

Jesus of Nazareth preached primarily in Galilee and Judaea. His message centered on a call to repentance, the imminent coming of the Kingdom of God, and, according to tradition, he performed acts of healing. His followers regarded him as the Messiah, the "Anointed One" of God, which corresponded to prevailing Jewish expectations of a liberator from political subjugation. The Roman authorities—particularly under the prefect Pontius Pilate (26–36 CE)—viewed religious movements with messianic claims as potentially subversive. Consequently, Jesus was sentenced to death by crucifixion, a penalty typically reserved for slaves and political rebels.

Following Jesus' execution, a nascent Christian community took shape in Jerusalem. Initially, its members still considered themselves part of Judaism. This early community was led by James the Just, a relative of Jesus, who functioned in a role similar to that of a bishop. Over time, however, the Christian doctrine extended beyond its Jewish roots. A pivotal figure in this expansion was Paul of Tarsus (c. 5–64 CE), a Roman citizen and former persecutor of Christians, who became the most fervent missionary of the new faith following a profound conversion experience. Paul established numerous congregations across the Eastern Mediterranean—in cities such as Antioch, Ephesus, Philippi, Corinth, and Rome. His epistles, later included in the New Testament, are crucial sources for understanding early Christian theology and ecclesiastical organization.

By the 50s CE, Christian communities existed in several cities across the Roman Empire. These groups were often socially distinct from the broader urban populations, drawing primarily from the lower strata of society—slaves, freedpersons, women, and ethnically diverse individuals. Christian gatherings typically took place in private homes, known as *domus ecclesiae* or house churches, which were adapted residential spaces. While this early phase lacked a standardized liturgy or a fixed scriptural canon, core beliefs such as the resurrection of Jesus and the expectation of his return were central.

Initially, Roman authorities responded only sporadically and locally to the rise of Christianity. There is no evidence of systematic persecution by the Roman state in this early period. The first recorded imperial action against Christians occurred under Emperor Nero (r. 54–68 CE). In 64 CE, a catastrophic fire ravaged Rome, the cause of which remained uncertain. According to Tacitus (Annals XV, 44), Nero deflected suspicion by blaming the Christians. This led to brutal executions: Christians were crucified, burned alive, or thrown to wild beasts. However, these measures were localized acts of repression, not indicative of an empire-wide persecution.

Under the Flavian dynasty and the so-called Adoptive Emperors, Christians again sporadically attracted imperial scrutiny. Notably, during the reign of Domitian (81–96 CE), Christians came under pressure. Domitian, who demanded semi-divine reverence and enforced traditional Roman religious practices, targeted opponents—sometimes for religious reasons. Although the extent of persecution under his reign remains debated, there is evidence suggesting a precarious situation for Christians refusing to participate in the imperial cult.

A significant primary source from this period is the correspondence between Pliny the Younger, governor of Bithynia and Pontus, and Emperor Trajan (r. 98–117 CE), dated around 112 CE. Pliny describes how he interrogated Christians, demanded they renounce their faith, and executed those who refused. He sought clarification from the emperor on how to handle the growing number of Christians. Trajan's reply was pragmatic: Christians were not to be actively hunted but were to be punished if formally accused and found guilty. This exchange reveals the Roman administrative approach—Christians were not prosecuted for their doctrine per se but for refusing to conform to Roman religious norms.

Despite intermittent repression, the Christian population steadily increased throughout the 2nd century CE. The missionary activity extended beyond the Greek-speaking Eastern Roman provinces. Christian communities, though initially small, established a firm presence in regions such as

Gaul, Germania, Africa Proconsularis, Hispania, and Britannia. Christianity's cultural appeal lay in its universality: it offered eternal life regardless of ethnicity, gender, or social class. Moreover, the communal support among Christians provided a sense of social security, especially during periods of political instability or economic distress.

The 3rd century CE saw intensified persecution. Notably, under Emperors Decius (r. 249–251) and Valerian (r. 253–260), persecution became systematic and empire-wide. In 250 CE, Decius issued an edict requiring all citizens to perform a public sacrifice to the emperor and Roman gods, verified by a *libellus* —a written certificate. Christians who refused were arrested, tortured, or executed. Many bishops, including Fabian of Rome, suffered martyrdom. Valerian continued this policy with two edicts in 257 and 258 CE, specifically targeting Christian clergy. Bishop Cyprian of Carthage was beheaded in 258 after refusing to return to pagan sacrifice.

The most severe and final wave of persecution occurred under Emperor Diocletian (r. 284–305 CE). A devout adherent of the Roman pantheon, Diocletian sought to restore imperial unity through the revitalization of traditional cults. In 303 CE, he issued a series of edicts ordering the destruction of Christian churches, the burning of sacred texts, and the imprisonment of clergy. This "Great Persecution" lasted until approximately 311 CE and resulted in significant casualties, although enforcement varied widely across regions. The persecution was particularly fierce in Egypt, Palestine, and Asia Minor, while comparatively mild in Gaul. The historian Eusebius of Caesarea chronicled these events in his *Ecclesiastical History*, though from a distinctly Christian perspective.

Paradoxically, the persecutions contributed to the further spread of Christianity. The memory of the martyrs became a foundational component of Christian identity. Their graves became pilgrimage sites; their names were incorporated into liturgy and calendars. The collective remembrance of suffering cultivated a theology of endurance and faithfulness that endowed the nascent religion with a profound sense of legitimacy. In subterranean catacombs, especially in Rome, Christians created burial chambers adorned with wall paintings, symbolic motifs (such as the fish and the Chi-Rho monogram ☧), and early depictions of biblical scenes.

By the 4th century CE, Christianity had become increasingly integrated into Roman society. Numerous cities now had established Christian congregations with permanent episcopal seats. The episcopacy emerged as the central administrative structure of the Church, often modeled after Roman governmental systems. Bishops such as Ambrose of Milan and Gregory Thaumaturgus began to play prominent public roles, acting as advocates for their communities in dealings with civic authorities.

Theological schools also developed, notably in Alexandria, where Origen (c. 185–254) pioneered allegorical interpretations of Scripture and explored the relationship between philosophy and faith. In North Africa, Tertullian (c. 160–220) articulated the concept of *trinitas*—the Trinity—and authored fervent apologetic works against Roman persecution. Early Christian literature thus played a dual role: it solidified theological foundations and established boundaries against competing religious ideologies and heresies such as Gnosticism and Montanism.

Even prior to Constantine's conversion in the early 4th century, Christianity had become a widespread religion across the Roman Empire, with an estimated 5 to 8 million adherents out of a total population of approximately 50 to 60 million. Christians lived amidst a religiously pluralistic society teeming with diverse cults—from the worship of Isis and Mithras to philosophical movements like Stoicism. The exclusivity of Christian worship, particularly its rejection of the imperial cult, rendered it both an object of fascination and a source of suspicion.

In conclusion, early Christianity, from the 1st to the early 4th century CE, underwent a profound transformation from a Jewish sect into a distinct, trans-cultural religion. This evolution was characterized by periods of persecution and expansion, adaptation to Roman administrative models, theological differentiation, and the emergence of a unique cultural identity. Paradoxically, the hardships faced by Christians strengthened their communal cohesion and missionary resolve—ultimately laying the foundation for the sweeping religious transformation that would redefine the Roman Empire in the 4th and 5th centuries CE.

8.2 Constantine the Great and the Edict of Milan (313)

The rise of Constantine the Great and the promulgation of the Edict of Milan in AD 313 mark a pivotal turning point in the history of the Roman Empire and the religious evolution of Europe. This period initiated the transformation of Christianity from a persecuted minority faith into a privileged and ultimately dominant religion within the Empire. Understanding the significance of Constantine and his religious policy requires a detailed examination not only of the immediate events leading up to 313 but also of the broader political and ideological consequences of his actions. These developments are closely linked to the political and military upheavals of the late third and early fourth centuries, particularly to the so-called Tetrarchy and the power struggles associated with it.

The Tetrarchy, introduced by Emperor Diocletian in AD 293, was an attempt to stabilize the governance of the vast Roman Empire by instituting a system comprising two Augusti (senior emperors) and two Caesares (junior emperors). Diocletian ruled as Augustus of the East, while Maximian controlled the West. Their respective Caesars were Galerius and Constantius Chlorus. Constantius Chlorus governed the western provinces of Britannia, Gaul, and Hispania and was the father of the future emperor Constantine. However, following Diocletian's abdication in 305, this system quickly descended into rivalry and civil war.

Constantine was born in AD 272 in Naissus (modern-day Niš in Serbia). His mother, Helena, is thought to have been the daughter of an innkeeper from Bithynia, while his father Constantius rose under Diocletian to the rank of Caesar and, in 305, to Augustus of the West. Upon Constantius's death in Eboracum (York) in 306, the legions in Britain unilaterally acclaimed Constantine as Augustus. This proclamation was not recognized by all members of the Tetrarchic system, but it positioned Constantine as one of several competing claimants in an increasingly fragmented empire.

From 306 to 312, multiple emperors vied for supremacy: Constantine in the West, Maxentius in Italy, Galerius in the East, and both Licinius and Maximinus Daia in the Balkans and eastern regions. Maxentius, the son of former Emperor Maximian, had declared himself emperor in Rome in 306 without official recognition by the Tetrarchy. The subsequent years were marked by continuous struggles for legitimacy and military dominance.

Between 306 and 312, Constantine focused on securing Gaul and the Rhine frontier. He led several successful military campaigns against Germanic tribes, particularly the Franks and Alamanni. Simultaneously, he embarked on administrative reforms and began to portray himself increasingly as a protector of Christianity, even though he had not yet officially converted. His policies were pragmatic: he extended protection to the Christian Church, appointed Christians to high offices, and communicated with Christian communities as a benevolent patron.

In 312, a decisive confrontation occurred between Constantine and Maxentius in the context of the ongoing civil war for control of Italy. Constantine led an army of approximately 40,000 to 50,000 soldiers from Gaul across the Alps into Italy. On his march toward Rome, he secured key victories, including those at Turin and Verona. The climactic battle took place on October 28, 312, at the Milvian Bridge (Pons Milvius) north of Rome.

The Battle of the Milvian Bridge is one of the most famous engagements of Late Antiquity—not only because of its military outcome but also due to its profound religious significance. According to Christian sources, especially Eusebius of Caesarea and Lactantius, Constantine experienced a vision the night before the battle: a sign appeared in the sky—either a cross or the Chi-Rho monogram (☧)—accompanied by the inscription *in hoc signo vinces* ("In this sign, you will conquer"). Constantine reportedly instructed his soldiers to paint this symbol on their shields. In the ensuing battle, he decisively defeated Maxentius's numerically superior forces. Maxentius drowned in the Tiber during the retreat.

This victory secured Constantine's position as sole ruler of the Western Roman Empire. He entered Rome in triumph on October 29, 312, but notably declined to perform the traditional visit to the Capitoline Temple of Jupiter Optimus Maximus. This symbolic act has been widely interpreted as a deliberate break with pagan tradition. Although Constantine continued to tolerate the official cults of the Empire, his political orientation from that point onward was unmistakably favorable to Christianity.

A defining moment in the religious history of the Empire was the issuance of the so-called Edict of Milan, proclaimed jointly by Constantine and Licinius in February 313. Their meeting likely took place in Mediolanum (modern Milan) on the occasion of Licinius's marriage to Constantine's sister, Constantia. The Edict itself is not preserved in any official Latin version, but survives in a Greek summary included in Lactantius's *De mortibus persecutorum* and Eusebius's *Historia ecclesiastica* (IX, 9). The content of the decree is, however, unambiguous: it guaranteed freedom of worship for all religions, with a particular emphasis on the rights of Christians.

The Edict of Milan did not merely tolerate Christianity—as the Edict of Toleration issued by Galerius in 311 had begun to do—but constituted a comprehensive act of religious equality. It mandated the return of previously confiscated Church property, recognized the Christians' right to public worship, and granted them legal parity with adherents of other cults. In a remarkable phrase, Constantine and Licinius declared that "we, too, may enjoy the favor of the divine majesty." This statement reveals that Constantine regarded divine support—not solely for Christians but for the entire Empire—as a source of imperial blessing.

The Edict had far-reaching consequences for the institutional development of Christianity. Within a few years, Christians began to practice their faith openly. New churches were constructed, especially in Rome. Among the most significant early projects was the Lateran Basilica (today known as San Giovanni in Laterano), the first monumental Christian church in the city. Its foundations were laid around 313–314. Soon thereafter followed major constructions such as the Old St.

Peter's Basilica on the Vatican Hill (construction beginning circa 319) and the Basilica of Saint Paul Outside the Walls along the Via Ostiensis. These buildings served not only as religious centers but also as visible expressions of the Church's emerging social status.

Constantine's support for the Church extended far beyond the Edict of Milan. He provided the Church with financial endowments from the imperial treasury, granted bishops administrative authority in matters such as inheritance law, and increasingly equated the Church hierarchy with urban administrative institutions. The bishop of Rome, in particular, began to assume greater prominence, even though Constantine himself did not recognize papal primacy in ecclesiastical terms. Nonetheless, he increasingly viewed himself as *episkopos tōn ektos*—"bishop of those outside the Church"—meaning a guardian of unity and doctrinal truth, even in theological matters.

One immediate consequence of the Edict and the Church's new status was the intensification of internal theological disputes. As early as the 310s, doctrinal controversies arose, especially concerning the nature of the Trinity and the person of Christ. The Arian controversy, initiated by the teachings of the Alexandrian priest Arius—who questioned the full divinity of Christ—divided congregations in the eastern provinces. Constantine, as a ruler, sought to preserve ecclesiastical unity, viewing the Church as a unifying force within the Empire. This concern would soon culminate in the Council of Nicaea—a theological and political outcome made possible by the groundwork laid in 313.

Constantine's personal relationship with Christianity was complex. He did not receive baptism until shortly before his death in 337, likely administered by Bishop Eusebius of Nicomedia. Nevertheless, from 313 onward he actively promoted Christianity, introduced Christian symbols on coinage, and adopted a monotheistic worldview in public inscriptions. His favored emblem remained the sun god, *Sol Invictus*, for some time, but this was gradually supplanted by the Christogram. His increasing identification with Christianity also manifested in legislative measures against certain pagan practices, including restrictions on sacrifices and prohibitions of specific oracular rituals.

Thus, the Edict of Milan inaugurated a new phase in Roman religious policy. It did not yet establish Christianity as the state religion—that would occur later under Theodosius I in 380—but it provided the legal, social, and cultural foundation upon which the Christian Church would rise to become a central pillar of the Late Roman state. The transformation initiated by Constantine was not merely religious; it represented a redefinition of imperial political structure and of the sacred self-conception of the Roman world.

8.3 The Council of Nicaea and the Formation of Christian Doctrine

The First Council of Nicaea in AD 325 represents a pivotal milestone in the history of Christianity and the Late Antique imperial church. Amid a period of profound transformation within the Roman Empire—particularly due to the increasing state patronage of Christianity under Emperor Constantine the Great—the council of Nicaea marked the first formal codification of doctrine in the form of an ecumenical creed. The attempt to forge doctrinal unity within a rapidly expanding and diverse religious community was not only the product of theological debate but also a reflection of the imperial administration's political interests in establishing a unified religious foundation to ideologically stabilize the Empire.

The immediate cause for the convocation of the council was the so-called Arian controversy, named after the Alexandrian presbyter Arius, who around 318/319 AD began to publicly disseminate his own teachings. Arius upheld a Christology grounded in the absolute uniqueness and incomparability of God the Father. From this theological premise, he concluded that the Son—Jesus Christ—although divine and exalted, was subordinate to the Father and not of the same essence (*homoousios*). The Son, Arius asserted, was a creature—though the first of all creatures—"created out of nothing." This position stood in stark contrast to the increasingly dominant theological trend that identified the divinity of the Son as fully and substantially equal to that of the Father.

Arius' teachings provoked both support and fierce opposition. Most notably, Bishop Alexander of Alexandria condemned Arius and succeeded in having him excommunicated. However, the dispute quickly spread beyond Alexandria, engulfing large parts of the Eastern Roman Empire. Arian positions garnered considerable support, especially in the provinces of Syria and Palestine. Even within the imperial court—particularly in the East—Arius had powerful allies, such as Eusebius of Nicomedia, a prominent bishop and confidant of the emperor.

Constantine, who since the Edict of Milan (313 AD) saw himself as the guardian of Christian unity, recognized the Arian controversy as a serious threat to both the religious cohesion and political stability of the Empire. While previous decades had demonstrated that the persecution of Christians could destabilize imperial rule, internal division within the Christian church now posed a similar danger. To avert an impending schism, Constantine resolved in 325 to convene an imperial synod that would clarify theological disputes and establish doctrinal unity. He invited bishops from all parts of the Empire

—East and West alike—to attend a council at Nicaea (modern-day İznik in Turkey), a city in the province of Bithynia in Asia Minor, not far from Nicomedia, then the imperial residence.

The council opened in June 325 AD and brought together approximately 250 to 320 bishops—the exact number remains debated, with Athanasius of Alexandria later citing 318, perhaps in symbolic reference to the number of Jewish scholars in the legend of the Septuagint. The majority of the participants hailed from the Eastern provinces of the Empire, particularly Egypt, Syria, Palestine, and Asia Minor. The Western representation was minimal, consisting of a few bishops from Gaul, Italy, and North Africa; Pope Sylvester I, Bishop of Rome, was unable to attend due to illness and sent two presbyters in his stead.

The formal organization of the council rested with the emperor, who personally attended the deliberations but refrained from issuing theological rulings. His role was that of a moderator and guarantor of peace. The initial sessions of the council, likely presided over by Bishop Hosius of Córdoba—Constantine's theological advisor—saw the presentation of arguments from the contending parties. Arius and his supporters, notably Eusebius of Nicomedia, sought to defend their doctrinal positions, but encountered vigorous opposition.

The leading opponent of Arianism at the council was the deacon Athanasius of Alexandria, who would later become bishop of the same city and a central figure in Trinitarian orthodoxy. Athanasius passionately argued for the full divinity of the Son and insisted on the use of the term *homoousios* ("of the same essence") to describe the relationship between Father and Son. This term was contentious, as it had not been part of earlier theological discourse and was criticized as overly philosophical or even Sabellian (modalist). Nonetheless, it emerged as the decisive term in defining the new orthodoxy.

The principal outcome of the council was the so-called *Nicene Creed* (*Nicaenum*), which was adopted by an overwhelming majority and included the following formulation:

"We believe in one God, the Father Almighty, Maker of all things visible and invisible.
And in one Lord Jesus Christ, the Son of God, begotten of the Father, only-begotten—that is, from the essence of the Father—God from God, Light from Light, true God from true God, begotten, not made, of one essence (homoousios) with the Father, through whom all things were made [...]"

With this wording, Arian theology was explicitly rejected. The council issued an *anathema* against all "who say there was a time when the Son was not," and against those who claimed that the Son was "created out of nothing" or was "of a different substance or essence" than the Father.

In addition to the creed, the council promulgated twenty so-called *canons* (disciplinary decrees), which addressed ecclesiastical regulations. These included provisions regarding the ordination of bishops, the conduct of the clergy, the celebration of Easter (which was to be established independently of the Jewish Passover), and rules for dealing with the *lapsi*—Christians who had renounced their faith under persecution. The Meletian Schism in Egypt, concerning the recognition of legitimate ecclesiastical authority, was also addressed.

Particularly contentious were the debates surrounding the date of Easter. In the Eastern provinces, Easter was often celebrated on the same day as the Jewish Passover (14th of Nisan), while in the West it was customary to observe Easter on a Sunday. The council opted unanimously for the Western practice—a decision that would have long-lasting consequences for the Christian liturgical calendar and the chronology of church festivals. The precise calculation of Easter would, in the following centuries, be determined through astronomical tables and became a central concern of ecclesiastical chronology.

After intense deliberations, the council likely concluded in July 325. Of the attending bishops, all but a few—namely Arius, Theonas of Marmarica, and Secundus of Ptolemais—signed the Nicene Creed. These dissenters were banished by imperial order, and Arius' writings were burned. The council's resolutions were communicated in official letters to the provincial bishops and, in some cases, summarized in imperial rescripts.

However, despite the seemingly definitive conclusions of the council, doctrinal consensus proved short-lived. Within just a few years, the tide began to turn. Eusebius of Nicomedia regained favor with Constantine, and in 328 Arius was recalled at the emperor's behest. Athanasius, though a staunch defender of the Nicene position and now Bishop of Alexandria, soon found himself embroiled in conflicts with Arian-leaning clerics and was exiled no fewer than five times between 335 and 366.

This sequence of events illustrates that the Council of Nicaea marked less an endpoint than the beginning of a centuries-long process of doctrinal clarification. The debate over Trinitarian theology continued to dominate theological discourse throughout Late Antiquity, particularly at the subsequent councils of Serdica (343), Rimini (359), and Constantinople (381). At the latter, the *Niceno-Constantinopolitan Creed*, an expanded version of the Nicene Creed, was formulated, definitively establishing Trinitarian orthodoxy.

Despite ongoing controversies, the First Council of Nicaea constituted a historical novelty: for the first time in Christian history, an assembly of bishops, under imperial patronage, had articulated a universal creed. The term *ecumenical* (Greek:

oikoumenikos – "concerning the whole inhabited world") assumed a theological meaning in this context. Constantine himself envisioned the council as the foundation of a "catholic" (universal) church that would serve as the ideological cornerstone of the Empire. The concept of a dogmatically unified church under imperial protection became the model for the later Byzantine state church.

Legally, Nicaea also set new standards: the council's canons were later incorporated into Roman legal collections, including the *Codex Theodosianus* (438) and the *Codex Iustinianus* (529–534). Thus, ecclesiastical norms became part of Roman law—a development that documents the growing fusion of church and state in the Late Antique and early Byzantine Empire.

Finally, Nicaea initiated the institutional framework for a series of subsequent ecumenical councils whose decisions would shape the theological and canonical foundations of the Christian churches for centuries. In total, the ancient church recognized seven ecumenical councils, beginning with Nicaea I (325) and culminating in Nicaea II (787), which addressed the issue of icon veneration.

The events of Nicaea therefore vividly demonstrate the close interweaving of doctrinal formation, political authority, and ecclesiastical institutionalization in Late Antiquity. The effort to achieve unity through theological precision became a defining feature of a religion that had transformed from a persecuted sect into the central ideological force of a world empire.

8.4 Christianity as the State Religion (Theodosius I.)

The year AD 380 marks a pivotal turning point in the religious history of the Roman Empire. With the promulgation of the *Edict of Thessalonica* (*Edictum Thessalonicum*), also known as *Cunctos populos*, issued on 27 February in the city of Thessalonica, Emperor Theodosius I officially and exclusively declared Nicene Christianity to be the state religion of the Roman Empire. This edict represented the culmination of a multi-decade process of Christian consolidation and ecclesiastical-political institutionalization in the context of Late Antiquity. Unlike Constantine the Great, who had merely legalized and favored Christianity, Theodosius advanced significantly further: not only did he elevate Christianity above all other religious traditions, but he actively persecuted religious practices that lay outside the doctrinal boundaries sanctioned by the imperial Church—especially traditional pagan cults and divergent Christian doctrines such as Arianism.

Theodosius I, born on 11 January 347 in Cauca (modern-day Coca in Spain), hailed from a Christian, senatorial family. His father, Flavius Theodosius, was a prominent and successful general, known for his campaigns against various barbarian groups. Following the death of Emperor Valens at the Battle of Adrianople in 378, Theodosius was appointed *Augustus* of the Eastern Roman Empire by Emperor Gratian in 379. From the outset of his reign, he was confronted with the pressing question of how to manage the religious fragmentation of his domain both politically and ideologically.

While in the West, under Gratian, public life was increasingly characterized by a Christian identity—Gratian notably renounced the title *Pontifex Maximus* in 382, a title traditionally associated with the highest office of the pagan priesthood—the Eastern Empire remained marked by strong Arian influences. Theodosius, himself a staunch supporter of the Nicene Creed, received baptism in 380 by Bishop Acholius of Thessalonica, explicitly affirming the doctrinal formula established at the

Council of Nicaea in 325. His baptism occurred during a period of grave illness, a common reason in Late Antiquity for postponing baptism until adulthood.

The *Edict of Thessalonica* employed forceful language to declare that henceforth only "the faith which the divine Apostle Peter transmitted to the Romans" was to be recognized as legitimate. The edict explicitly named Bishop Damasus of Rome and Bishop Peter of Alexandria as the chief authorities of this "Catholic faith," thereby reinforcing the link between papal authority and imperial legislation. In a significant move, all divergent Christian groups—including, most notably, Arians, Donatists, and other so-called "heretics"—were not only denounced as false believers but classified as enemies of the state. They were barred from using church buildings, their assemblies were forbidden, and their assets confiscated.

In the years that followed, Theodosius expanded his religious policy systematically. In 381, he convened the Second Ecumenical Council in Constantinople, which reaffirmed the Nicene Creed and further developed it into the *Niceno-Constantinopolitan Creed*, thereby establishing the Trinitarian faith as the binding doctrinal foundation of the imperial Church. Additionally, the Bishop of Constantinople was recognized as second in precedence after the Bishop of Rome, further centralizing the Church's hierarchical structure.

Simultaneously, comprehensive measures were taken against pagan religions. As early as 382, under Gratian, the Altar of Victory had been removed from the Senate House in Rome, provoking outrage among pagan senators. Theodosius not only continued but intensified this course. In 391, he issued a law that criminalized all public pagan sacrifices and banned attendance at pagan temples. The use of incense, the erection of statues, the consultation of oracles, and even the decoration of homes for traditional festivals were defined as offenses against the order of the *religio publica*.

One of the most dramatic manifestations of this policy was the systematic closure and destruction of pagan temples. Between 391 and 392, the Eastern Empire witnessed a veritable wave of iconoclasm, spurred by imperial legislation and local ecclesiastical mobilization. The most notable incident was the destruction of the Serapeum in Alexandria in 391, one of the most significant religious sites in Roman Egypt. This act, initiated by Bishop Theophilus of Alexandria and executed by groups of Christian monks, had both theological and symbolic significance: it marked the deliberate cultural displacement of paganism from public life.

But not only paganism fell victim to this policy. Internal Christian dissenters—particularly Arians—also faced state repression under Theodosius. Arian bishops were deposed, their congregations dispossessed, and their religious services banned. In Constantinople, where Arians had previously dominated the ecclesiastical landscape, Theodosius appointed Gregory of Nazianzus as bishop in 380, representing the Nicene Orthodox position, despite strong resistance from segments of the population. These actions were part of a broader program to unify and subordinate religious structures to imperial authority.

Another element of this transformation was the codification of ecclesiastical policy within imperial legal collections. Many statutes in the *Codex Theodosianus*, compiled under Theodosius II from 429 onward, can be traced back to laws issued during the reign of Theodosius I. These regulations included the punishment of heretics, the expropriation of pagan temple proprietors, and privileges granted to clergy, such as tax exemptions, immunity from civil litigation, and rights of inheritance.

The societal ramifications of these developments were profound. Whereas Christianity under Constantine had primarily established itself in urban centers, Theodosius's policies led to a significant expansion of church structures into rural areas (*pagi*). Numerous new bishoprics were founded, especially in Gaul, Hispania, and North Africa. Christianity increasingly became the dominant cultural and social force, deeply embedded in everyday life through institutions such as schools, poor relief, pilgrimage, and monasticism.

In the social sphere, the elevated role of Christianity triggered a transformation of elite culture. Whereas educated elites in the 2nd and 3rd centuries had often emphasized classical learning, rhetoric, and philosophy, under Theodosius, familiarity with Christian Scripture, patronage of the Church, and closeness to the episcopate became defining traits of aristocratic identity. Many senators were baptized and sponsored the construction of churches, the acquisition of relics, or the founding of episcopal sees. Honorific titles such as *vir clarissimus* or *vir illustris* were soon complemented by ecclesiastical roles such as *comes ecclesiae* or *defensor ecclesiae*.

In the sphere of public cult, traditional pagan festivals such as Saturnalia, Lupercalia, or Parilia lost their societal prominence. In their place, Christian feast days such as Easter, Pentecost, and the commemorations of martyrs gained prominence. These were celebrated through liturgical processions, scriptural readings, and homilies, often held in monumental basilicas that now supplanted temples as the primary sites of public worship. A striking example of this shift is the Basilica of St. John Lateran, initiated under Constantine and expanded under Theodosius into the principal church of Rome.

The veneration of saints also rose dramatically in importance under Theodosius. The relics of martyrs were translated into ornate shrines—*martyria*—which functioned both as pilgrimage destinations and as liturgical centers. This contributed to the establishment of a widespread network of Christian holy sites throughout the empire. Cities such as Trier, Milan, Antioch, and Jerusalem emerged as major religious centers of both spiritual and economic significance.

Politically, the institutionalization of Christianity as the state religion introduced a new balance of power between emperor and Church. While the emperor continued to regard himself as *episkopos ektos* ("bishop from outside"), certain bishops—most notably Ambrose of Milan—claimed moral authority over the ruler. This was most evident in the so-called *Penitential Conflict* of 390, when Ambrose denied the emperor access to the church following the massacre at Thessalonica, in which imperial troops killed thousands of citizens. Theodosius submitted to this ecclesiastical censure and appeared in public penance, clad in penitential garments—an unprecedented event in Roman imperial history.

Upon the emperor's death on 17 January 395 in Milan, Theodosius I left behind a complex and ambivalent legacy. On the one hand, he laid the foundations for a unified imperial Church and firmly entrenched Christianity at the heart of Roman state identity. On the other hand, his policies paved the way for increasing persecution of religious minorities and growing internal polarization within Christianity itself. In the centuries that followed, the influence of bishops continued to grow, as did the entrenchment of Christian norms in Roman law, education, administration, and everyday culture.

CHAPTER 9: LATE ANTIQUITY AND THE DIVISION OF THE EMPIRE (284–476 AD)

9.1 Diocletian's Reforms and the Tetrarchy

When Diocletian was proclaimed emperor in AD 284 amid a moment of profound political instability, the Roman Empire had already endured half a century of internal crises and external threats. The so-called "Crisis of the Third Century" (AD 235–284), which began with the assassination of Emperor Severus Alexander, had shaken the empire to its core through a seemingly endless succession of emperors, usurpations, military dictatorships, and territorial losses. In this turbulent context, Gaius Aurelius Valerius Diocletianus, an officer of Illyrian origin, entered the stage of world history. His reign not only ushered in a period of decisive reform but also initiated a fundamental reorganization of imperial rule, known as the *Tetrarchy*, or "rule of four."

Diocletian was proclaimed *Augustus* of the East by his troops on 20 November AD 284 in Nicomedia (modern-day İzmit in Turkey) following the death of Emperor Numerian. However, it was not until the spring of 285 that he eliminated his rival Carinus, who ruled in the West. Carinus was reportedly killed at the Battle of the Margus (modern-day Morava in Serbia) by one of his own officers, thereby facilitating Diocletian's unchallenged accession to power. Even at this early stage, Diocletian displayed remarkable political acumen, proving himself a deft consolidator of power who adeptly employed both military force and political maneuvering.

One of the most pressing challenges facing Diocletian was the untenable military situation along the frontiers. In the East, the Sassanid Empire posed a continuous threat to Roman Mesopotamia, while in the West, Germanic tribes such as the Alamanni, Franks, and Juthungi repeatedly breached the Rhine and Danube frontiers. Internally, the empire suffered from administrative disarray, rampant inflation, currency debasement, and increasing dominance of the military in political affairs. Furthermore, the legitimacy of the imperial office had been eroded by a multitude of rival claimants and short-lived emperors.

Diocletian's first major reform was the division of imperial authority. In AD 285, he appointed his long-time ally Maximian as *Caesar*, and in 286 elevated him to the rank of *Augustus*, thus establishing a diarchic model of governance in which Diocletian administered the East and Maximian the West. The formal proclamation occurred in Mediolanum (modern Milan), which Maximian designated as his western capital. While Diocletian governed from Nicomedia in the East, Maximian operated mainly from Trier and Milan in the West.

The full implementation of the *Tetrarchy* took place in AD 293. Diocletian appointed two additional men as *Caesares* (junior emperors): Galerius in the East and Constantius Chlorus in the West. This four-emperor system aimed to ensure political stability, administrative efficiency, and clear lines of succession. Each *Augustus* nominated a *Caesar*, who was both a designated heir and an autonomous military and administrative leader within their respective territory. This structural reform was revolutionary: for the first time, imperial authority was deliberately and systematically distributed across multiple rulers, each responsible for a specific geographic region of the empire. Galerius was assigned the Balkans and the Eastern provinces with his capital in Sirmium, while Constantius Chlorus governed Gaul and Britain from his base in Trier.

The legitimacy of this new imperial order was reinforced by a sophisticated system of propaganda, ritual, and religious symbolism. Diocletian increasingly styled himself as *dominus et deus* ("lord and god"), thereby openly distancing himself from the republican façade that previous emperors had at least nominally upheld. He rarely appeared in public, donned imperial purple robes with a diadem, and introduced the *adoratio*—a formalized act of kneeling and prostration—in court ceremonies. This sacralization of the imperial office served not only ideological purposes but also functioned as a means of consolidating power. It elevated the emperor above mere mortals, rendering the institution of emperorship sacred and unassailable, thereby reinforcing the Tetrarchic succession mechanism.

In parallel with the reform of the imperial image, Diocletian thoroughly reorganized the administrative structure of the empire. He subdivided the larger provinces into smaller, more manageable units. Under his reign, the number of provinces nearly doubled to approximately 100. These provinces were grouped into larger administrative units called *dioceses*, each overseen by a *vicarius*, who was in turn subordinate to one of the four *praetorian prefects*. This hierarchical structure greatly enhanced administrative oversight and improved the efficiency of tax collection. It laid the foundational framework for the later Byzantine administrative system.

Special attention was also given to the reform of the taxation system. During the reign of Emperor Gallienus (r. 253–268), rampant inflation had reached its zenith, causing the imperial currency system to collapse. In response, Diocletian launched a comprehensive coinage reform in AD 301. He introduced new gold coins (*aurei*), silver coins (*argentei*), and bronze coins (*folles*), all based on standardized weights and purities. Combined with his fiscal reforms, these monetary measures aimed to restore economic stability and predictability.

In the same year, Diocletian issued the famous *Edict on Maximum Prices* (*Edictum de Pretiis Rerum Venalium*), which survives in stone inscriptions found in places such as Aphrodisias in Asia Minor. The edict established maximum prices for over 1,000 goods and services, ranging from grain and textiles to wages for laborers. Its purpose was to curb inflation and stabilize the economy. However, the edict proved largely ineffective. Instead of economic stabilization, it led to the rise of black markets and scarcity of goods. This early attempt at state-controlled pricing ultimately failed due to lack of enforcement and eroding public confidence in imperial institutions.

Another major area of reform under Diocletian was the military. While the frontiers were nominally protected by the *limes* systems, increasing threats from Persians, Goths, and various Germanic tribes necessitated new defense strategies. Diocletian reinforced the frontier troops (*limitanei*) and invested in permanent military installations in the border regions. Additionally, he established mobile field units (*comitatenses*), which could be rapidly deployed from central bases to threatened areas. This dual system of stationary and mobile forces provided greater strategic flexibility and became a key feature of later Roman military doctrine.

Despite some internal tensions, the Tetrarchy initially functioned effectively. Constantius Chlorus led successful campaigns against the Alamanni (296) and in Britain (296–298), while Galerius, after initial setbacks, achieved a decisive victory in 298 over the Sassanid king Narseh at the Battle of Satala. The subsequent Peace of Nisibis secured Roman control over important territories in Armenia and Mesopotamia.

Diocletian also enjoyed considerable domestic success. In AD 297, he suppressed a revolt in Egypt led by the usurper Domitius Domitianus. After retaking Alexandria, Diocletian reorganized the strategically and economically vital province, implementing reforms in both taxation and administration. In Egypt, he adopted a quasi-pharaonic image, aligning himself in inscriptions with the ancient rulers of the Nile.

A darker aspect of Diocletian's rule was the final major persecution of Christians in the Roman Empire. In AD 303, he promulgated a series of edicts aimed at dismantling the Christian institutional structure. Churches were destroyed, sacred texts were burned, and Christians who refused to perform sacrifices to the Roman gods were subjected to persecution, torture, or execution. The persecution was particularly intense in Nicomedia and the eastern provinces, while it was more lenient in the West under Constantius Chlorus. These measures were motivated by the belief that Christianity threatened the traditional Roman order. Ironically, the persecutions ultimately strengthened the Christian movement by fostering martyrdom and ideological cohesion.

In AD 305, Diocletian undertook an unprecedented step in Roman history: he voluntarily abdicated the throne. On 1 May, he resigned his office at his palace in Split (modern-day Diocletian's Palace in Croatia), while Maximian did the same in Milan. The *Caesares*, Galerius and Constantius Chlorus, were elevated to *Augusti*, and two new *Caesares*—Severus and Maximinus Daia—were appointed. Diocletian believed he had institutionalized the Tetrarchic system on a permanent basis. However, this peace proved short-lived. Following the death of Constantius Chlorus in Eburacum (York) in 306, his troops proclaimed his son Constantine as emperor, bypassing the formal succession structure. The ensuing conflicts would quickly undermine the Tetrarchy.

Nevertheless, Diocletian's reforms laid the foundation for Late Antiquity and the Byzantine Empire. The sacralization of the imperial office, the administrative reorganization, fiscal and monetary reforms, and military restructuring all endured well beyond his resignation, even though the Tetrarchy as a governing model did not survive. Diocletian not only transformed the Roman Empire institutionally but also ideologically. His reign marked a decisive shift from the classical Roman world to the structures and mindsets of Late Antiquity, where authority and power were conceptualized in new and lasting ways. His rule from AD 284 to 305 stands as a radical turning point—not an end, but the beginning of a new phase in Roman history.

9.2 Constantinople and the Eastern Empire

Following the abdication of Diocletian in AD 305, the tetrarchic system he had devised rapidly entered a phase of disintegration. The unexpected death of Augustus Constantius Chlorus in AD 306 at Eburacum (modern-day York) derailed the intended succession plan, as his son Constantine—later known as Constantine the Great—was proclaimed emperor by the troops against the will of the remaining tetrarchs. This event ignited a new cycle of power struggles, from which Constantine eventually emerged as the sole ruler of the Roman Empire. His reign from AD 306 to 337 marks a profound turning point in the Empire's history. With the foundation of Constantinople as the "New Rome" in the East, Constantine laid the institutional and cultural foundations for the eventual division of the Empire into Western and Eastern halves. The "Eastern Roman Empire"—still referred to by contemporaries as the *Imperium Romanum*—gradually developed into a distinct political and cultural entity.

Constantine was born in AD 272 or 273 in Naissus (present-day Niš in Serbia). His grip on power after 306 was initially precarious, as he faced challenges from rival emperors and usurpers such as Maxentius in Italy and Licinius in the East. Following his decisive victory over Maxentius at the famed Battle of the Milvian Bridge on October 28, 312—which culminated in the capture of Rome and the elimination of his opponent—Constantine turned his attention to consolidating control over the eastern provinces. In AD 324, he defeated Licinius first at Adrianople and then in the naval Battle of Chrysopolis on the Bosporus. These victories left Constantine as the uncontested sole ruler of the Roman world.

The choice of location for his new imperial capital was of immense strategic and symbolic significance. Although Diocletian had previously elevated Nicomedia to the status of eastern imperial residence, Constantine envisioned more than a mere seat of government. He aimed to establish a second Rome—a center not only of administration but also of imperial ideology. In 324, he selected the ancient city of Byzantium, originally a Greek colony founded in the 7th century BC, strategically located at the crossroads of Europe and Asia, nestled between the Sea of Marmara, the Bosporus, and the Black Sea. The official inauguration of the newly established city, initially named *Nova Roma* ("New Rome"), took place on May 11, AD 330. However, the name "Constantinople"—City of Constantine—soon became the prevailing designation during the emperor's own lifetime.

The planning and construction of Constantinople followed a coherent ideological and administrative vision. Constantine commissioned the construction of temples, basilicas, a Senate house, a hippodrome, and an imperial forum flanked by colonnades and adorned with monuments. Particularly notable was the so-called Column of Constantine, crowned by a statue of the emperor depicted as the sun god *Sol Invictus*. The ongoing religious transformation of the Empire was also reflected in the city's architecture: while many pagan elements remained present, Christian edifices emerged alongside them, including the first Hagia Sophia, or Church of Holy Wisdom, built between AD 325 and 360 as the *Basilica Constantiniana*.

Constantinople's elevation to the rank of capital was reinforced through a series of special privileges. A separate city Senate was established, granted formal equality with that of Rome. The city received its own *Praefectus urbi*, tasked with overseeing order and administration. Inhabitants, including officials and merchants, were incentivized to settle in the new capital through tax relief and settlement privileges. Constantine also instituted a grain supply system akin to the Roman *annona* to ensure food security for the population. In short order, Constantinople evolved into a political and cultural nucleus of the Empire—one that would, over the centuries, prove to be the more stable and enduring heir of Roman imperial legacy.

The death of Constantine on May 22, 337, initially led to a division of imperial authority among his sons—Constantine II, Constantius II, and Constans. This period was once again marred by rivalry and internecine conflict, culminating in Constantius II's sole rule from AD 353. He was followed, after a brief interlude, by Julian the Apostate (r. 361–363), the last pagan emperor to govern from Constantinople. Julian attempted a restoration of traditional Roman cults, but his initiatives were reversed following his death during a Persian campaign in AD 363. Under his successors—especially Theodosius I (r. 379–395) —Christianity finally attained dominance within the Empire. Theodosius I was the last emperor to rule over both the eastern and western halves of the Roman world. After his death in 395, the Empire was permanently divided between his sons: Arcadius in the East and Honorius in the West.

Constantinople now became the true heart of the Eastern Roman Empire, which increasingly operated independently of developments in the Western half. While the Western Empire crumbled during the 5th century under the strain of internal crises, military weakness, and barbarian invasions, the East retained political stability and economic strength. The imperial court in Constantinople could rely on a well-preserved administrative structure, a functioning tax system, and a dense network of cities and commercial hubs. Its location on the Bosporus provided not only access to the resources of Asia Minor and the Eastern Mediterranean but also offered substantial advantages in terms of military defense.

During the 5th century, Constantinople also emerged as a focal point of theological and doctrinal controversy. Debates surrounding the nature of Christ—including the disputes over Monophysitism and Nestorianism—along with the role of the Council of Chalcedon in AD 451, significantly influenced the intellectual and religious trajectory of the Eastern Empire. The Council, held just outside Constantinople, convened the leading bishops of the Christian world. It affirmed the doctrine of the dual nature of Christ—fully human and fully divine—a position endorsed by Emperor Marcian (r. 450–457). This dogmatic definition, however, deepened the rift between the orthodox Church in Constantinople and the Monophysite communities of Egypt, Syria, and Armenia—a division that would have long-term destabilizing effects on imperial cohesion.

Under emperors such as Theodosius II (r. 408–450) and Leo I (r. 457–474), the fortifications of Constantinople were significantly enhanced. Most notable were the Theodosian Walls, constructed between AD 412 and 422. This formidable triple-layered defense system—consisting of a moat, a lower outer wall, and a high inner wall with guard towers—rendered the city virtually impregnable. Indeed, Constantinople would not fall to external invaders until the 13th century, a testament to the strategic foresight and engineering prowess of its planners.

The Eastern Empire's economic foundations were likewise more robust than those of the West. Constantinople's location at key commercial crossroads—especially in the grain and silk trades—brought prosperity. The imperial bureaucracy maintained the stability of the gold coinage system, particularly the *solidus*, a high-quality gold currency introduced by Constantine, which remained a standard for international trade well into the Middle Ages. This monetary stability enabled the East to finance its armies and maintain public order through consistent wages and grain distributions.

Cultural life in Constantinople also flourished. The University of Constantinople, established in AD 425 under Theodosius II, became a major center of Greco-Roman education. Studies in philosophy, rhetoric, and theology defined the intellectual atmosphere. The city's libraries—notably that of the Patriarchal Palace—amassed and preserved the corpus of ancient knowledge, much of which would later be lost in the West. In this sense, Constantinople served not only as the political capital of the Empire but also as its cultural memory.

When the Western Roman Empire came to an end in AD 476 with the deposition of the last emperor, Romulus Augustulus, by the Germanic general Odoacer, the Eastern Roman Empire continued to exist unbroken. At that time, Emperor Zeno (r. 474–491) reigned in Constantinople. He observed the events in the West with detachment and formally acknowledged Odoacer as a governor. Thus, while 476 marked the end of the Western imperial office, it did not signify the demise of the Roman Empire itself. In the self-perception of the Eastern emperors, the idea of *Imperium Romanum* endured. Constantinople now stood as the sole center of Roman power—an empire that would, in the coming centuries, continue under the name "Byzantium," a term only coined in modern historiography.

In sum, Constantinople was far more than a new capital; it

represented both a symbolic and practical rebirth. From the perspective of Late Antiquity, it was the place where Roman heritage was preserved, reimagined, and developed further. The Eastern Empire, with Constantinople at its pulsating heart, emerged from the shadow of the West and assumed its intellectual and political legacy—not as a successor but as a continuation. The "Eastern Roman Empire" was, in truth, the Roman Empire by another name: Hellenized in culture, legitimized by Christianity, organized through a sophisticated bureaucracy, and safeguarded by formidable military structures—and it would endure for nearly another millennium.

9.3 Economic Decline, Defense Crisis, the Migration Period, and Invasions (Huns, Goths)

The economic decline of the Roman Empire during Late Antiquity was a gradual yet devastating process, whose effects were deeply entwined with an increasingly overstrained defensive structure and the dramatic population movements known as the Migration Period. Between the late 3rd and the late 5th centuries AD, the Empire fell into a profound crisis, which manifested in its economic infrastructure, monetary system, fiscal policies, and military capabilities. Concurrently, external pressures intensified—particularly the migration of Germanic and Central Asian tribes such as the Goths and the Huns—placing growing strain on the already fragile structure of the Western Empire. These developments, in their complex interplay, precipitated the gradual disintegration of the Western Roman Empire, while the Eastern Empire—economically and militarily more stable—endured.

Economic difficulties had already begun to show tangible effects in the 3rd century AD but escalated dramatically in the following centuries. Central to this process was the erosion of the urban tax base, which had supported the Roman administrative and military system for centuries. While the Empire relied on an annual tax revenue of approximately 200 million sesterces, the productive population steadily declined due to wars, epidemics—such as the Cyprian Plague (251–270 AD)—and rural depopulation. The once-flourishing urban economy increasingly gave way to subsistence agriculture in the countryside. More and more farmers retreated to their estates, which, through tenancy contracts (coloni arrangements), effectively devolved into a form of serfdom. The term *colonus* thus transformed from denoting a free tenant to a hereditary, bonded laborer.

The monetary system clearly reflected the ongoing crisis. The hyperinflationary fiscal policies of the 3rd century—particularly under Emperor Gallienus (r. 253–268)—had severely undermined public trust in silver and bronze coinage. Although Emperor Diocletian temporarily stabilized the currency with his coinage reform in 294 AD—introducing the *Argenteus* (silver) and the *Follis* (bronze)—the underlying structural problem remained: the state's need for revenue grew as the population sank deeper into poverty. Especially problematic was the fact that many taxes were no longer collected in coin but in kind—an indicator of the progressive breakdown of the monetary economy. This system of tax-in-kind (the *annona* system) increased the burden on rural populations and deepened the disparities between wealthy regions (notably in Gaul, Northern Italy, and the East) and peripheral provinces such as Britain or North Africa.

Roman tax policy became institutionalized in the *Capitatio-Iugatio* system, which linked personal and land taxation. However, frequent failures of the census, corruption among local tax collectors, and inflated assessment targets significantly increased the real burden. The *curiales*—local magistrates who were personally liable for municipal tax payments—increasingly sought to evade their responsibilities, either by fleeing or by entering the clergy. Between 350 and 400 AD alone, the number of urban officeholders is estimated to have declined by around 30%. The imperial administration responded with coercive measures but could not halt the structural erosion of its fiscal base.

Parallel to the economic decline, the Empire's defense crisis intensified. Under Diocletian, the Roman army had expanded to over 400,000 troops—about 300,000 in the mobile field army (*comitatenses*) and 100,000 in the stationary border troops (*limitanei*). These massive military expenditures required immense resources—financially and logistically. Yet the more unstable the economy became, the harder it was to adequately pay and supply the armies. Furthermore, strategic priorities shifted: the focus moved from offensive frontier policies to defensive responses to incursions and migrations, evidenced by the construction of massive border fortifications such as the Danubian limes and the fortified chains along the Rhine.

In the 4th century, the security situation changed fundamentally with the onset of the so-called Migration Period. The initial impetus for these vast movements came from the Huns—a nomadic Central Asian people who, around 370 AD, crossed the Danube frontier and displaced the resident Germanic peoples, especially the Goths. The Goths, divided into the Tervings (later Visigoths) and the Greuthungs (later Ostrogoths), requested asylum in the Roman Empire in 376. Emperor Valens permitted the Tervings to settle south of the Danube, but due to mismanagement, hunger, and mistreatment by Roman officials, tensions escalated into rebellion.

The Battle of Adrianople on August 9, 378, was both a military and psychological disaster for the Roman Empire. Without awaiting reinforcements from his nephew Gratian,

Valens attacked the Gothic camp and was decisively defeated. An estimated two-thirds of the Roman army—some 15,000 to 20,000 soldiers—were killed, including Valens himself, making him the first emperor to die in battle since Decius in 251. This defeat exposed the limits of late Roman military power and forced the Empire into negotiations with the Goths. From this point on, numerous Germanic tribes were settled within the Empire as *foederati* (federated allies)—a policy that brought short-term relief but long-term instability.

The integration of the Goths under Emperor Theodosius I into the Roman army created a precarious duality: on one hand, the Goths were offered military ranks and payment; on the other, they remained largely autonomous units only nominally under Roman command. After Theodosius's death in 395 AD, the Gothic leader Alaric turned against the Empire. Between 395 and 410, he led several campaigns through Greece, Italy, and eventually against the city of Rome itself. The incursion of the Visigoths culminated in the sack of Rome on August 24, 410—the first capture of the city since the Gallic invasion in 390 BC. This event had immense symbolic impact and shattered confidence in the invincibility of Rome. Contemporary authors such as Jerome lamented: *"Si Roma perit, mundus perit"* ("If Rome falls, the world falls").

While the West was overrun by Goths, Vandals, Alans, and Suebi, a new and even more aggressive actor emerged after 430: the Huns under Attila. From 434, Attila ruled the Huns jointly with his brother Bleda, and he consolidated power through demands for tribute from the Eastern Roman Empire and through military expansion. After allegedly murdering Bleda in 445, Attila embarked on nearly a decade of conquest across the Danube basin, the Balkan Peninsula, and modern-day Hungary. In 447 alone, the Huns destroyed over 70 cities in Thrace and Moesia, including Serdica (Sofia), Marcianopolis, and Philippopolis. The *Notitia Dignitatum* attests to the catastrophic effects on the provincial administration—entire administrative districts ceased to exist.

Despite massive annual tribute payments of 2,100 pounds of gold from Emperor Theodosius II (from 443 AD onward), Attila turned his attention westward. In 451, he invaded Gaul with a force estimated at over 200,000 men, including Hunnic cavalry, East Germanic vassals, and even Roman deserters. The decisive clash occurred at the Battle of the Catalaunian Plains on June 20, 451, where the Western Roman general Flavius Aetius, in alliance with the Visigothic king Theodoric I, confronted Attila. Although the battle was indecisive, it marked the end of Attila's advance into Gaul. Theodoric was killed, and Attila withdrew, only to return in 452 to ravage Northern Italy, razing Aquileia to the ground. It was only through a diplomatic mission led by Pope Leo I that Attila was persuaded to retreat. Following his death in 453, the Hunnic Empire quickly disintegrated due to internal power struggles—a temporary relief for Rome, albeit a fleeting one.

Meanwhile, the Western Roman administration was collapsing. By the mid-5th century, the Western Roman army consisted almost entirely of mercenaries and Germanic contingents. The central imperial authority, already weakened by a rapid turnover of ineffective emperors (nine emperors ruled between 455 and 476 alone), was marginalized by powerful regional figures such as Ricimer and Orestes. The Vandals, under their king Geiseric, had captured Carthage in 439, severing the vital grain supply from North Africa—once the backbone of Roman provisioning. The term "vandalism" became historically linked to their sack of Rome in 455 by Geiseric's fleet.

The final phase of the Western Empire was marked by a complete loss of control over its provinces. In 468, a massive naval expedition led by Emperor Leo I to reconquer Carthage failed disastrously—over 1,100 ships carrying 100,000 men were destroyed off Cape Bon by the Vandals. Internally, the tax system had collapsed. The Roman historian Sidonius Apollinaris lamented in 460 that in Gaul, "there is scarcely anyone left who can still pay taxes." Once-thriving cities such as Trier, Cologne, and Arles fell into decay or were occupied by Germanic groups.

The last Western Roman emperor, Romulus Augustulus, was deposed in 476 AD by the Germanic military leader Odoacer. Odoacer ostentatiously renounced the imperial title and sent the imperial regalia to Constantinople. This event marked the formal end of the Western Roman Empire, though de facto it had already ceased to function effectively years earlier. Odoacer ruled Italy as king in the name of the Eastern Roman emperor but remained essentially independent. The Eastern Roman Empire endured—economically and militarily consolidated under emperors such as Zeno (r. 474–491) and Anastasius I (r. 491–518).

In conclusion, the economic decline of the Western Empire, combined with a dysfunctional fiscal and military system, initiated a profound internal collapse. The Roman administration, characterized by centralization and bureaucracy, proved unable to adapt to changing social and military realities. The Migration Period—with the Goths, Huns, and Vandals at its center—acted as a catalyst rather than the sole cause of the Empire's fall, accelerating the demise of an already fragile system. The fall of the Western Roman Empire was thus not a sudden catastrophe but a slow dissolution under the weight of internal weaknesses and external shocks. While the Roman Empire continued in the East, the West was lost forever.

9.4 The Fall of the Western Roman Empire in 476 AD – Causes and Consequences

The fall of the Western Roman Empire in 476 AD represents one of the most dramatic and symbolically charged moments in Roman history. This event marks the definitive end of the Western imperial office and the formal collapse of the western half of the Empire. The causes of this decline were multifaceted and stemmed from a long series of internal weaknesses and external pressures that had accumulated over centuries. The consequences of the fall of the Western Roman Empire were profound for both the Western world and the entire Mediterranean region, significantly shaping the course of European development during the Early Middle Ages.

The immediate cause of the Empire's collapse was the deposition of the last Western Roman Emperor, Romulus Augustulus, on September 4, 476 AD by the Germanic military leader Odoacer, who held command over the Roman troops in Italy. This occurred at a time when the Western Empire was plagued by numerous political, military, and economic crises that had steadily worsened over the preceding decades. The formal act of deposing Romulus Augustulus and returning the imperial insignia to the Eastern Roman Emperor Zeno, who in turn showed no intention of intervening in Italian affairs, symbolized the final loss of Western imperial authority. This gesture marked the end of the Roman imperial tradition in the West, which had formed the backbone of the Roman state for nearly five centuries.

However, the disintegration of the Western Empire was not the result of a sudden collapse, but rather the outcome of a long, gradual decline that had begun in the third century and continued through the fourth and fifth centuries. Already under the emperors of the third century, when the Empire was confronted with a multitude of internal and external crises—from the so-called "Soldier Emperors" to the "Crisis of the Third Century"—the Western part of the Empire was increasingly weakened. These years were marked by persistent power struggles, political intrigue, and military defeats. The continuous threat posed by external enemies such as the Germanic tribes, the Persians, and later the Huns, as well as incessant civil wars and political upheavals, deeply destabilized the Empire.

Another crucial factor contributing to the fall of the Western Empire was the progressive weakening of the Roman central government. The administrative apparatus became increasingly corrupt and inefficient, while military power was gradually concentrated in the hands of individual generals and Germanic federate troops (foederati), who constituted the majority of the army. These foederati were originally recruited as auxiliary forces to defend against external threats. Over time, however, they grew into a significant political and military force within the Empire, frequently supplanting the Roman decision-makers in both influence and authority.

Political instability in the West intensified following the division of the Empire by Emperor Theodosius I in 395 AD, when he assigned the western half to his son Honorius and the eastern half to Arcadius. This division led to increasing isolation and weakness in the West, while the East—especially the Eastern Roman Empire (Byzantium)—benefited from a more centralized administration and a more robust economic base. As military conflicts and barbarian invasions increasingly strained the Western Empire, the Eastern Empire emerged as the more stable and resilient successor state.

A further factor that accelerated the disintegration of the Western Empire was the structural transformation of its military. In the later imperial period, the army increasingly relied on mercenaries, who often lacked any personal loyalty to the Roman state. Particularly the Germanic peoples, employed as foederati, gained significant political and military influence. By 476 AD, when Odoacer, a Germanic military commander, seized power in Italy, this was widely seen as the direct result of this development. Odoacer, initially an officer in the Roman army, led a group of Germanic soldiers in rebellion against Romulus Augustulus and eventually deposed him. The fact that a former Roman officer of Germanic origin could assume power in Rome underscores the Roman central government's loss of control over military affairs and highlights the reversal of political dynamics in the West.

However, the deposition of Romulus Augustulus not only signified the end of the imperial office in the West but also marked the conclusion of a distinct political and cultural era. The fall of the Western Roman Empire represents the transition from Classical Antiquity to the Early Middle Ages. The Western world entered a new historical phase characterized by the growing dominance of Germanic cultures. While the Western Roman state collapsed, Germanic peoples such as the Ostrogoths, Vandals, Franks, and Lombards gradually assumed control over the former Roman provinces.

One of the immediate consequences of the Empire's fall was the fragmentation of its territory into a multitude of Germanic kingdoms. Odoacer himself ruled Italy as King, nominally recognizing the sovereignty of the Eastern Emperor, although this recognition had little practical effect. In other regions of the West—such as Hispania, Gaul, and North Africa—Germanic kingdoms arose on the ruins of the Roman administrative system. These new states were in many ways shaped by Roman culture and governance, but the political and social upheaval resulted in a fundamental reconfiguration of Western Europe.

Moreover, the fall of the Western Empire entailed the collapse of much of the Roman infrastructure and administrative organization in the West. The once-great Roman cities fell into decline, and the vast network of Roman roads—which had connected the Empire—was no longer maintained. Trade and cultural exchange, which had flourished under the Pax Romana, deteriorated significantly. The centralized bureaucratic system disintegrated, and in many areas a new form of governance emerged, increasingly dominated by local Germanic chieftains and landed aristocrats.

The fall of the Western Roman Empire also had long-term consequences for Roman identity. In the centuries following the collapse, many Roman values and institutions survived in the eastern part of the former Empire, especially in the Eastern Roman (Byzantine) Empire. There, the culture of classical antiquity continued to flourish, and Constantinople became a bastion of Roman heritage and governance. In contrast, much of Roman life and tradition faded in the West, as the Germanic kingdoms developed their own cultural and political systems. Nevertheless, the legacy of Rome endured in certain respects—most notably in the organization of the Christian Church and the Roman legal tradition, both of which continued to exert influence in medieval Europe.

CHAPTER 10: THE EASTERN ROMAN EMPIRE (BYZANTIUM) AND THE ROMAN LEGACY

10.1 The Continuation of the Empire in Constantinople

The fall of the Western Roman Empire in 476 CE, marked by the deposition of the last Western Roman Emperor, Romulus Augustulus, by the Germanic military leader Odoacer, is often regarded in classical historiography as the end of the Roman Empire. However, this perspective is overly simplistic. In Constantinople, the capital of the Eastern part of the empire, Roman statehood not only survived as a relic but continued as a powerful, politically relevant, and culturally vibrant successor state—what is today commonly referred to as the Byzantine Empire. Importantly, this entity always regarded itself as the "Roman Empire," and its rulers consistently styled themselves as Roman Emperors (*basileus tōn Rhōmaiōn*) until its very end.

The survival of the Roman state in Constantinople was not a matter of mere historical coincidence, but the result of long-term structural developments, strategic adaptability, and the city's unique geographical location on the Bosporus, which conferred significant military and economic advantages.

As early as the reign of Emperor Diocletian (284–305), the empire's administrative structure had undergone a fundamental transformation. Diocletian introduced the Tetrarchy, dividing the empire into four administrative units, each governed by an Augustus and a subordinate Caesar. This system aimed at more effective control over the vast territories and served as an institutional precursor to the later division between East and West. It was, however, under Constantine the Great that the East emerged as a lasting center of imperial authority. In 330 CE, Constantine established a new capital on the site of the ancient Greek city of Byzantion: Constantinople, or "New Rome." Through monumental constructions such as the Forum of Constantine, the Hippodrome, and early Christian churches, he endowed the city with imperial splendor that would endure for centuries.

Following the death of Theodosius I in 395, the empire was permanently divided between his two sons: Honorius in the West and Arcadius in the East. While the Western Empire succumbed over the subsequent decades to internal turmoil, economic decline, and external invasions, the Eastern Empire stabilized under the rule of Arcadius (r. 395–408) and later his son Theodosius II (r. 408–450). In 413, Theodosius II initiated the construction of the famed Theodosian Walls—massive fortifications that would protect Constantinople for centuries. These defenses, consisting of double walls, towers, and a sophisticated gate system, became one of the most formidable military structures of antiquity.

By the fifth century, the Eastern Roman Empire had emerged as a distinct political entity. Under Emperor Leo I (r. 457–474) —the first emperor crowned by the Patriarch of Constantinople —the Byzantine emperorship began to ideologically distance itself from Western Roman traditions. Leo asserted imperial authority over the powerful *magister militum* Aspar, a critical step in the consolidation of imperial power in Byzantium.

The reign of Emperor Zeno (r. 474–491) further underscored this shift. Zeno's interactions with Odoacer and later with Theoderic the Great, who in 493 established the Ostrogothic Kingdom in Italy, illustrate the East's assumption of responsibility for the Roman legacy. By officially recognizing Theoderic as the governor of Italy, Zeno effectively relieved the Eastern Empire of direct involvement in the West while maintaining a nominal claim to universal rule.

Under Emperor Anastasius I (r. 491–518), the Eastern Roman Empire experienced a period of administrative reform and economic consolidation. Anastasius introduced a new taxation system, abolishing the burdensome *chrysargyron* tax—a levy that had weighed heavily on commerce—and replaced it with more efficient fiscal mechanisms. His most significant contribution, however, was the monetary reform that introduced the *follis*, a large copper coin, thereby stabilizing the Byzantine currency system. Through disciplined financial management, Anastasius generated budget surpluses, enabling the funding of military and infrastructure projects without imposing excessive new taxes.

The true apogee of the Late Antique Eastern Roman Empire began with the accession of Justinian I in 527. Under his rule (527–565), the empire underwent both territorial expansion and internal transformation. Through ambitious military campaigns, Justinian reclaimed North Africa from the Vandals (533–534), Italy from the Ostrogoths (535–554), and parts of Hispania. His reign was equally marked by monumental architectural projects, extensive legal codification, and religious centralization. The construction of the Hagia Sophia, completed in 537, stood as a crowning achievement and enduring symbol of Christian-Roman imperial authority. The *Codex Iustinianus*, compiled in 529 by the jurist Tribonian, along with the *Digest* in 533, systematically codified Roman law and would go on to shape the legal traditions of continental Europe for centuries.

Nevertheless, Justinian's rule was not without crises. The Nika Riots of 532 devastated large portions of Constantinople and resulted in the deaths of approximately 30,000 people. These uprisings revealed the latent instability of urban life and the volatility of the *demes*—chariot-racing factions with political influence. Additionally, the Justinianic Plague, which arrived from Egypt in 541 and recurred in waves until the 8th century, significantly weakened the empire. The demographic collapse and economic disruptions led to a sharp decline in urban population and fiscal capacity.

Following Justinian's death, a period of relative stagnation ensued. The reign of his successor Justin II (r. 565–578) was marred by military defeats and increasing pressure from the Persians and the Avars. A semblance of stability returned only under Emperor Maurice (r. 582–602), who pursued an active foreign policy, especially in the Balkans, where he sought to repel Slavic incursions. Maurice was also the first Byzantine emperor to attempt to establish a dynastic principle by naming his son Theodosius as co-emperor—a move that ultimately failed when Maurice was overthrown by the military officer Phocas in 602.

Phocas's seizure of power triggered a major political and military crisis. Sasanian King Khosrow II exploited the upheaval as a pretext for a full-scale war against Byzantium. Under his command, the Persians captured Syria, Palestine, and Egypt between 611 and 626—regions that had long been the empire's most prosperous provinces. In 626, Constantinople itself came under siege by a coalition of Avars and Persians, but the city withstood the assault—a turning point in imperial history.

Deliverance came under Heraclius (r. 610–641), one of Byzantium's most significant emperors. Launching an extraordinary military counteroffensive between 622 and 628, Heraclius penetrated deep into Persian territory, defeated the enemy at Nineveh in 627, and triumphantly returned the True Cross, previously taken from Jerusalem. However, this victory was soon eclipsed by a new threat. Beginning in 634, Arab armies, unified by Islam, launched invasions into the eastern provinces. By 642, the empire had irretrievably lost Syria, Palestine, and Egypt—regions of immense economic, religious, and cultural importance. This loss constituted a major rupture, forcing the empire to fundamentally redefine itself.

In the 7th and 8th centuries, the empire underwent profound transformation. The formerly urban character of the Late Antique state gave way to a more rural society. The administrative and military apparatus was restructured through the *theme* system, which integrated civil and military authority within regional districts. This reform, initiated under Heraclius and expanded by his successors, was instrumental in ensuring the empire's survival. Linguistically, too, change was underway: Latin was gradually replaced as the administrative language by Greek, which became the lingua franca of the empire. This transition was complete by the time of Heraclius, who was the first emperor to formally adopt the title *basileus*.

Despite continuous external threats—from the Bulgars in the Balkans to the Arabs in Asia Minor—the empire endured. The Arab sieges of Constantinople in 674–678 and again in 717–718 were both repelled through a combination of strategic ingenuity, the deployment of "Greek fire," and the formidable Theodosian fortifications. The second siege, under Caliph Umar II, was decisively broken by Emperor Leo III (r. 717–741), affirming Constantinople's resilience and status as an impregnable capital.

During this period, the Byzantine capital was not only a military bastion but also a center of cultural and religious innovation. Within its walls, a distinctive imperial-Christian ideology developed, portraying the emperor as divinely appointed. The imperial palace, the Hagia Sophia, and the Senate represented continuity with Roman traditions, while iconography, liturgy, and court ceremony cultivated a unique Byzantine identity.

The continued existence of the Empire in Constantinople was thus the result of a multitude of interlocking factors: a favorable geopolitical location, stable administrative and military structures, a vibrant urban culture, and not least, the capacity for ideological renewal. Even though the Empire increasingly distanced itself from its Latin, Western Roman origins over time, it nevertheless remained, for its contemporaries—and for many centuries—the *Imperium Romanum.*

Constantinople not only survived the fall of the West but became, for many centuries, the dominant capital of an empire that carried forward the Roman idea, transforming and adapting it to new realities. This continuity of imperial authority, urban infrastructure, legal order, and cultural self-perception makes the survival of the Empire in Constantinople one of the most significant chapters in European history.

The Byzantine self-conception as the "Roman Empire" was a central ideological foundation of the Eastern Roman Empire and shaped its self-image, administration, law, religion, culture, and foreign policy for over a millennium. The inhabitants of the Empire did not consider themselves "Byzantines"—a term coined only in modern times—but *Rhomaioi* (Ῥωμαῖοι), that is, Romans. This identity was not an empty reference to tradition but was lived with deep conviction and actively defended in dealings with other political entities. The "Roman" aspect of their identity expressed a historical, legal, political, and also theological claim that understood the Byzantine Empire as the direct and legitimate continuation of the *Imperium Romanum*—not as a successor state, but as an enduring reality.

A key reason for this self-understanding was the uninterrupted institutional survival of central Roman structures following the relocation of the power center to Constantinople under Constantine the Great in 330 CE. The capital was deliberately conceived as *Nova Roma*, or "New Rome," a concept reflected not only in the urban architecture—with senatorial buildings, a forum, triumphal arches, and a city layout based on Roman models—but also in the replication of political structures. The Senate was revived in Constantinople, and imperial institutions such as the Praetorian Prefecture, the *comes rei militaris* office, and the notaries were preserved and further developed. Latin continued to be used as the administrative language until the 7th century, and many legal texts, including those under Justinian I, were still composed in Latin. It was only under Emperor Heraclius (r. 610–641) that Greek officially became the language of government—a shift that more accurately reflected cultural realities but did not diminish the Empire's Roman self-perception.

One of the most significant expressions of this identity was the imperial title. The Byzantine emperors held the title *Imperator Romanorum* (Greek: *Basileus tōn Rhōmaiōn* – βασιλεὺς τῶν Ῥωμαίων) until the end of the Empire in 1453. This title was not merely a formal relic, but symbolized a universal claim to both secular and spiritual authority in line with the Roman imperial idea. When Charlemagne was crowned "Emperor of the Romans" (*Imperator Romanorum*) by the Pope in Rome in the year 800, the Byzantine side responded with diplomatic protest. From Constantinople's point of view, this was an illegitimate appropriation of a title that rightfully belonged only to the Eastern Roman Emperor. Only under the Treaty of Aachen (812) was Charlemagne grudgingly acknowledged as "Emperor"—but never with the addition "of the Romans."

This distinction remained clear in diplomatic correspondence: only the Byzantine emperor was "the Emperor" (*ho basileus*), while other monarchs—whether in the West, in Persia, or later in the Caliphate—were referred to as *rex* or *archon*. The protocols of Byzantine diplomacy were designed to emphasize the supremacy of the Roman Emperor. This is evident, for example, in *De Ceremoniis* by Emperor Constantine VII (10th century), a work on court etiquette that explains in detail how foreign envoys were received and how their rank was classified within the imperial hierarchy.

The Roman legal tradition was also actively preserved and further developed. Justinian's *Corpus Iuris Civilis*, consisting of the *Codex*, the *Digesta*, the *Institutiones*, and the *Novellae*, remained the basis of Byzantine legal life for centuries. Later legal codes such as the *Ecloga* (741), composed under Leo III and incorporating stronger moral-theological elements, or the *Basilika* (9th century), a Greek translation and expansion of Justinian's code, testify to the continued engagement with Roman legal tradition. Even in the late Middle Ages, Byzantine law schools studied and commented on the *Digesta*, which in turn influenced later Western European canonical and secular law.

The Roman character was also reflected in the urban structure. Constantinople was a typical Late Antique metropolis in Roman style: it possessed a hippodrome, aqueducts, baths, a forum, multiple basilicas, and administrative buildings modeled on Roman precedents. The city's population lived in multi-story *insulae*-like apartment blocks, and there was a sophisticated provisioning system involving grain imports, bread distributions, and aqueducts. The organization of urban life remained influenced by the Roman model, as did the tax and supply systems, which were based on census data, land taxation, and payments in kind—concepts that derived directly from the late Roman administration.

The military organization also retained Roman elements for a long time. Although the legions disappeared in Late Antiquity, the term *stratiotēs* for soldier and the division into mobile field armies (*comitatenses*) and border troops (*limitanei*) persisted in modified form until the 7th century. With the restructuring into *theme* armies under Heraclius, new units were created, but their names (e.g., *tagmata*) and ranks (*strategos*, *drungarios*) still drew on Roman military concepts.

Finally, Orthodox theology also played a significant role in the self-conception as the "Roman Empire." The Church was an integral part of the state, and the Byzantine emperor saw himself as *Pontifex Maximus*, the supreme protector of the Church—a position established in Late Antiquity by Constantine the Great. Christian Orthodoxy was not seen as a contrast to Roman identity but as its spiritual fulfillment. The Byzantine Empire was viewed as the "New Israel," chosen to preserve the true Christian doctrine. In this sense, ancient Rome and the heavenly Jerusalem merged into a sacral, legitimized imperial ideal, reflected in imperial coronation ceremonies, iconographies of imperial power, and the theological concept of *symphonia*, the harmonious relationship between Church and State.

Another piece of evidence for this self-conception is the persistent refusal of the Byzantine rulers to accept the term "Byzantine." In Byzantine sources, Constantinople is always referred to as "the City" (*hē polis*) or "New Rome," and the Empire itself as *Basileia tōn Rhōmaiōn* ("Empire of the Romans"). Even in legal and theological texts, the identity as "Roman" remained unshakable—an example being the work *De Administrando Imperio* by Emperor Constantine VII, which describes the global order under the leadership of the Roman emperor.

The population of the Empire, both in the capital and in the provinces, also understood themselves as part of the "Roman" world. Travelers, merchants, and pilgrims were still reporting in the 12th century on the self-designation of inhabitants of Anatolia, Greece, or Asia Minor as *Rhomaioi*. Arab and Persian sources also refer to the Eastern Roman Empire as "Rum"—a clear indication of how enduringly the Roman identity was perceived even outside the Empire.

In summary, the Byzantine self-perception as the "Roman Empire" was not a mere historical reminiscence, but an active political, legal, and cultural project. The rulers, elites, and citizens of the Empire saw themselves as guardians of a unique civilizational heritage that did not end with the fall of the Western Roman Empire in 476 CE but found a new, equally legitimate and enduring form in Constantinople. This consciousness endured for centuries, profoundly shaped Byzantine foreign and domestic policy, and formed the foundation for the ideological, cultural, and religious continuity with which Byzantium saw itself as the true and final *Imperium Romanum*—until its conquest by the Ottomans in 1453.

10.2 Justinian I: Codex Iustinianus and Architectural Policy

The rise of Justinian I to the imperial throne of the Eastern Roman Empire in A.D. 527 marked one of the most pivotal turning points in the history of Byzantium and the late antique Mediterranean world. Born around A.D. 482 in Tauresium, in the Roman province of Dacia Mediterranea (near modern-day Skopje in North Macedonia), Justinian emerged from humble origins and ascended to the highest echelons of political power through the patronage of his uncle, Justin I, who had become emperor in A.D. 518. Upon assuming power, Justinian embarked on a comprehensive political, legal, and cultural program aimed not merely at preserving the Roman Empire, but at actively restoring it—territorially as well as institutionally. At the heart of this ambitious renewal project were two major undertakings: the legal codification of Roman law, culminating in the *Codex Iustinianus* and the broader *Corpus Iuris Civilis*, and a monumental building program intended to transform Constantinople into a symbol of imperial majesty and Christian glory.

Justinian's legal reform constituted a milestone in the history of jurisprudence. For centuries, Roman law had accumulated in a confusing and unwieldy body of edicts, statutes, legal opinions, and juristic writings. Previous emperors, such as Theodosius II, had already attempted to systematize this legal corpus—most notably with the *Codex Theodosianus* of A.D. 438. However, Justinian aimed to go further. In A.D. 528, he commissioned a legal committee under the leadership of the praetorian prefect Tribonian to collect, review, and systematically organize all still-valid imperial constitutions (*leges*) dating back to the reign of Emperor Hadrian (r. 117–138).

The result was the *Codex Iustinianus*, first published in A.D. 529. This codex not only curated and ordered imperial enactments but also represented the first formal expression of the emperor's exclusive legislative authority. Yet this was merely the beginning. In a subsequent phase, Justinian appointed an expanded commission to systematically process classical Roman jurisprudence, especially the works of eminent jurists such as Ulpian, Gaius, Papinian, and Paulus. This effort culminated in the publication of the *Digest* (or *Digesta*, also known as the *Pandectae*) in A.D. 533. The *Digest* consisted of 50 books and included approximately 9,000 extracts selected from over 2,000 legal treatises. Concurrently, an elementary legal textbook, the *Institutiones*, was composed to serve as a foundational text for legal education. Together with a revised edition of the *Codex* (the *Codex Iustinianus repetitae praelectionis*) in A.D. 534 and the subsequent *Novellae* (new laws), these texts formed the *Corpus Iuris Civilis*—a compilation rediscovered in medieval Western Europe that became the cornerstone of continental civil law systems well into the modern era.

This codification was not merely a legal endeavor; it constituted a political manifesto. Justinian conceived of himself as God's earthly representative, governing an empire imbued with divine law. The *Codex Iustinianus* integrated secular and ecclesiastical norms—particularly in areas such as marriage law, family law, and property rights—thereby reinforcing the notion of a sacred imperial office. The *Digest* contains numerous passages that theologically legitimize the emperor's authority, articulating the concept of a *sacrum imperium*.

Simultaneously with this legal reform, Constantinople—the political and spiritual heart of the Eastern Roman Empire—was transformed into an architectural testament to Byzantine grandeur. Especially after the catastrophic Nika Riots of A.D. 532, which resulted in the destruction of large parts of the city and the deaths of tens of thousands, Justinian initiated a monumental building program designed to reaffirm his political authority and divine legitimacy. At the center of this program was the reconstruction of the *Hagia Sophia*, whose construction began on February 23, A.D. 532, and was completed in a remarkably short time, with its consecration taking place on December 27, A.D. 537.

The new *Hagia Sophia* (Ἁγία Σοφία – "Holy Wisdom"), designed by the architects Anthemios of Tralles and Isidore of Miletus, surpassed all previous church buildings in scale and complexity. Its central dome reached over 55 meters in height and spanned approximately 31 meters in diameter—a technical marvel of late antique engineering. Contemporary sources report that upon entering the completed basilica, Justinian exclaimed, "Solomon, I have surpassed thee!"—an explicit reference to the biblical Temple of Solomon as the supreme symbol of sacred kingship.

The *Hagia Sophia* was not merely an architectural achievement; it was a theological statement in stone. The dome symbolized the heavens, while the richly decorated interiors, adorned with golden mosaics, reflected light in ways that evoked a palpable sense of divine presence. The basilica served as the patriarchal cathedral of Constantinople and the central venue for imperial liturgy, including coronations and receptions of foreign envoys. Through its construction, Justinian projected his role as the protector of Orthodoxy, especially after the doctrinal upheavals caused by Arianism and the Monophysite controversy, which had deeply divided the religious fabric of the empire.

In addition to the *Hagia Sophia*, Justinian oversaw the construction or renovation of numerous other buildings. The Church of Saints Sergius and Bacchus, built between A.D. 527 and 536 and possibly serving as a prototype for the *Hagia Sophia*, is notable among these. The *Hagia Eirene* ("Holy Peace") was also rebuilt during his reign. In the provinces, Justinian commissioned the construction of churches, fortresses, and administrative complexes—such as the imposing city walls of Dara in Mesopotamia (modern southeastern Turkey), a key bulwark against the Sassanid Empire.

Civil infrastructure projects were also vigorously pursued under Justinian's rule. Aqueducts, cisterns, bridges, roads, and administrative buildings were repaired or newly built across the empire. A prime example is the massive cistern beneath Constantinople—the *Yerebatan Sarnıcı* or "Basilica Cistern"—constructed around A.D. 532. Capable of holding approximately 80,000 cubic meters of water, and supplied by aqueducts from the Belgrad Forest, the cistern ensured the city's water supply during sieges and exemplified Justinian's concern for urban welfare and resilience.

Justinian's architectural policies left a lasting imprint not only in the imperial core but also in distant provinces. In Ravenna, for instance, which was restored to imperial control after the reconquest of Italy by General Belisarius, grand basilicas decorated with Byzantine mosaics were constructed. Chief among these are *San Vitale* (completed A.D. 547) and *Sant'Apollinare in Classe* (consecrated A.D. 549). The renowned mosaic of Justinian in *San Vitale*, depicting him surrounded by court officials and soldiers, visually encapsulates his dual role as both secular ruler and spiritual leader.

This architectural program was inseparable from Justinian's universalist vision of emperorship. He viewed himself as a successor to Augustus and Constantine, endeavoring to reshape his capital—both physically and ideologically—into a "New Rome." In this symbolic politics, ancient Roman traditions were fused with the Christian-Byzantine worldview. The *Codex Iustinianus* and the monumental ecclesiastical architecture functioned together as complementary manifestations of imperial order—one in legal form, the other in stone.

However, these vast undertakings placed a severe strain on the empire's finances. The suppression of the Nika Revolt alone had entailed substantial costs, compounded by Justinian's extensive military campaigns in both the East and West. Consequently, the imperial administration pursued an aggressive fiscal policy, particularly under the tax officials John of Cappadocia and Peter Barsymes. Their methods were reputedly harsh yet effective: temple treasures and aristocratic wealth were confiscated, and tax liabilities were assessed down to the individual level, often to the brink of insolvency. These measures provoked discontent among the elite and contributed to the resurgence of religious opposition, especially among the Monophysite communities in Syria and Egypt.

Despite these adversities, Justinian's legal and architectural legacies proved to be of immense historical significance. Although the *Corpus Iuris Civilis* was not fully adopted in late antiquity, it remained in force in Constantinople and later reemerged in Western Europe from the 11th century onwards, notably at the University of Bologna. Through canon law and Roman common law, it profoundly influenced the legal systems of France, Germany, and Italy and laid the foundations for Enlightenment thought and the codifications of the 19th century, such as the *Code Civil* and the *Bürgerliches Gesetzbuch* (BGB).

Likewise, Justinian's architectural heritage resonated far beyond his own era. The *Hagia Sophia* remained the largest church in Christendom until the fall of Constantinople in 1453 and inspired countless sacred edifices—from *San Marco* in Venice to the *Blue Mosque* in Istanbul. Its centralized domed design became a defining model for Orthodox ecclesiastical architecture throughout the eastern Mediterranean, the Balkans, Georgia, and Russia.

Justinian's reform program was the expression of an emperor acutely aware of his historical mission—to not merely preserve the Roman Empire, but to revitalize it on a new foundation. His legal codification constituted a "perpetual guarantee" of Roman legal norms; his architectural achievements embodied imperial authority in enduring stone. In the synthesis of law, theology, and architecture, the Byzantine Empire under Justinian reached its highest ideological and symbolic intensity—a legacy that would shape the medieval world and continue to resonate into the modern age.

10.3 Christian Orthodoxy and Separation from the West

The development of Christian Orthodoxy in the Eastern Roman Empire (Byzantium) and its gradual separation from the Latin West constitutes a central aspect of the religious, cultural, and political history of the Middle Ages. This chapter aims to trace in detail how the Greek Orthodox Church emerged within the Byzantine Empire, how it diverged from the Western Church in terms of dogma, liturgy, and institutional structures, and what conflicts, councils, and theological developments contributed to this division. The narrative follows a chronological approach and considers both religious debates and political power struggles between the Emperor and the Papacy, as well as cultural differences that culminated in the schism between East and West.

Already in the 4th century AD, before the final collapse of the Western Roman Empire, divergences began to emerge between East and West concerning theological interpretation, liturgical practice, and ecclesiastical organization. A decisive factor was the question of language: while Latin remained the dominant ecclesiastical language in the West, Greek increasingly asserted itself in the East. This did not only lead to the development of distinct theological vocabularies, but also caused substantial difficulties in mutual understanding at major ecumenical councils. An early example of such tensions was the Council of Chalcedon in 451, which formulated the so-called Chalcedonian Creed. This council, which declared the doctrine of two natures in Christ—one divine and one human in a single person—as the orthodox position, was accepted by the majority in the East, but rejected by many Oriental Churches, such as the Coptic and Syriac traditions. This already marked the beginning of internal divisions within Eastern Christianity itself.

The following centuries were characterized by a growing estrangement between the Eastern and Western Churches. In the Eastern Roman Empire, a specific understanding of the relationship between Church and State evolved under the influence of the imperial office. In the so-called "Caesaropapism," the Emperor was not only viewed as the secular ruler but also as the supreme protector and even active co-regent of the Church. This close interweaving of sacred and secular authority fundamentally differed from the Western concept of ecclesiastical independence, especially as represented by the Papacy in Rome. From the 5th century onward—particularly under Pope Leo the Great (r. 440–461)—the Roman pontiffs claimed universal jurisdiction over the entirety of Christendom. In contrast, the Byzantine emperors and the Patriarchs of Constantinople favored a synodal structure and the principle of Pentarchy, which held that the five patriarchates of Rome, Constantinople, Alexandria, Antioch, and Jerusalem were to be considered equal in honor and authority.

In the 6th century, under Emperor Justinian I (r. 527–565), the conflict assumed new dimensions. Justinian championed the ideal of *symphonia*—a harmonious cooperation between Church and State, in which the Emperor was considered the secular arm of God. His direct intervention in theological disputes—for example, the condemnation of the so-called "Three Chapters" at the Second Council of Constantinople in 553—led to serious tensions with the West. Pope Vigilius (r. 537–555) initially refused to accept the imperial decisions but was arrested in Constantinople and forced into compliance. This episode starkly revealed the extent of Byzantine imperial power over ecclesiastical matters, as well as the underlying weakness of the Papacy at this juncture.

The 7th century witnessed further theological controversies, most notably surrounding the doctrine of Monothelitism—the belief that Christ possessed only one (divine) will. This teaching was supported by several Byzantine emperors, including Heraclius (r. 610–641) and Constans II (r. 641–668), as a conciliatory gesture toward non-Chalcedonian Christians in the East. However, resistance arose both in the East and the West. Pope Martin I (r. 649–655) condemned Monothelitism at a synod in Rome in 649 and was subsequently arrested by Byzantine troops, brought to Constantinople, and put on trial. This event caused a profound rift between Rome and Byzantium. It was not until the Third Council of Constantinople (680–681) that the controversy was resolved, with the official condemnation of

Monothelitism and the reaffirmation of the doctrine of two wills in Christ (Dyothelitism).

In addition to theological disputes, liturgical differences further widened the gap. The Greek liturgy developed under the influence of the Church Fathers Basil the Great (d. 379) and John Chrysostom (d. 407), whose liturgical rites are still used in the Eastern Church today. These rites differ fundamentally from the Latin Mass in terms of language, ritual, Eucharistic theology, and liturgical music. Byzantine iconography—with its emphasis on the veneration of sacred images (icons)—also diverged from the Western tradition, which initially displayed a more reserved attitude toward religious imagery. This contrast became especially acute during the period of the so-called Iconoclasm.

Iconoclasm was introduced under Emperor Leo III (r. 717–741), who issued an edict in 726 ordering the destruction of icons. The movement continued, with interruptions, until 843, and deeply divided Byzantine society into Iconoclasts (opponents of images) and Iconodules (defenders of icons). Under Empress Irene (r. 797–802), and at the Second Council of Nicaea in 787, icon veneration was officially restored. The Western Church, especially under Pope Hadrian I, viewed the entire controversy with concern. While the West never officially questioned the use of images, it regarded imperial interference in doctrinal matters as overstepping legitimate authority.

A dramatic rupture in East-West relations occurred in the year 800, when Pope Leo III crowned Charlemagne as Emperor of the Holy Roman Empire. This coronation was perceived as a provocation by Byzantium, which still claimed the exclusive right to the Roman imperial title. The Byzantine court viewed the Western imperial coronation as illegitimate. As a result, a profound political and ecclesiastical rift emerged. It was not until 812 that Emperor Michael I officially recognized

Charlemagne as *basileus*—but not as the legitimate Roman Emperor in the full sense. This dual imperial claim entrenched the separation between a Latin West and a Greek Orthodox East.

The situation further deteriorated in the 9th century. The so-called Photian Schism (863–867) marked a new peak in the conflict. Patriarch Photius of Constantinople was appointed by Emperor Michael III, despite the fact that Pope Nicholas I refused to recognize the appointment. In response, Photius convened a synod in which he condemned certain Western innovations, especially the *Filioque* clause—the addition to the Nicene Creed which states that the Holy Spirit proceeds not only from the Father but also from the Son. Although this clause had arisen in the West as early as the 6th century, it was viewed in the East as illegitimate and heretical. Although the Photian Schism was formally resolved in 879, deep-rooted mistrust persisted.

The 11th century ultimately brought the final rupture. The Great Schism of 1054 marks the formal division between the Eastern and Western Churches. The causes were manifold: theological differences (such as the *Filioque*), disputes over liturgy, canon law, and jurisdiction. The conflict reached its climax when the papal legate Humbert of Silva Candida placed a papal bull of excommunication on the altar of the Hagia Sophia against Patriarch Michael I Cerularius (r. 1043–1058). The Patriarch responded with a counter-excommunication. Although these mutual excommunications were later viewed by some as unlawful, the breach proved irreversible. Since then, two distinct Churches have existed: the Roman Catholic Church in the West and the Greek Orthodox Church in the East.

This division was not only theological and ecclesiastical in nature, but also reflected differing mentalities and self-conceptions. While the Western Church, under the influence of the Papacy, developed a juridical-hierarchical structure, Eastern Orthodoxy emphasized mystery, liturgy, and the continuity of tradition. In Byzantium, the Emperor was seen as divinely appointed guardian of Orthodox doctrine, and the Patriarch as *primus inter pares* ("first among equals") within a synodal church system. After the schism, this structure became a defining feature of Eastern Christian identity.

In the cultural and artistic spheres, the schism manifested in divergent architectural styles (e.g., domed structures such as the Hagia Sophia versus Romanesque basilicas), in saint veneration, in liturgical music (Byzantine chant versus Gregorian chant), and in theological literature. Byzantine theology—represented, for instance, by John of Damascus (7th/8th c.) and Symeon the New Theologian (10th/11th c.)—developed a mystical spirituality that contrasted sharply with the scholastic rationalism of the Latin West.

Henceforth, the Byzantine Empire considered itself the true "Roman Empire" with the only legitimate, orthodox Church. This notion persisted even after the fall of Constantinople in 1453 and continues to influence the self-identification of many Orthodox Churches today.

In conclusion, the separation between East and West was not the result of a sudden rupture but rather the outcome of centuries of cultural, linguistic, theological, and political divergence. Its roots extend deep into Late Antiquity, and its consequences still shape the Christian world to this day.

10.4 Military Conflicts with the Persians and Arabs

Between the 6th and 8th centuries CE, the Eastern Roman Empire—commonly referred to in historiography as the

Byzantine Empire—was confronted with a series of profound military conflicts that fundamentally altered its geopolitical position, economic strength, and cultural identity. The two most significant foreign threats during this period were the Sasanian Empire to the east and, from the early 7th century onwards, the rapidly expanding Arab Caliphates. The confrontations with these powers profoundly shaped the Byzantine state in structural, military, and ideological terms. These wars demanded enormous resources, led to significant territorial losses, and culminated in a long-term military stalemate with the Islamic powers. The following chapter provides a detailed chronological overview of these conflicts, focusing on key events, military strategies, and quantitative data on troop strengths, casualties, and territorial changes.

Military engagements with the Sasanian Empire had already begun during the early centuries of Byzantine history but escalated to new levels during the reign of Emperor Justinian I (r. 527–565), and especially under his successor Justin II (r. 565–578) and subsequent emperors. After a brief peace treaty in 532—referred to as the "Eternal Peace"—concluded between Justinian and the Sasanian king Khosrow I (r. 531–579), hostilities resumed as early as 540. The trigger was Justinian's expansion of Byzantine influence in Armenia and the Caucasus, which Khosrow interpreted as a breach of the treaty. In that year, Khosrow invaded Syrian territory with an army estimated at around 30,000 men and sacked the major city of Antioch on the Orontes. The city, which had an estimated population of 200,000 prior to its fall and was one of the most significant urban centers of the East, was devastated, and large portions of its population were deported.

The subsequent years were marked by a series of retaliatory campaigns across Mesopotamia, Armenia, and the southern Caucasus. Between 540 and 562, intense military operations occurred, focusing particularly on the fortresses of Dara (heavily fortified by the Byzantines) and Nisibis. Byzantine commanders such as Belisarius, Germanus, and Narses achieved some tactical victories, but failed to secure lasting territorial gains. Eventually, in 562, a new peace agreement was signed for a duration of 50 years, stipulating that Byzantium would pay an annual tribute of 30,000 solidi (approximately 450 kg of gold) to the Sasanians—a payment that effectively functioned as protection money.

Under Emperor Justin II, this fragile peace quickly unraveled. He discontinued the tribute payments, prompting the Persians to resume hostilities in 572 under Khosrow I. The result was a prolonged war lasting until 591—one of the longest individual conflicts of the era. During this time, military leadership was restructured, most notably under General Philippicus and later under the energetic Maurice, who became emperor in 582. Maurice successfully ended the conflict through an alliance with the Sasanian usurper Khosrow II. After Khosrow II was overthrown in 590, he fled to Constantinople, where Maurice reinstated him to the Persian throne with Byzantine support. In return, Byzantium received substantial territorial gains in Armenia and Upper Mesopotamia, including control of Dara and Martyropolis. This marked the apogee of Byzantine power in the East.

However, this favorable situation proved short-lived. Following Maurice's assassination in 602 by the usurper Phocas (r. 602–610), Khosrow II declared war on the new regime—ostensibly to avenge Maurice, but in reality to pursue Sasanian expansionist aims. The ensuing war (602–628) became one of the most devastating conflicts of Late Antiquity. Under the leadership of generals Shahrbaraz and Shahin, the Sasanians launched a vast campaign of conquest: between 603 and 614, most of Syria, Palestine, and Egypt fell under their control. In 614, Jerusalem was captured, and the True Cross—one of Christianity's most revered relics—was taken to Ctesiphon. This symbolic blow to the Christian world caused outrage throughout Byzantium and the Latin West.

From 616 to 619, Egypt was conquered—a catastrophic loss for the Byzantine Empire, which was heavily dependent on the grain shipments from the Nile Valley. At the time, Egypt supplied roughly one-third of the grain consumed in the Eastern Empire and included major cultural and economic centers such as Alexandria, with an estimated population of 300,000. These losses led to the collapse of the grain trade, soaring food prices, and widespread famine in Constantinople and Asia Minor.

A turning point came with the accession of the vigorous Emperor Heraclius (r. 610–641), who initially faced enormous challenges: an empty treasury, low troop morale, and a destabilized eastern frontier. Beginning in 622, Heraclius personally led a series of military campaigns into the Sasanian heartlands. He adopted a novel strategy—rather than maintaining a defensive posture along the borders, he launched deep incursions into Persia proper, targeting Armenia, Azerbaijan, and eventually even the vicinity of Ctesiphon. In the decisive Battle of Nineveh in December 627, he defeated the Sasanian general Shahrbaraz. The collapse of Sasanian resistance was hastened by internal political turmoil: in 628, Khosrow II was overthrown and executed. His successor, Kavad II, immediately sought peace, restoring all Byzantine territories and returning the True Cross to Jerusalem. Byzantium appeared to have achieved a decisive victory.

Yet the exhaustion from this protracted war left the empire vulnerable to a new and unforeseen threat: the Islamic expansion following the death of the Prophet Muhammad in 632. As early as 634, Muslim armies under Caliph Abū Bakr and his successor ʿUmar ibn al-Khaṭṭāb advanced into Byzantine Syria. In 636, the pivotal Battle of Yarmouk took place. A Byzantine force commanded by General Theodore Trithurios—

numbering between 40,000 and 80,000 troops—was decisively defeated by a smaller Muslim force of 25,000 to 40,000 under Khālid ibn al-Walīd. Despite numerical superiority, the Byzantine forces suffered from poor coordination and low morale. This defeat marked the end of Byzantine control in Syria.

Between 638 and 642, the Byzantines lost Palestine, Damascus, and finally Egypt. Alexandria, the jewel of Byzantine Africa, fell in 641 after several sieges. The loss of Egypt proved particularly devastating. The Arab commander ʿAmr ibn al-ʿĀṣ swiftly integrated the province into the Caliphate. Egypt would become a major granary for the Islamic world in the ensuing centuries—a resource loss that Byzantium never recovered. A final Byzantine attempt to retake Egypt in 646 was decisively repelled.

At the same time, Arab incursions increasingly targeted Asia Minor and even Constantinople itself. Under Caliph Muʿāwiya I (r. 661–680), founder of the Umayyad dynasty, the Caliphate launched a naval expansion and systematic raids on the Aegean coast. Between 674 and 678, the first Arab siege of Constantinople took place. Although prolonged and intense, the siege failed—largely due to the effective use of "Greek Fire," an incendiary weapon akin to a primitive flamethrower. A peace treaty was eventually concluded, temporarily halting the attacks but obligating Byzantium to pay an annual tribute to the Caliphate. Around 679, this tribute amounted to approximately 3,000 gold solidi, 50 horses, and 50 slaves per year.

In the aftermath, the situation on the eastern frontier gradually stabilized. While further peripheral territories such as Cilicia were lost, the emperors of the Isaurian dynasty, particularly Leo III (r. 717–741), reorganized the empire's defenses. During the second Arab siege of Constantinople (717–718) under Caliph Sulaymān, the Byzantines once again successfully defended their capital. Allied with the Bulgarians and fortified by robust city walls and Greek Fire, they inflicted heavy losses on the invading Arab fleet—estimated at up to 1,800 ships—largely due to storms, epidemics, and superior defensive tactics. After a year of failed assaults, the siege was lifted. This marked a significant turning point: for the first time, Byzantium had effectively halted Islamic expansion.

Nevertheless, warfare with the Arabs continued intermittently for centuries, especially in Eastern Anatolia and Cilicia. In the 740s, the Byzantine general Artabasdos briefly regained some fortresses. Between 750 and 900, a strategic equilibrium developed between Byzantium and the Abbasid Caliphate, which had supplanted the Umayyads in 750. During this period, Byzantium introduced a new military-administrative system known as the *theme* system (*themata*), integrating military and civilian functions in regional units—a reform directly shaped by the lessons learned from centuries of frontier warfare with Persians and Arabs.

The military conflicts with the Persians and Arabs may be understood as a transitional epoch in Byzantine history. The Eastern Roman Empire lost approximately two-thirds of its eastern territory, shrinking from roughly 3.5 million to about 1.2 million square kilometers between 600 and 700 CE. It was compelled to abandon its expansionist posture and adopt a defensive strategy. Yet, its repeated ability to recover in the face of existential threats stands as a testament to its extraordinary structural resilience. The Arab–Byzantine border wars shaped the political and cultural landscape of the Eastern Mediterranean for centuries, leaving an enduring legacy in both military organization and regional identity.

CHAPTER 11: THE ROMAN LEGACY IN EUROPE AND THE RECEPTION OF ANTIQUITY

The cultural, linguistic, and administrative imprint of the Roman Empire constitutes one of the most enduring legacies of antiquity. In particular, the Latin language, the Roman legal system, and Roman administrative structures formed the backbone of European civilizations for centuries. The roots of this legacy stretch deep into the republican and imperial phases of Roman history and exerted a fundamental influence on both the Middle Ages and the modern era.

The dissemination of the Latin language began during the early Roman Republic and intensified as Rome expanded beyond the Italian Peninsula. By the 4th century BCE, Latin had become firmly established in Latium as a language of administration and public communication. The *Lex Hortensia* of 287 BCE, which granted plebiscites (resolutions of the Plebeian Assembly) the force of law for all Roman citizens, was of course proclaimed in Latin, thereby reinforcing its status as the official language of law. With the continued territorial expansion of Rome, Latin gradually became the *lingua franca* across vast areas of Europe.

By the end of the 3rd century BCE, Latin had spread throughout central Italy. However, its true internationalization began after the Second Punic War (218–201 BCE), when Rome emerged as the dominant power in the western Mediterranean. In the newly conquered provinces, such as Hispania following the defeat of Carthage or Gallia Narbonensis, which was declared a Roman province in 121 BCE, a slow yet continuous process of Romanization of the local populations commenced. This

Romanization was not only military and administrative in nature but also linguistic. The establishment of colonies—such as *Emerita Augusta* (modern-day Mérida) in 25 BCE—resulted in the settlement of Roman veterans who spoke Latin as their native language and embedded it into local social structures. The *municipium* system, further developed during the imperial period, required local elites to adopt Latin in administration and legal affairs.

Under Augustus (27 BCE–14 CE), Latin was consolidated as the standard means of communication within the western provinces, supported by a well-organized educational system and a flourishing literary culture. By the reign of Emperor Claudius (41–54 CE), Latin was not only used by the elite but had also permeated the lower social strata in large parts of Gaul. In his *Annales*, Tacitus describes how Germanic and British elites sent their sons to Rome to be trained in rhetoric and the Latin language—a testament to the prestige and attraction of Roman education and language.

The influence of the Latin language was closely tied to Roman law. Roman jurisprudence began with the *Twelve Tables* (*Lex Duodecim Tabularum*) of 451 BCE, the first written codification of Roman law. This legislation regulated civil, criminal, and family law and was composed in archaic Latin, facilitating its diffusion among the free citizens of early Rome. As the Republic developed, the *ius civile* (civil law) became increasingly differentiated, particularly through the activities of the praetors, who from 367 BCE held judicial powers and issued the *Edictum Perpetuum*, a systematic collection of legal principles.

Under Augustus and his successors, Roman law evolved into a complex legal system that was codified and systematized by renowned jurists such as Gaius, Ulpian, and Papinian. Gaius's *Institutiones*, written around 160 CE, would later serve as the foundation for Justinian's legal reforms. The spread of Roman law in the provinces was facilitated by the extension of Roman citizenship, which by the *Constitutio Antoniniana* in 212 CE was granted to all free inhabitants of the empire. From this point onward, the *ius civile* acquired universal validity as the foundation of legal practice across the empire, rendering the *ius gentium*—originally devised for non-citizens—largely obsolete.

By the 3rd century CE, Roman law had become the normative foundation for administration, judiciary, and social organization. Under Emperor Diocletian (284–305), extensive administrative reforms were implemented, including changes to the legal system. The expansion of the imperial bureaucracy divided the empire into smaller administrative units called *dioeceses*, whose officials—primarily *praesides* and *vicarii*—applied Roman law as the binding standard. This centralization was continued under Constantine the Great (306–337), who further reinforced the emperor's legislative authority and increased the central oversight of judicial processes.

In Late Antiquity, particularly in the 5th and 6th centuries CE, Roman law entered a decisive phase of transformation. In 438 CE, Emperor Theodosius II promulgated the *Codex Theodosianus*, a comprehensive compilation of imperial legislation since Constantine I, valid throughout both the Eastern and Western Roman Empires. Even more significant was the codification under Emperor Justinian I (527–565), who created the *Corpus Iuris Civilis*, comprising the *Codex Iustinianus*, *Digestae*, *Institutiones*, and *Novellae*. This monumental legal achievement would remain the foundation of European jurisprudence for centuries.

The Justinianic legal corpus was rediscovered in the 11th century in Bologna, where jurists such as Irnerius began to study it, thereby laying the groundwork for the so-called *ius commune* —a common legal system that gained validity across medieval Europe. The *Codex Iustinianus* became not only a central text in legal education at emerging universities but also a practical legal foundation for princes, cities, and courts throughout Europe. Especially within the Holy Roman Empire, Roman law —alongside canon law—became the dominant legal source, though it was often combined with local customary laws (e.g., the *Sachsenspiegel* in the 13th century).

Parallel to legal continuity, the administrative system of the Roman Empire also served as a long-lasting model. Even in the Republic, Roman governance was based on the division of responsibilities between magistrates and the Senate, with consuls, praetors, and censors holding key offices. With the establishment of provinces from the 3rd century BCE onwards and the appointment of the first *proconsules*, a provincial administration emerged that aimed at long-term integration. Each province was governed by a magistrate responsible for tax collection, legal jurisdiction, and public order. This structure was further developed under Augustus, who distinguished between imperial and senatorial provinces and introduced the office of *procurator Augusti*.

Administration became increasingly professionalized: whereas in the early Republic, offices were primarily held by aristocrats, the Principate saw the emergence of structured career paths (*cursus honorum*) and specialized branches of administration. The expansion of the road network—for example, the construction of the Via Appia, begun in 312 BCE—allowed for more efficient communication between Rome and the provinces, greatly facilitating centralized control and tax collection.

The *Tetrarchy*, introduced by Diocletian, and its subdivision of the empire into four administrative units reflected the evolution of an increasingly centralized bureaucratic state. The Roman model of a hierarchical administrative apparatus, based on a multitude of specialized officials—such as the *magister officiorum*, *comes sacrarum largitionum*, or *praefectus praetorio*—was adopted and further developed in both Byzantine and Carolingian administration. During the Frankish period (8th–9th centuries), many Roman administrative terms and practices were preserved: the title *comes* (count), for example, was directly derived from the Late Roman *comes rei militaris* or *comes sacrarum largitionum*. The territorial divisions into *civitates*, *pagi*, or *dioeceses* were also retained in early medieval territorial organization.

The use of Latin as the language of chancery persisted beyond the fall of the Western Roman Empire in 476 CE and remained the undisputed official and ecclesiastical language throughout the Carolingian period (from 751 onwards). Even the *Carolingian Renaissance* under Charlemagne (r. 768–814) was deeply inspired by the idea of reviving Roman heritage. Under the leadership of Alcuin, the palace school in Aachen introduced a standardized form of Latin writing—the *Carolingian minuscule*—which would later influence the humanist script and the development of the printing press. The Latin educational system, with rhetoric, grammar, and jurisprudence as its core disciplines, was preserved in cathedral schools and institutionalized in the universities of the 12th century.

Latin remained the dominant language of Europe's *Republic of Letters*, legal practice, liturgy, and administration until the 18th century. In England, laws continued to be written in Latin until 1733; in the German-speaking lands, this persisted well into the 17th century. Courts such as the Imperial Chamber Court (*Reichskammergericht*) employed Roman-canonical terminology and legal methodology.

During the transition from antiquity to the Middle Ages, profound transformations occurred in society, politics, and religion. Yet, particularly in the Church, in liturgical life, as well as in architecture and urban planning, clear continuities can be discerned that are unmistakably rooted in Roman heritage. While the political structure of the Western Roman Empire disintegrated after the 5th century CE, many Roman traditions survived within ecclesiastical organization and practice, as well as in urban forms and building techniques. The Roman Church —structurally grounded in Roman administrative models— became the principal bearer of cultural and intellectual continuity, and its liturgy and architecture bore witness to the survival of the ancient world within the Christianized medieval order.

The influence of the Roman Empire on the Christian Church was already clearly evident in the 4th century. After Constantine the Great proclaimed religious freedom through the Edict of Milan in 313, the Church began to be rapidly integrated into the Roman state system. From that point on, the emperor saw himself as the protector of Christianity (*Pontifex Maximus*), and the Church gradually adopted administrative, legal, and representative elements of Roman governance. This was especially apparent in the structure of the ecclesiastical hierarchy, which closely mirrored the Roman provincial organization: bishops occupied a position equivalent to that of Roman provincial governors (*praesides*), archbishops corresponded to higher officials of the dioceses, and the bishop of Rome—the pope—assumed the rank of *primus inter pares*, a status rooted in his prominent position within the former Roman capital.

In the 5th century, after the fall of the Western Roman Empire in 476 AD, the Church effectively took over the role of the state in many regions. The Roman Catholic Church became the principal bearer of Roman identity, administration, and continuity. The liturgical orders of the Western Church, especially the Roman Mass, developed under the influence of ancient ceremonial forms, such as those employed during triumphal processions, official inaugurations, or sacrificial rites. Thus, the structure of the Christian Mass—with entrance procession, readings, offering, a central culminating rite, and dismissal—was strongly shaped by the model of Roman state rituals. Elements like the *Ordo Missae*, which can first be documented in the 6th century, were based on Roman administrative language and logic. The use of Latin as the liturgical language persisted throughout the Middle Ages and thus became an essential vehicle for cultural continuity between Antiquity and the Middle Ages.

Pope Gregory I (reigned 590–604), known as "the Great," played a decisive role in solidifying Roman liturgy. Under his leadership, the Roman liturgy was standardized, later becoming known as the "Gregorian liturgy." Gregory collected and organized liturgical chants and initiated the systematic documentation of liturgical practices. The Gregorian chant named after him evolved from older, locally varied Roman singing traditions, which in turn had both Jewish and Roman ceremonial origins. Roman liturgy also shaped sacred architecture—for example, through the eastward orientation of altars or the design of the apse, where a bishop's throne was often placed—a motif derived from the Roman judicial basilica.

Roman influence was also reflected in the very structure of church buildings. The early Christian basilica was a direct continuation of the Roman judicial and market basilica. The Constantinian Basilica of St. John Lateran in Rome, begun in 313, became the model for numerous medieval churches. Its elongated form with a central nave, side aisles, and a semicircular apse served the liturgy, which depended on processional movement and hierarchical spatial organization. In the Carolingian Empire, especially under Charlemagne (reigned 768–814, emperor from 800), the deliberate cultivation of ancient models took place. The Palatine Chapel in Aachen, consecrated in 805, adopted the central architectural form of Roman rotundas and referenced elements from Constantine's Church of the Holy Sepulchre in Jerusalem and the Church of San

Vitale in Ravenna—the latter a Byzantine structure with strong Roman influences.

The role of Roman architecture in medieval urban planning should not be underestimated. Many European cities continued to develop on the layout of Roman settlements. The *cardo* and *decumanus* structure (north-south and east-west axes) was preserved for a long time in cities such as Cologne (*Colonia Claudia Ara Agrippinensium*), Trier (*Augusta Treverorum*), and Arles (*Arelate*). In these cities, the forum, theater, and baths remained central points of urban life—sometimes repurposed, sometimes converted. Churches were often erected on the foundations of ancient temples or administrative palaces, and Roman city walls, such as those in Autun, London, or Lugo, were incorporated into medieval fortifications.

The reuse of Roman building materials—known as *spolia*—was widespread in the early Middle Ages. In Ravenna, for example, ancient columns and capitals from Constantinople and Rome were installed in churches like San Vitale (consecrated in 547). Even the original St. Peter's Basilica in Rome (built in the 4th century, later replaced) contained *spolia* from Roman temples and basilicas. This practice continued during the Middle Ages, especially in times of scarce resources, such as in the 9th and 10th centuries. At the same time, the *spolia* contributed to aesthetic continuity and symbolized the connection between the new Christian empire and ancient Rome.

A particularly striking example of Roman influence on medieval urban planning is the city of Lucca in Tuscany. The Roman amphitheater, built there in the 1st century AD, served in the Middle Ages as the foundation for the Piazza dell'Anfiteatro. Its elliptical shape was retained, and the stands were built over with residential houses—a typical example of the transformation of ancient monuments into elements of medieval urban life. Likewise, the city of Florence, originally a

Roman military camp (*castrum*), still shows traces of the Roman grid system in the street layout of its old town. In Rome itself, the Roman Forum largely fell into ruin during the Middle Ages, but many ancient buildings were repurposed as churches —for example, the Pantheon (since 609 known as *Santa Maria ad Martyres*) or Hadrian's Mausoleum (now Castel Sant'Angelo), which at times served as a papal fortress.

Symbolically, too, the Roman legacy had a profound impact on medieval conceptions of rulership. The title "Emperor" (*imperator Romanorum*) was bestowed upon Charlemagne by Pope Leo III in the year 800, with the Carolingian ruler consciously stepping into the succession of Roman emperors. The idea of *renovatio imperii* (renewal of the empire) was linked in architecture with a return to Roman building traditions. Roman construction techniques such as barrel vaults, round arches, and *opus caementicium* (Roman concrete) experienced a revival during the Carolingian and Ottonian periods, although often without reaching the technical sophistication of ancient Roman times.

The liturgy remained strongly influenced by the Roman model even in the centuries following Gregory the Great. During Holy Week, symbolic acts recalling Roman triumphal rites were repeated—for example, the Palm Sunday procession. The Gregorian calendar, introduced under Julius Caesar in 45 BC, remained the basis for both ecclesiastical and civil timekeeping until its reform by Pope Gregory XIII in 1582. That a papal calendar, created over 1500 years earlier, would become the binding structure for time itself testifies to the deep-rooted influence of Roman structures on medieval thought.

Schools and monasteries served as custodians and transmitters of ancient education. The Benedictine Rule, formulated around 529 AD by Benedict of Nursia, adopted the clear structure and discipline of Roman military and administrative systems. In the monasteries' scriptoria, Roman texts were copied, commented upon, and interpreted within liturgical contexts. Cicero, Virgil, Livy, and other authors remained part of the intellectual canon —preserved and transmitted by a Church that saw itself as a continuation of the Roman Empire.

In the High Middle Ages, particularly from the 11th century onward, there was an intensified return to Roman architectural principles in what became known as the Romanesque style. Massive construction methods, the use of round arches, piers, domes, and an axial ground plan with transept and crossing all derive directly from Roman prototypes. In Cluny III, consecrated in 1130, Roman formal rigor was fused with Christian monumentality. The goal was to create a house of God that expressed the grandeur of the Heavenly Jerusalem—and thereby also the greatness of the Roman heritage—in architectural form.

Christian liturgy and medieval urban planning are hardly conceivable without the Roman Empire. What Rome developed in its late period in terms of administration, ceremonial practices, and architecture was not merely preserved but also transformed. The medieval Church adopted both the external forms of Roman rule and its intellectual structure. In church interiors, in the calendar, in the Mass, and in the urban landscape of Europe, Rome lived on—not as a dead past but as a living foundation of a new, Christian world. This dual legacy —Roman and Christian—formed the cornerstone of European civilization during the Middle Ages.

The era of Humanism and the Renaissance in Europe, spanning the 14th to 16th centuries, marked a decisive turning point in European history, closely linked to the rediscovery and reinterpretation of the Roman legacy. After centuries of medieval dominance by the Christian Church as the bearer of knowledge and culture, Europe experienced a renewed focus on the sources of antiquity—an awakening that began in Italy and quickly spread across the continent. Rome was rediscovered not only as a historical city but above all as a political and cultural model, becoming the epitome of a glorious past that served as a paradigm for contemporary models of governance and society.

Humanism, whose roots lie in the late 13th and early 14th centuries, placed the revival of classical education, ancient languages, and philosophical traditions at its core. Prominent figures such as Francesco Petrarca (1304–1374) are considered pioneers of this movement. Petrarch traveled to Rome in search of ancient manuscripts to collect and study. His discoveries of ancient texts, including letters by Cicero, created a bridge between the Middle Ages and antiquity. Petrarch recognized Rome as the "Eternal City," the source of knowledge, political order, and artistic perfection. In his writings, he described the ruins of Rome as monuments of a glorious past that should be preserved and revived.

In the 15th century, the engagement with Roman culture intensified. Humanists such as Lorenzo Valla (1407–1457) devoted themselves to the critical analysis of ancient sources. In 1440, through philological studies, Valla demonstrated that the so-called Donation of Constantine — a document that granted the Church extensive temporal powers — was a forgery. This revealed how Humanism was not solely aimed at aesthetic and literary rediscovery, but also at political and legal reforms rooted in the Roman origin of power. The return to original Latin texts enabled a critical reception of Roman legal and state doctrines and the formulation of new political ideas.

The Renaissance itself, which spread during the 15th and 16th centuries primarily in Italy but also in other parts of Europe, combined this humanistic education with artistic and architectural innovation. Rome became the center of this cultural revival. After the devastations and decline of Late Antiquity and the Middle Ages, the city experienced a remarkable rebirth under the popes of the Renaissance period. Pope Nicholas V (reigned 1447–1455) initiated extensive construction projects to make Rome shine as a new capital of Christianity and as the heir of the Roman Empire. He founded the Vatican Library in 1448 and promoted the restoration of ancient monuments such as the Colosseum.

His successor, Pope Sixtus IV (reigned 1471–1484), adorned the Vatican with frescoes and palaces and initiated the construction of the Sistine Chapel (completed in 1483). Its wall and ceiling paintings, later executed by Michelangelo and other artists, became a symbol of the fusion of ancient artistic ideals with Christian theology. The humanistic spirit of this era led many Renaissance artists and scholars to view Rome as a model of harmony, proportion, and order, one they sought to surpass in their own works.

Rome's political significance was also reassessed. During the Renaissance, the idea of a unified empire ruled by an emperor — reminiscent of the ancient Roman Empire — gained new momentum. Emperor Maximilian I (reigned 1493–1519) sought to present himself as an heir to Roman imperial traditions and summoned scholars to legitimize his rule through Roman legal traditions. Charles V (reigned 1519–1556) also considered himself a successor to the Roman emperors and defended the "Holy Roman Empire of the German Nation" as the legitimate legal successor of the ancient empire.

Rome now functioned as a cultural model far beyond Italy. The idea of the "Eternal City" permeated European political thought. Renaissance rulers endeavored to align and shape their own concepts of governance according to the principles of the Roman Republic and the Principate. For example, the French kings Louis XI and Francis I adopted Roman legal principles to centralize their administration. The Reformation, which began in the 16th century, also referred critically to Roman church structures, questioning liturgy and canon law in light of Roman models.

Architecturally, Renaissance ideas were heavily influenced by Roman antiquity. The architect Filippo Brunelleschi (1377–1446) initiated the revival of classical column orders, proportions, and perspective as found in ancient Roman architecture. The dome of Florence Cathedral (completed in 1436) became a symbol of the new union between ancient technology and modern innovation. In Rome itself, Donato Bramante began planning the new St. Peter's Basilica (from 1506), creating a structure that combined the ideals of the ancient Roman temple with Byzantine architecture into a new monumental Christian center.

The urban structure of Rome was also deliberately used during the Renaissance as a symbol of political and cultural power. Pope Julius II (reigned 1503–1513) initiated the redesign of the city with wide streets, public squares, and monumental buildings to make Rome visibly the center of the Christian world and heir to the ancient empire. The Via dei Fori Imperiali, a road built in the 20th century directly over ancient forums, had its precedents in Renaissance urban planning, which consciously integrated ancient urban structures into the new cityscape.

The cultural impact of Rome's legacy persisted into the modern era. During the Baroque period — especially in the 17th and 18th centuries — Rome once again became a magnet for artists and intellectuals from across Europe who drew inspiration from the masterpieces of antiquity and the Renaissance. The founding of the Accademia di San Luca (1593) symbolized the institutionalization of the Roman artistic tradition. Artists such as Gian Lorenzo Bernini and Francesco Borromini shaped the urban landscape with baroque churches and palaces that, in their monumentality and dynamism, echoed ancient models while simultaneously reinterpreting them.

Politically, Rome remained a symbol of legitimacy and continuity even in the early modern period. The papal curia considered itself the guardian of the Roman heritage, especially in the field of canon law, codified in the *Corpus Iuris Canonici*, which continued to play a central role well into the 20th century. Monarchs such as Louis XIV of France referred to the Roman tradition to legitimize their absolute rule, while emerging Enlightenment republics — such as the United States after 1776 — looked to the Roman model of republican virtues and the separation of powers as an inspiration.

In the 19th century, in the context of rising nationalism and Romanticism, Rome became a symbol of historical and cultural identity that shaped both Italian unification and Europe's collective memory. The unification of Italy in 1870, when Rome was declared the capital, reflected the political reunification on the basis of a shared historical legacy. Artists, poets, and historians of the 19th century — such as Johann Wolfgang von Goethe and Heinrich Heine — visited Rome as a pilgrimage site of European culture and expressed deep admiration for its ancient and Renaissance splendor.

The idea of Rome as a political and cultural model was not abandoned in modern Europe. During the fascist rule in Italy under Benito Mussolini (1922–1943), the "rebirth of Rome" was employed as propaganda. Ancient monuments were restored, and new grand avenues like the Via dei Fori Imperiali were constructed to equate the power and grandeur of the fascist regime with that of the ancient empire. At the same time, Rome remained a source of inspiration for scholars, artists, and politicians — a symbol of continuity in times of profound social and political transformation.

Today, the Roman legacy continues to be present in Europe's cultural memory. The principles of Roman legal order, republican governance, and artistic aesthetics remain foundational to many European institutions and cultural identities. The rediscovery of Rome in Humanism and the Renaissance was more than just a historical revival: it was a fundamental impulse that led Europe to reflect on and redefine its own history and identity. Rome became — and remains — a political and cultural model whose significance has endured across millennia.

CLOSING WORDS

At the end of this journey, I would like to sincerely thank you for your time and attention. It is a great honour for me that you chose to embark on this adventure with me. Your interest and curiosity are what make writing so meaningful.

If you enjoyed this book, I warmly invite you to explore my other works as well. Each one represents another step along my creative path, and I hope they will bring you just as much insight and enjoyment.

Should you find a moment, I would be truly grateful if you shared your thoughts and impressions in an honest review on Amazon. Your feedback is not only of great importance to me, but also to other readers in search of new literary explorations.

Once again, thank you for your support and your interest. I wish you many enriching and inspiring hours of reading ahead!

Copyright © 2025 Eric Rump

All rights reserved.

ISBN: 9798293278930

Imprint

contact:

Eric Rump

Hauptstraße 30

09306 Königshain Wiederau

Germany

rumperic@gmail.com

Printed in Dunstable, United Kingdom